LOOKING AFTER MISS ALEXANDER

States, People, and the History of Social Change
Series editors Rosalind Crone and Heather Shore

The States, People, and the History of Social Change series brings together cutting-edge books written by academic historians on criminal justice, welfare, education, health, and other areas of social change and social policy. The ways in which states, governments, and local communities have responded to "social problems" can be seen across many different temporal and geographical contexts. From the early modern period to contemporary times, states have attempted to shape the lives of their inhabitants in important ways. Books in this series explore how groups and individuals have negotiated the use of state power and policy to regulate, change, control, or improve people's lives and the consequences of these processes. The series welcomes international scholars whose research explores social policy (and its earlier equivalents) as well as other responses to social need, in historical perspective.

LOOKING AFTER
MISS ALEXANDER

*Care, Mental Capacity, and the Court of Protection
in Mid-Twentieth-Century England*

JANET WESTON

McGill-Queen's University Press
Montreal & Kingston • London • Chicago

© McGill-Queen's University Press 2023

ISBN 978-0-2280-1467-6 (cloth)
ISBN 978-0-2280-1468-3 (paper)
ISBN 978-0-2280-1583-3 (ePDF)
ISBN 978-0-2280-1584-0 (ePUB)
ISBN 978-0-2280-1609-0 (OA)

Legal deposit first quarter 2023
Bibliothèque nationale du Québec

Printed in Canada on acid-free paper that is 100% ancient forest free
(100% post-consumer recycled), processed chlorine free

The open access edition of this book was funded by the
Wellcome Trust

Library and Archives Canada Cataloguing in Publication

Title: Looking after Miss Alexander : care, mental capacity, and the
    Court of Protection in mid-twentieth-century England / Janet
    Weston.
Names: Weston, Janet, author.
Series: States, people, and the history of social change ; 7.
Description: Series statement: States, people, and the history of social
    change ; 7 | Includes bibliographical references and index.
Identifiers: Canadiana (print) 20220390010 | Canadiana (ebook)
    20220390088 | ISBN 9780228014676 (cloth) | ISBN 9780228014683
    (paper) | ISBN 9780228015833 (ePDF) | ISBN 9780228015840 (ePUB) |
    ISBN 9780228016090 (OA)
Subjects: LCSH: Alexander, Beatrice (Beatrice Ruth)—Mental health. |
    LCSH: Great Britain. Court of Protection. | LCSH: Mental health
    laws—Great Britain—History—20th century.
Classification: LCC KD3412 .W47 2023 | DDC 344.4104/4—dc23

To my parents:
Patricia Weston
and
John Weston (1943–2021)

CONTENTS

❁

FIGURES

※

PREFACE

Miss Beatrice Ruth Alexander, a retired housekeeper, was found incapable of managing her affairs in 1939, shortly before her sixtieth birthday. Some five years earlier she had inherited a beautiful large home in rural Dorset and a comfortable pension from her late employer, but friends and neighbours had become increasingly concerned that this windfall was more than Miss Alexander could manage. A local family of ill repute had moved into the house with her, and seemed to exercise considerable control over her money and movements. When pressed, Miss Alexander vehemently denied that she needed help. The neighbours agreed that there was nothing really wrong with her in medical terms; she was just a timid person who could easily be dominated by more forceful personalities.

Her situation prompted the intervention of an office of the courts, sometimes known as the Lunacy Office. This office found her incapable of managing her own property and affairs as a result of mental infirmity, and placed the Official Solicitor in charge of her inheritance. A woman with some nursing experience, Kate Wortt, was hired to live with Miss Alexander and to keep an eye on her, under the supervision of the Official Solicitor and the overarching control of the head of the Lunacy Office: the Master in Lunacy. This arrangement continued for the next twenty-five years, until Miss Alexander became increasingly frail and unwell and required more care than Miss Wortt – herself nearly eighty years old by this time – could provide. Miss Alexander spent her final years in a private nursing home and died in 1969, a few weeks after her ninety-first birthday, having remained legally 'incapable' throughout the last thirty years of her life.[1]

This book is about the curious events in 1939 that saw Miss Alexander declared 'incapable', and the arrival into her life of individuals and institutions, like Miss Wortt, the Official Solicitor, and the Lunacy Office, whose stated aim was to look after her. It is about the quirks of fate and unusual decisions that guided this particular chain of events, and the legal and social structures that enabled them. It asks what this turbulent time in the life of one woman might reveal about mid-twentieth-century mental health law and associated ideas of citizenship, vulnerability, and care. And, by reflecting closely on Miss Alexander's story, it also examines some of the values, assumptions, imaginative leaps, and emotional responses involved in interpreting her life, in the past when her mental capacity was assessed, and in the present, in the process of history writing itself.

I first encountered the Court of Protection and ideas of mental capacity through my work in the charity sector in the 2000s, in the context of statutory wills and disputes over testamentary capacity. I observed, and very occasionally participated in, the discussions and negotiations that took place when someone seemed to have been unable to make a will, usually because they were severely affected by dementia. At what point did confusion, forgetfulness, disorientation for time and place, and difficulties with communication interfere with someone's ability to understand and meaningfully engage in the process of making important decisions about their own affairs? Once that point was reached, who should be able to estimate their wishes and decide on their behalf? Over a decade later, having sidled into a completely different career but remaining curious about the Court of Protection and this notion of mental capacity, I discovered the first of twelve well-stuffed cardboard files in The National Archives in London dedicated to Miss Alexander.

Many of these kinds of files, I had learned, contained only brief legal documentation. Those found incapable were usually referred to in cursory terms as 'the Patient', and sparse details about their lives were given by anonymous authors filling in the blanks on pre-printed forms. In contrast, Miss Alexander's files were alive with personalities. Letters and lengthy reports put forward opinions, questions, problems, and requests, not only at the time Miss Alexander was found incapable, but also throughout the decades that followed. Miss Alexander was almost always 'Miss Alexander' in these written records of her final three decades. Along with her name came some small sense of her as an individual, with passions and fears, inspiring affection and frustration, and with a full life taking place just out of sight, beyond the reach of this paperwork about her mental incapacity. Like the officials in London who puzzled over the problems that her situation presented, I came to know her a little, not intimately and not as an impersonal Patient, but as Miss Alexander.

The process of making sense of the labyrinthine legal structures, terms, and procedures that governed the events of Miss Alexander's later life was lengthy. It made me realise that I was not the only one unfamiliar with the history of the Court of Protection and mental capacity law. Histories of mental health law tend to focus on processes of involuntary confinement and treatment in asylums and hospitals, while legal histories have barely touched the practices of the twentieth century. This book therefore provides a preliminary account of one of the missing pieces of this picture: the development of mental health law dealing with mental capacity during the twentieth century. As legal historians and scholars have rightly observed, the law surrounding mental capacity is a highly disparate field and can be called upon in almost any set of circumstances in which people have dealings with one another,[2] but it seemed to me that the twentieth century archives of the Court of Protection provided one valuable point of access.

What follows will therefore be of interest to those concerned with the history of law and mental health, but this book also picks up on a number of wider themes. I have connected Miss Alexander's story to some of the developments and ideas in circulation during the mid-twentieth century, to do with the proper role of the state and its citizens. As others have argued, the administration of the law is far from politically neutral; it is part and parcel of the workings of the state and reflects dominant beliefs about how its citizens should behave.[3] Miss Alexander's mental capacity to manage her own affairs was considered by an office that was part of the professionalising and growing civil service, and its work interacted with some of the ideas and changes behind the developing welfare state. With Miss Alexander being found incapable, her ability to exercise the freedoms supposedly available to all citizens was assessed and found wanting, and some of those freedoms were removed from her. In their decisions and activities, the individuals and institutions involved in Miss Alexander's life therefore reflected and enacted ideas about the state and its citizens.

Miss Alexander's story also offers an entry point for thinking about histories of vulnerability and care. These two concepts more commonly take centre stage within sociological and socio-legal research than history,[4] but I argue that both were extremely important to the work of the Lunacy Office and Official Solicitor, and by extension, to Miss Alexander. Those found incapable of managing their own affairs were seen as vulnerable to harm, particularly from financial abuse or exploitation. Attention to vulnerability meant looking beyond illness and considering Miss Alexander's situation in its wider context, but this attention was weighted with unspoken assumptions about what caused vulnerability and who might experience it. Views of Miss Alexander's vulnerability shaped the care that was provided to her, which was inextricably linked to control. Miss Alexander received care in her home, and her story begins to flesh out our understanding of unpaid community-based care and supervision in the twentieth century, but this was also part of a larger realm of care work that involved the legal system and the civil service. Her story can help us to adopt a more capacious understanding of care that includes all of these caring (and controlling) activities.

By focusing on Miss Alexander and the people and institutions most directly involved in her encounter with capacity law, I build on recent work in modern social and cultural British history that exploits the potential of individual and small stories.[5] Such stories can suggest new ways of understanding large-scale or long-term developments in the past, challenging received wisdom. They can also prompt valuable reflection on the work of historical research and the ways in which history is then presented to its readers. Small stories like Miss Alexander's foreground some of the issues that accompany all historical reasoning and writing: accounting for individual foibles and sheer luck as well as structural patterns of continuity and change, dealing with incomplete evidence and archives that distort as much as they reveal, using imagination in combination with this evidence and knowledge gleaned elsewhere to fill in the blanks, and the influence of contemporary and personal concerns (and feelings) over analysis and interpretation.

By touching on such issues as they have played out in relation to this particular story, I make a case for a kind of history writing that is not afraid of the unknowable, and embraces its debts to imagination as well as insight and knowledge. This is how history turns traces of the past into something meaningful; it is also how history can include stories and people that left little trace at all. To do this, to acknowledge the place of creativity, uncertainty, and subjectivity in the writing of history without losing sight of the facts and evidence that historical events and actors leave behind, is a 'middle ground' worth claiming.[6]

Making sense of Miss Alexander's life has involved reading records that relate to hundreds of other people found incapable over the first six decades of the twentieth century, and getting to know some of the individuals, families, professionals, and practices that were involved in this branch of the law. It also brought me into contact with some of the scholars and activists working hard to improve laws and practices surrounding mental capacity and vulnerable adults today. These encounters have highlighted to me how difficult it can be to find just and practical ways forward when individual lives fail to match the liberal ideal of the autonomous adult. Miss Alexander's story is important, at least in part, because it prompts us to think carefully about this ideal, about whether and how she was enabled to look after herself, and about what it might mean to look after one another.

⚜

ACKNOWLEDGEMENTS

The research for this book was funded by a Wellcome Trust Research Fellowship in Medical Humanities (grant reference number 209884/Z/17/Z), and I am extremely grateful for everything that this fellowship provided: a good salary to pay the bills, generous research expenses, additional funding to compensate for disruption caused by COVID-19, and perhaps most importantly, a relatively long period of job security that gave me not only time, but confidence. Counterfactuals may be a risky business, but it seems highly unlikely that I would have been able to write this book (or to carry on masquerading as a historian at all) without it.

I held this fellowship at the Centre for History in Public Health, London School of Hygiene and Tropical Medicine (LSHTM), and am grateful to all of my colleagues there, especially Alex Mold and Ingrid James, for their advice and support. Beyond LSHTM, thanks are due to colleagues and friends who have provided encouragement, suggestions, and valuable information and insight at various stages of this project, particularly Joanna Bourke, Beverley Clough, Hazel Croft, Louise Hide, Alex Ruck Keene, Denzil Lush, Hilary Marland, Emma Milne, Lucy Series, and Susie Shapland. I would also like to acknowledge the anonymous reviewers for their constructive (and reassuring) comments; I hope they recognise the impact that their excellent ideas have had on the final product, and will forgive the rest.

No less significant has been the impact of the questions and reflections generated by all those involved in *Power and Protection*, two short films and events about the Lunacy Office. Special thanks to Charlie Barnes, creative director of Dead Earnest Theatre, who was the driving force behind this: the films (including one about Miss Alexander) are available at www.lshtm.ac.uk/research/centres-projects-groups/power-and-protection. I would also like to thank the hardworking staff at The National Archives in London, who dealt admirably with my many Freedom of Information requests plus a pandemic, and Chris Loftus at the University of Sheffield's Special Collections and Archives, who speedily scanned a good chunk of their Robert Saunders collection for me. I am also very grateful to Richard Baggaley at McGill-Queen's University Press for his feedback as the book inched towards completion.

Finally, I owe huge thanks to Owen Roberts for countless conversations over many years about Miss Alexander, about the technicalities of the law and the vagaries of the civil service, and especially about how impossible it is to write a book. Owen, I hope you like it.

ABBREVIATIONS

BUF   British Union of Fascists
DVAMW Dorset Voluntary Association for Mental Welfare
LCV   Lord Chancellor's Visitor
MAD   Management and Administration Department,
       Royal Courts of Justice
SSC   Sheffield Special Collections
TNA   The National Archives, London
WI   Women's Institute

LOOKING AFTER MISS ALEXANDER

❀

INTRODUCTION

For most of us, most of the time, we take our day-to-day freedom to make decisions for ourselves for granted. Faced with countless large and small questions about our personal lives and relationships, our finances, our health and medical care, and our plans for the future, we are constantly making choices. Some of these choices may be very much informed by the expectations, wishes, and suggestions of those around us, but if they were challenged, these decisions would still be respected and upheld in law as our own – that is, unless our mental capacity to make our own decisions is questioned. The onset of illness, the diagnosis of mental illness or a learning disability, or even advanced age or unusual behaviour, can all prompt concern that we lack capacity, that we cannot manage our own affairs, and that our decisions are no longer legally valid.

Although this is a book about many non-legal things, its starting point is the law of England and Wales surrounding mental capacity. This was the legal framework encountered in 1939 by Miss Beatrice Ruth Alexander, a retired housekeeper whose story is at the heart of this book. Vital to this legal framework was the Court of Protection, previously known as the Lunacy Office, an institution which may be unique in the world as a 'specialist court charged with the determination of capacity'.[1] Simply put, the Court of Protection was, and still is, 'concerned with the ways in which decisions may lawfully be made on behalf of those who are unable to make decisions for themselves'.[2] Today, such decisions may concern medical treatment, from being vaccinated to withdrawing life support, or very personal matters such as entering into a marriage or sexual relationship, or transactions of a financial nature like making a will or selling a house.[3]

As the 1930s came to a close, Miss Alexander was one of about 20,000 adults in England and Wales who were under the auspices of the Lunacy Office as a result of being found incapable of managing their own 'property and affairs'. Exact numbers are elusive, but over the course of the twentieth century hundreds of thousands of people found themselves in this position.[4] In broad terms, 'property and affairs' meant anything to do with finances, from houses and businesses to savings accounts, insurance policies, even divorce settlements and family trusts. Responsibility for determining incapacity and then taking charge of someone's 'property and affairs' rested from the nineteenth century with the 'Office of the Master in Lunacy', or Lunacy Office. It was officially renamed the Court of Protection in 1947.[5] Day-to-day decision-making on behalf of those found incapable was delegated variously to family members, professional advisers, and state and welfare officials, known in different times and roles as committees, deputies, or receivers.

The diagnoses, symptoms, and states of mind of those found incapable of making their own decisions, and the terminology used to describe them, were varied and wide-ranging. They included alcoholism, brain damage, confusion, coma, delusions, dementia, depression, Down's syndrome, hallucinations, idiocy, imbecility, insanity, mania, melancholia, mental defect, old age, paralysis, schizophrenia, and senility. Those described in these terms and found incapable remained under the aegis of the Lunacy Office/Court of Protection for anything from a few months to a long lifetime. Although a minority successfully argued after a period of months or years that their mental state had improved and they were once again capable of looking after themselves, most remained legally incapable for the rest of their lives. The work of the Lunacy Office aimed to protect vulnerable people from exploitation, to safeguard their money and bring their affairs under control, and to facilitate the provision of all necessary care and comfort. It also represented a significant infringement of individual rights and freedoms.

Miss Beatrice Alexander became entangled with the Lunacy Office and capacity law in the summer of 1939, when she should have been enjoying a pleasant retirement. For twenty-five years she had been the loyal housekeeper of John Norton, a divorced doctor, moving with him in 1924 from London to the idyllic village of Chilfrome in Dorset when he retired. Dr Norton died after ten quiet years in Chilfrome, and Miss Alexander would ordinarily have been facing the need to find a new position and a new home. But it transpired that Dr Norton had remembered her in his will, leaving to her his beautiful house, the Old Rectory, and the income from his substantial investments. Just five years later, the Official Solicitor was appointed to act as Miss Alexander's receiver: the person taking control of her 'property and affairs'. According to outside observers, Miss Alexander had fallen under the influence of a disreputable family who took advantage of her modest wealth and her gentle nature for their own financial gain. A neighbour alerted the Lunacy Office, legal wheels were set in motion, and Miss Alexander's life was transformed.

TELLING SMALL STORIES

The story at the centre of this book is an unusual one. What happened to Miss Alexander is a 'small history': a retired housekeeper in a rural English village, of modest but comfortable means, was exploited financially by those she called friends.[6] This was not exactly an everyday experience, but nor is it very hard to imagine – especially since Miss Alexander was recently bereaved, newly affluent and alone, and by all accounts a very nervous and timid person. Her story takes a startling turn when legal proceedings were initiated, and the Lunacy Office stepped in to place the Official Solicitor in charge of Miss Alexander's inheritance. Miss Alexander was no 'lunatic'. She had no medical diagnosis or mental disorder, as far as anyone could see. She protested, denying any infirmity and asking to be left alone. Even so, she was found incapable in law of managing her property and affairs; her so-called friends were evicted from the Old Rectory, the home they had shared for many years with Miss Alexander; and her income was used to employ a nurse-companion, who moved in with her on a permanent basis. This was a startling degree of intrusion into her life. What made it possible?

The answer connects to another strange feature of the story: the Lunacy Office itself. It is out of place here in very concrete terms. According to most histories of mental health law, it had effectively ceased to exist a few decades before these tumultuous events at the Old Rectory.[7] Asylums and secure hospitals loom large in visions of historical mental health law and care, but this strange 'office' has faded into obscurity. Not only is its starring role in Miss Alexander's later life a surprising guest appearance from an actor thought to have retired long ago, its style of intervention is also strikingly at odds with existing historical accounts of mental health law in England over this period. These accounts usually depict the middle decades of the twentieth century as an era of 'medicalism', during which medical expertise in matters of mental infirmity was generally preferred to legal control.[8] Yet the Lunacy Office's actions seem to focus narrowly on legal methods of compulsion and control, with little interest in medical developments concerning the mind.

Even in the context of the wider caseload of the Lunacy Office, Miss Alexander's story stands out as unusual. Most of those coming under the auspices of the Lunacy Office were in hospitals or nursing homes, not living independently in their own home. Most cases were initiated by next of kin, prompted by some financial issue that needed resolution, not nosy neighbours worried about abuse. Few prompted any disagreement, let alone formal protest, from the supposedly incapable persons themselves. What can close attention to one exceptional story deliver, beyond a string of surprises? 'Atypical or extreme cases', to borrow the language of social science, 'often reveal more information because they activate more actors and more basic mechanisms in the situation studied'.[9] In other words, this strange case is useful because its very strangeness prompted people to get involved, asking questions, testing boundaries, pursuing every possible avenue, and, importantly for historical research, frequently putting pen to paper to explain themselves as they did so. As an extreme case, it provides a partial view of other lives and Lunacy Office cases in general, although it is not representative of them. Importantly, its idiosyncrasies are themselves significant. They act as signposts to certain features of the Lunacy Office and, more broadly, the society in which Miss Alexander lived, that might otherwise go unnoticed: features that influenced all Lunacy Office cases to some extent, and make Miss Alexander's particular experiences much more intelligible.

Drawing on the methods of microhistory, all of the unusual features of Miss Alexander's story can be read as clues that demand close attention and explanation. Their strangeness suggests that some part of the bigger picture is missing, that there is 'a gap between our mindset' or understanding of the past, 'and that which is revealed' by the archival sources to have happened. These oddities could be 'a sign of a larger, but hidden or unknown, structure' within which they will make sense.[10] Miss Alexander's three-decade-long encounter with the Lunacy Office may seem surprising from the vantage point of the early twenty-first century (and it may have surprised some of its protagonists at the time, too), but it happened nonetheless. What version of the past can account for it?

These anomalies begin to make sense in a context of persistent legalism and compulsion within mental health law, in which medicine retained a fairly minor role well into the 1950s. They are indicative of a close association between mental health law, and social care and welfare, a relationship often overshadowed by historians' attention to the role of psychiatry and the hospital within modern responses to mental illness. The little-noticed survival and growth of the Lunacy Office, and Miss Alexander's encounter with it, also make sense in relation to ideas – often highly gendered – within the emerging welfare state about citizenship, vulnerability, and care. And finally, these strange events draw attention to the role of chance and coincidence in shaping the past, in which individual foibles and biases collide with opportunities and institutions to produce sometimes unexpected sequences of events.

A fuller understanding of Miss Alexander's encounter with the Lunacy Office has required me to pay close attention to both institutions and individuals. For individuals, the digitisation of sources such as census records and newspapers have provided access to much more information than would have been possible to locate even just a decade or two ago. This enables what historian Julia Laite has described as a 'collectivity of stories', which helps to illuminate the bigger picture by situating multiple individual people as interconnected and essential components of it.[11] Although Miss Alexander is the focus here, I pick up threads of other stories too: the employer who made her financially independent, the neighbour who alerted the Lunacy Office, the officials who visited and evaluated her, the nurse-companion who lived with her, and, importantly, the Lunacy Office itself, an institution with a curious story of its own.

This focus on Miss Alexander and those around her encourages attention to individual agency. People made decisions that were highly contingent, informed by personal peccadillos or unique confluences of events. They were also guided by the overarching historical processes and structures that shaped the boundaries of the possible. Legal decisions were pushed this way and that by 'agency, creativity, and chance' as much as by formal rules and the words of statute, as Miss Alexander's story makes plain.[12] There are tensions, inherent within social history and exacerbated by this close focus on a small story, between paying attention to individual people and their experiences, and paying attention to the larger context and structures that shaped their horizons.[13] It is in part to strike a balance between these two aspects that I look closely at the Lunacy Office and to a lesser extent the Official Solicitor's office, as well as Miss Alexander and her circle. Agency, creativity, and chance are not unbounded. Laws, policies, and social norms all played a role in shaping events, and here the Lunacy Office is central. Miss Alexander's story only makes sense in conjunction with the story of this unusual institution, and together they offer scope to combine individual experience with institutional and structural considerations.[14]

Piecing together and presenting a convincing account of why people behave as they do requires imagination and powers of persuasion. This is just as true for the neighbours, friends, doctors, welfare officers, and legal experts who weighed up Miss Alexander's situation in the mid-twentieth century as it is for the historian in East London sifting through their archival traces seventy years later. In both instances, much about Miss Alexander remained ambiguous, unknown, and unknowable. The beliefs and feelings of the interpreters come into play. Far from being a simple application of facts and rules, the use of capacity law to regulate Miss Alexander's life required imaginative work to account for her behaviour in ways that were useful and meaningful. In conversation with a wider world of people and ideas, this work drew on shared assumptions – about 'normal' behaviour, happiness, safety; about what constituted a valuable citizen, a successful society, a well-organised state – and promoted certain ways of seeing the world.[15] Ultimately, one account won out, but different legal decisions were possible. Different arguments could have been made; different versions of Miss Alexander could have proved persuasive. Although legal adjudication has to fulfil certain requirements to be accepted as such, this still leaves plenty of room for variation.[16]

Historical research and writing about Miss Alexander is much the same. Historians have long acknowledged the role of imagination in creating a picture of the past, although the point at which there is 'too much' imagination within historical writing is debateable and often highly context dependent.[17] Imagination is especially integral to micro-historical approaches, albeit with 'careful rules' of evidence and the need to make it plain when conclusions are speculative.[18] In this story, uncertainty abounds. Facts themselves are far from certain – even, as suggested above, the legal fact of Miss Alexander's mental incapacity. The vexed question of Miss Alexander's mental state is its own obstacle: her judgement and rationality were called into doubt; her thoughts and motives may be particularly difficult to grasp. The same is true of others in the story as well, whose actions were guided by their professions, personalities, political allegiances, family ties, past experiences, and present emotions. Such uncertainty is especially prominent when focusing on people, but it is not entirely absent from interpretations of organisations and larger structures too. Historical reasoning is rarely final.

There is, therefore, no definitive version of this story. This is far from fatal: as Carolyn Steedman has observed, history writing is itself a way of writing about and through indeterminacy. Any retelling will miss the mark. Miss Alexander's story 'could be told in a dozen different ways, each with faithful and proper adherence' to the sources and to what was said and done, but none will exactly replicate that which happened.[19] Deciding which way to tell the story is not only a creative act, but, as Hannah Johnson has pointed out, a personal and political one. Historical interpretation draws on the cultural contexts, emotional investments, and 'ethical presuppositions' of the teller, all of which are often unarticulated.[20] My version of Miss Alexander's story reflects my own imaginative horizons, reactions, and goals. One such goal is to show that history writing can dwell on uncertainty and ambiguity, and illuminate the role of imaginative creativity and emotional investment, without forfeiting facts or producing accounts that are any less persuasive.

THE LUNACY OFFICE

Before going any further, it is worth explaining the legal context, in broad strokes. Even those who are well versed in twenty-first-century Court of Protection work or the lunacy inquisitions of the more distant past tend to be unfamiliar with their twentieth century counterpart. This is largely because capacity law in the twentieth century was bookended by what looked like dramatic statutory breaks, leaving it disconnected from past and present alike. The first such bookend was the Lunacy Act of 1890, which gave the sense of an ending. Historian Akihito Suzuki, in the leading work on nineteenth-century Commissions in Lunacy, stated it plainly: this Act 'effectively ended a legal procedure that had been used for more than five hundred years'.[21] The procedure in question was the cumbersome lunacy inquisition, through which fairly small numbers of people were found 'lunatic' or 'idiot' and had 'committees' placed in charge of their personal or financial affairs.

The second bookend arrived 115 years later, in the form of the Mental Capacity Act of 2005. This marked a new beginning by creating what is known as a superior court of record, called the Court of Protection. The job of this twenty-first-century Court of Protection is to 'make decisions on financial or welfare matters for people who can't make decisions at the time they need to be made',[22] and it has been described as a 'hinge point in the shift from the old to the new rhetoric' in the field of capacity law and a 'blank canvas' onto which a brand new legal approach to mental capacity could be painted.[23] Its newness was its defining quality, tending to overshadow the fact that the Act also terminated the existence of an old Court of Protection which had carried out many (although not all) of the same duties.

This old Court of Protection, pre-dating the 2005 Act, was in fact the selfsame entity as the Lunacy Office of the nineteenth century. Its changes of name over the intervening years helped to place its continued existence in the shadows. As the term 'lunacy' fell from favour in the early twentieth century, to the extent that it was officially banished from statutes and regulations in 1930, the Lunacy Office was renamed in the blandest possible terms in 1928 as the 'Management and Administration Department'.[24] 'Management and Administration' reflected the business of the office, albeit obliquely, and was too anodyne to prompt any objections. To the amusement of the master of the department at the time, its initials also spelled MAD. This name was not popular. After protracted discussion and negotiation, those who did not find it amusing to work for the 'MAD' were relieved to see it renamed again in 1947 in more dignified terms: 'Court of Protection'.[25] In summary, the Lunacy Office (or 'Office of the Master in Lunacy', or 'MAD') in the first half of the twentieth century, and the Court of Protection in the second half, were all one and the same thing.

A further reason for the lack of attention to the old Court of Protection and its administration of capacity law was the very private nature of its work. The Court of Protection in the early years of the twenty-first century had something of a reputation for being mysterious or clandestine, or the 'most sinister', 'secret court' in Britain, as a series of shrill newspaper headlines proclaimed in 2015 to 2016.[26] Yet it was probably less 'secret' by then than it had been for well over a century. Throughout the twentieth century its predecessor had conducted its business behind firmly closed doors, in rooms in London's Royal Courts of Justice until the 1950s, and thereafter from premises on Store Street in Bloomsbury, on the edge of the city's legal district. Despite its new name, it was not strictly speaking a court but an office of the courts, and its decision makers were not strictly judges, although they enjoyed similar powers. Their decisions were not recorded in newspapers or law reports, and hearings were not open to the public. If not quite shrouded in secrecy, they were certainly veiled in the name of discretion. This veil helped to conceal the administration of capacity law from public attention: there was no significant legislative change, no enquiries to investigate its workings, no high profile cases or scandal. Until the very end of the century, it generated no substantial interest from policy makers. As concern about breaches of patients' rights and the ideas of anti-psychiatry began to affect mental health law and practice in the second half of the century, the Lunacy Office/Court of Protection quietly continued, seemingly untouched.

A lack of profile or public attention is also down to the fact that the Lunacy Office did not deal with law and medicine at their most visibly coercive. Its business was *not* involuntary confinement or treatment. Those who came under its remit were not all housed together in institutions, but dispersed across specialist and general hospitals, nursing homes, and private residences, as their individual circumstances dictated. There was no physical manifestation of determinations of incapacity to manage one's property and affairs: no single place where its impact could be seen. It is also fair to say that the office intervened in the affairs of relatively small numbers of people. With barely more than 30,000 'open cases' at its busiest in the late 1940s, its 'patients' (as they were always called) were fewer in number than the *50,000 Outside the Law* in institutions under the Mental Deficiency Acts, for whom the National Council of Civil Liberties advocated in their 1951 report of that name. Its activities concerned fewer than the 60,000 older people in the 'back wards' of mental hospitals, for whom the Aid for the Elderly in Government Institutions group began to campaign in the 1960s, and very much fewer than the 150,000 hospitalised under the Lunacy and Mental Treatment Acts when the Percy Committee made its enquiries in the 1950s.[27]

Yet the number of those on the receiving end of its interventions had risen dramatically since the start of the century, and its powers were significant. The Lunacy Office was responsible for determining whether someone was indeed incapable of managing their affairs, and could then decide the future of those who were so found. The family members or officials who were appointed as 'receivers' managed the day-to-day aspects of an 'incapable' person's finances, but had to account to the Lunacy Office/Court of Protection on a regular basis and had to seek specific permission for anything out of the ordinary. The 'property' that receivers were charged to manage ranged from one small bank account to large businesses, investments, farms, houses, and frequently also debts and payments to family members. Decisions that receivers and Lunacy Office staff made on behalf of those found incapable involved bills and medical expenses, financial support for dependants, investments, management of rental properties, restructuring family trusts, pursuing and settling legal disputes, and estate planning; they also touched on practical concerns such as where a person should live, given that this was likely to involve financial decisions and expenditure of some kind. For Miss Alexander, additional decisions made on her behalf concerned who she should live with, and, by extension, the kind of life that she would lead.

THE ARCHIVES AND MISS ALEXANDER

As a young woman, Beatrice Alexander won prizes for her butter making, including a silver rose bowl. This is very nearly the only fact that I have discovered about her early years, beyond the barest outline of a biography.[28] Census data prevent Miss Alexander from being entirely 'archivally invisible' during these years, in Marisa Fuentes elegant phrase, but they give little away.[29] They tell me that she was born in 1878 in Norfolk to Dennis and Ruth Alexander, both also Norfolk born and raised. She was their first child, soon followed by Arthur, then Frank, Granville, Helen, Louis, Ernest, Kenneth, Dennis junior, and finally John, the baby of the family, born in 1898 when Beatrice was twenty years old.

At some point between 1906, when she is fleetingly named in a Norfolk newspaper article reporting on the annual agricultural show, and 1911, when she appears in the census of that year, Miss Alexander moved to London and took up a job as housekeeper for Dr John Norton.[30] The position was clearly a successful one for her, given its longevity. When Dr Norton retired from medical practice and moved to Chilfrome in Dorset in 1924, she moved with him and remained there until Dr Norton's death ten years later. In his will, Dr Norton left his estate to Miss Alexander for her lifetime. Miss Alexander received all of his household goods outright, and was able to continue living at the Old Rectory for as long as she wanted. She also received a comfortable income from the late doctor's investments, which were held on trust and managed by his executors, the Midland Bank, for her benefit. Five years later, in 1939, the files in the London National Archives about Miss Alexander and her incapacity begin.

As with all archives, these records are oddly detailed in some respects and frustratingly opaque in others. At least one crucial report from the summer of 1939 is missing, but even an archive that contained every conceivable item of official paperwork would be incomplete in other ways. Notably, within the twelve files dedicated to recording the events of Miss Alexander's thirty-year encounter with the Lunacy Office, there are only two short letters written in her own hand. These are accompanied by barely a handful of references elsewhere to comments that she made or wishes that she expressed. These are files *about* Miss Alexander, but as is so often true of legal (and medical or state) archives, she appeared only because something exceptional and distressing had happened to her.[31] These 'exorbitant circumstances' removed her from the everyday and propelled her into the orbit of a legal system with narrow, pre-defined interests. Their archival traces provide 'no pathway to her thoughts' and present profound challenges to any attempt to reconstruct, recount, or recuperate her life.[32]

Placing Miss Alexander somewhere near the centre of this book in spite of her archival absence draws on Fuentes' approach to 'ephemeral archival presences'. Fuentes makes a compelling case for the political and ethical importance of what she describes as 'ek[ing] out extinguished and invisible but no less historically important lives' – in other words, finding ways of writing about those who are almost or entirely eliminated by archival sources, and elucidating the distortions and silences of these archives themselves.[33] Miss Alexander's experiences were nothing like those of the enslaved women about whom Fuentes writes so eloquently, but Fuentes's approach is informative, and Miss Alexander's life and experiences do matter. Miss Alexander becomes visible only when and because she lost the legal status accorded to most adults, which recognises them as self-governing and autonomous; in possession of certain rights and responsibilities. Archival material about her inevitably distorts and sidelines as a result, giving priority to the final thirty years of her life and not the first sixty, to her 'weaknesses' and not her strengths, paying little attention to her own opinions, her friends, her interests, her passions, her daily life. But there is still scope to shift its weight, to use it as the starting point rather than the final word, and to consider the events it describes from different perspectives.[34] Not only does this prompt critical reflection on the material itself, acknowledging uncertainty; it also includes Miss Alexander herself, someone who was found incapable, within this history of capacity law.

The files about Miss Alexander are part of what is described as a random sample of 2 per cent of Official Solicitor cases. In 1934, five years before his appointment as Miss Alexander's receiver, Official Solicitor Alexander Gilchrist stated that he acted in this capacity for about 1,700 people, meaning that about thirty of these files might be included in such a sample.[35] Prior to the Public Records Act 1958 and its requirements for retention, though, files relating to such appointments were typically destroyed ten years after the case came to an end. Unsurprisingly, then, there are very few files dating back as far as the 1930s or earlier. The number of files currently open for inspection is smaller still, since files containing information about persons who may still be alive are not made available to researchers. Altogether, this means that Miss Alexander is one of only twenty-two people, from the entire twentieth century, whose Official Solicitor files concerning mental incapacity are currently available to view.[36]

Fortunately for curious historians, there are a further 258 case files dealing with mental incapacity available from the records of the Lunacy Office/Court of Protection itself, including a larger number from earlier decades. These records are reportedly a 'two per cent sample ... selected to illustrate both the administration of patients' estates and their medical histories',[37] but it seems likely that the process of selection (and the proportion saved for posterity) was rather more haphazard than this suggests. Although some documents of record such as court orders were retained separately, most case files were routinely destroyed after ten years. However, when the Lunacy Office relocated from London to Cambridge at the start of the Second World War, an assortment of its recently closed files was left in an attic at the Royal Courts of Justice and subsequently forgotten. These accidental survivors were rediscovered in

1973 and deposited with the Public Records Office, as The National Archives was previously called.[38]

There is, therefore, an abundance of files that were closed in 1938 to 1940, the oldest of which was opened in 1901. The Court of Protection archive also includes a collection of files closed in 1983, when many dormant files relating to people who had died many years ago were reviewed and finalised. These two cohorts are joined by at least three files that were specifically chosen for permanent retention because of their perceived interest to future researchers,[39] and a smattering of files closed in other years, whose retention could have been either accidental or intentional. In fact, this eclectic collection might be a reasonably good random sample, especially for the period to 1940. It is complemented by administrative material scattered across the archives of the Lord Chancellor's Office, which was responsible for these judicial entities, and together these collections form the foundation of this book. I have also drawn on the published legal literature concerning capacity, along with newspapers and genealogical materials available from Ancestry.co.uk.

The potential for legal records to contribute to histories of madness has not gone unrecognised. Historians have highlighted the value of legal proceedings surrounding competence in its civil (rather than criminal) context as particularly useful for understanding madness as it was perceived beyond the medical sphere, in the home and the courtroom.[40] Even so, they are still rarely used. Historian of mental health James Moran has suggested that legal records have been sidelined by historians of madness in part because they do not 'fit squarely enough within the "therapeutic turn" that asylum documents have come to represent'.[41] Similarly, for Suzuki, they reveal rather more about 'lunacy from the family's viewpoint' than the physician's.[42] In fact, as this book suggests, legal records concerning mental capacity can contribute much more broadly as well: legal models of incapacity had much less to do with views of lunacy or madness than with ideas of citizenship, vulnerability, and care.

MENTAL HEALTH LAW AND CITIZENSHIP

Ideas about citizenship and the proper relationship between individuals and the state provide one way to make sense of Miss Alexander's story. As legal historian Ben Griffin has argued, there is considerable scope to integrate histories of the administration of non-criminal law into histories of the state.

Indeed, a long-standing reluctance to do so may be evidence of the enduring success of Victorian efforts to present the law as apolitical.[43] The Lunacy Office's administration of the law was connected to changing views of the proper role of the state, and the nature of citizenship. In very broad terms, these changing views have typically been characterised as a shift away from the individualistic ideals of the Victorian era in the first half of the twentieth century, towards a wider acknowledgement of the need for collective action. This was inspired in part by greater recognition of (or anxiety about) intransigent social problems that seemed to lie beyond the reach of individual effort. The state came to be seen as 'the embodiment rather than the antithesis of communal responsibility', as social historian Pat Thane has put it, and popular perceptions of the role of both the state and its citizens changed as a result.[44]

Historians of law and policy surrounding mental illness and mental deficiency have mapped legislative changes onto these broad trends. In terms of admission to and involuntary detention in asylums, the Lunacy Act of 1890 has been characterised as a 'legalistic' approach that firmly focused on protecting individual liberty, while the 1930 Mental Treatment Act marked a turning point towards prioritising the health of the nation rather than individual freedom, using state-supported medical expertise and voluntary channels to encourage treatment.[45] This trend was extended further by the Mental Health Act of 1959, described in one history of nursing as a 'high water mark of medical dominance'.[46] In this reading, the Mental Health Act of 1983 then signalled the reappearance of a focus on individual freedoms that had to be protected by law from the excesses of medicine, coinciding with the shrinkage of the welfare state.[47]

Similarly, the Mental Deficiency Act of 1913 has been described as part of the ideological shift away from individual liberty and towards collectivism, as 'mental defect' emerged as a social problem that required systematic, state-sponsored attention. This Act can be understood as part of the liberal welfare reforms of the early twentieth century, but scrutiny of mental deficiency law and policy also highlights conceptualisations of citizenship that easily enabled those deemed mentally defective to be excluded. As Mathew Thomson has shown, they were positioned as biologically different, lacking 'the mental ability to exercise liberty in a meaningful sense', meaning that their involuntary segregation and institutionalisation was acceptable.[48] This connects to work on the role of the 'psy' disciplines of psychology, psychiatry, and psychoanalysis in shaping ideas of citizenship as both status and practice.[49] Simply put, the idea of 'healthy minds' as a prerequisite for good citizens became increasingly influential, with a particular focus on childhood and the family as key elements in the production of psychologically mature citizens who could exercise their social responsibilities wisely. Immaturity, irresponsibility, and mental weakness came to be seen as problematic for the wellbeing of society as a whole.[50] For those deemed mentally defective, for whom cure was thought to be impossible, this problem was insurmountable.

The view from the Old Rectory in 1939 builds on and knits together these ideas. Capacity law did not deal with admission to mental hospitals or managing mental defect, but it drew together similar questions about individual freedoms, the role of the state and of medicine, and the requirements of citizenship. The Lunacy Office was still governed by the legalistic Lunacy Act of 1890, with no space for voluntarism. Although it enlisted medical expertise after a fashion, Miss Alexander's situation makes clear the curious position within legal decision-making that medical insight occupied. The 'medical dominance' of the mid-twentieth century is absent, although the office was not entirely insulated from widely circulating ideas about the boundaries of mental illness. The operation of the Lunacy Office also reflects growing state involvement in welfare. Its work and staffing increased dramatically, and the office itself came to rely on funding from the Treasury instead of meeting its own costs from the fees it collected from its patients. In its readiness to step inside the Old Rectory, placing a civil servant in charge of Miss Alexander's home and affairs, the Lunacy Office was mirroring the expansion of welfare services in other fields, channelled and funded by the state.

Miss Alexander's case is also symptomatic of the overlap between welfare services and desires to regulate the boundaries of citizenship. Findings of incapacity delivered care and control: although it could not demand segregation or institutionalisation, the Lunacy Office was very much in the business of supervision and restriction. It was prepared, for a time in the mid-twentieth century at least, to intervene when adults appeared to be irresponsible, immature, inexperienced, or weak of character, and unable to exert their rights and freedoms as citizens – and consumers.[51] Mental incapacity was more readily identified amongst women, and the Lunacy Office provides a clear example of the state adopting the role of a 'quasi-parental entity'[52] that perceived some people as being in much greater need of 'parenting' than others. The idea that a demonstrable ability to 'exercise liberty in a meaningful sense' was necessary for full citizenship permeated the corridors of the Lunacy Office, and Miss Alexander's Dorset village as well. Yet, in determining whether Miss Alexander could exercise her freedoms meaningfully, those involved in her case looked beyond her mental state as defined by illness or impairment, and contemplated her vulnerability in a much wider sense.

VULNERABILITY AND CARE

Contemporary analyses of law and policy surrounding mental capacity law and adult protection have made extensive use of theories of vulnerability. Much of this has been inspired by legal scholar Martha Fineman's proposal that 'the "vulnerable subject" must replace the autonomous and independent subject asserted in the liberal tradition'. For Fineman, vulnerability arises from embodiment, which makes it a constant feature of all human life. Alongside this universality is the fact that vulnerability is also 'particular: it is experienced uniquely by each of us', and a good part of this experience is shaped by the resources available to us. If attention to this vulnerable subject sat at the heart of social policy, Fineman argues, then societies would develop a more meaningful vision of equality, and a 'reorientation of political culture' towards this goal.[53]

Building on this, legal scholars have critiqued the law's focus on a narrow idea of mental capacity. Looking only for the presence or absence of mental capacity, such scholarship argues, 'may obscure from the legal gaze the power dynamics and situational factors which will impact on the individual'.[54] In other words, this approach looks only at the supposedly inherent vulnerability that comes with mental illness or disability, and may fail to see the full array of ways in which people are vulnerable to (or protected from) harm. Such vulnerabilities certainly might be affected by disability or illness, but can also be caused or exacerbated by someone's 'personal, social, political, economic and environmental situation', and by 'abusive interpersonal or social relationships, and socio-political oppression or injustice'.[55] A legal gaze that encompassed these factors would be able to identify vulnerability more usefully, and would be able to offer much better solutions to the problems that vulnerability raises. The idea of mental capacity as a matter of fact to be objectively discerned only individualises the issues at stake, and ignores the broader context that enables or inhibits a person's ability to function and thrive.[56]

The High Court in the twenty-first century has acknowledged certain contextual factors that may generate legally significant vulnerability in adults.[57] Miss Alexander's experience with the Lunacy Office is indicative of a similar recognition of the importance of a person's particular situation and context, albeit often unspoken and somewhat different in nature. The Lunacy Office paid little attention to illness: what was of much more interest was Miss Alexander's personal, social, and financial situation and particularly her interpersonal relationships. These contextual factors, considered alongside her character, were sufficient in 1939 to confirm that she was vulnerable to harm and exploitation. They also guided the kind of care that her receiver provided, within the parameters of the law and a largely paternalistic model of welfare. Importantly, perceptions of her vulnerability and the care it demanded were affected by the ideologies of those around her and their assumptions regarding citizenship, gender, and respectability, an aspect of the decision-making process that was not acknowledged at the time any more than it is today.

In making the case for vulnerability as a useful way to understand what happened to Miss Alexander, I reflect this very contemporary interest in the concept. The word 'vulnerable' is not used in the archived case files, in relation to Miss Alexander or anyone else. Nevertheless, I propose that Lunacy Office work drew on shared ideas of individual vulnerability as a state of heightened risk of harm. Histories of abuse in various guises have highlighted the problems that occur when terminology and concepts are in flux, especially those (like vulnerability) that are connected with rights, harms, and morality: such ideas are both malleable and powerful, and it becomes especially important to understand their definitions and the context in which such defining takes place.[58] For the Lunacy Office, particular people appeared especially likely to suffer harm if left to their own devices, and therefore required a receiver: in this sense, they were implicitly viewed as vulnerable. Given that mental capacity law focused at this time on 'property and affairs', harm was ostensibly only of a financial nature, but those involved were not blind to other kinds of harm that could and did occur alongside (or lead to) financial harm.

Complex ideas about what constituted vulnerability, what caused it, and what reduced it, are all visible in the workings of the Lunacy Office.

Vulnerability is not the only big concept at work behind the scenes in the Lunacy Office. Mental capacity proceedings and receiverships were a form of care and a form of control: two ideas rarely easy to separate in the context of mental health law, and often placed in opposition. Work on mental deficiency policy and practice has described a long-standing 'care/control paradox', in which the desire to control people and their behaviours sat uncomfortably alongside the desire to provide care to them.[59] In practice, the fulfilment of both desires could look the same: residence in an institution; close supervision in the community. Control is usually seen as a negative, associated with restricting individual freedoms and causing harm, while care is seen as a social and personal good, but in practice the two are not always so easily distinguished. Historical research addressing care has highlighted that, as Louise Hide and Joanna Bourke put it, 'care and harm can co-exist because the same behaviours and attitudes are conceptualised differently depending on the cultural context and perspective of the individual'.[60] From a slightly different viewpoint, work in the medical humanities has highlighted that, for those receiving support, a *lack* of restriction or constraint can be experienced as a lack of care.[61] Control is not always simply harmful, any more than care is always harmless.

Perceptions of Miss Alexander and her vulnerability affected the kind of care and control that was delivered to her. Historical and sociological scholarship on care has positioned it as a form of work with emotional as well as material components, often poorly valued thanks to its association with women and the domestic.[62] Histories of care in twentieth-century Britain have tended to focus on institutional settings such as hospitals and hostels, despite and alongside acknowledgements of the perennial importance of informal care provided in the home.[63] Miss Alexander's story offers an opportunity to remedy this, looking at care at the Old Rectory from her devoted companion, Miss Wortt. This care included supervision and control, and sat uneasily between paid employment and personal duty. Miss Alexander and the Lunacy Office offer a way to reconceptualise the history of care as well, by drawing attention to other kinds of care work that are rarely recognised as such since they are usually 'ascribed to men'.[64] Care for Miss Alexander was delivered by the Lunacy Office and the Official Solicitor in the administration of law and the management of property, as well as by Miss Wortt. As political theorist Joan Tronto has argued, this work 'is part of the realm of care' too.[65]

I became acutely aware of some of the difficulties surrounding care as a concept as I read the files about Miss Alexander. When I first encountered them, only a few of the twelve files about her were open to the public. The available papers ended abruptly in the midst of the Lunacy Office and Official Solicitor's initial foray into her affairs, and with an astonishing revelation about the neighbour who had been responsible for instigating legal proceedings in the first place. At that moment and in that light, the use of mental capacity law felt like an authoritarian intrusion into Miss Alexander's private business, in the interests of making her household conform to social norms: it felt like unwelcome control. Once later files became available and the events of 1939 took their place within a longer period of Miss Alexander's life, my view changed. It still seemed like control, but control that had brought care. This shifting interpretation was influenced by my own changing feelings: I became emotionally attached to Miss Alexander and some of those connected to her, particularly Miss Wortt, her nurse-companion. As I read, I worried about what would happen to them. Notes and jottings in the files, from officials who – like me – had not met these women and knew them only as a 'case', took on a new hue. Surely these officials also felt some connection, some concern? Perhaps their decisions and actions were themselves a form of care.

Care and control, like vulnerability, are not words that feature in the records about Miss Alexander. By bringing them into the story, I provide a partial and provisional account of what happened, full of contemporary and personal preoccupations. This is true of all history writing. By letting such preoccupations rise to the surface at times throughout this book, I want to add to efforts already in train elsewhere, where others have 'flouted the realist illusion customary in the writing of history', unsettled the finality with which much historical writing is presented, and disrupted the appearance of stability and coherence within archives (and legal records in particular).[66] Researching and writing about the past draws together knowledge and the unknowable, certainty and ambiguity, facts and speculation. The contemporary and the personal are central to how this is done, and to the story that emerges as a result.[67]

OUTLINE OF THE BOOK

In the next chapter, I build on these initial introductions to Miss Alexander and the Lunacy Office. As well as giving an account of the Lunacy Office's little-known survival, expansion, and conversion into the Court of Protection, this chapter explains the rather complex structures that led mysterious entities such as the Official Solicitor and Lord Chancellor's Visitors (LCVs) to become involved in Miss Alexander's affairs. Miss Alexander herself receives as much of a history and a life before the finding of incapacity as I have been able to uncover, but as the discussion makes clear, a great deal remains uncertain or unknown. Those involved in determining whether she was incapable of managing her own affairs were faced with uncertainty in a very different context, but a similar uncertainty nonetheless.

Chapter 2 turns to consider how Miss Alexander came to the attention of the Lunacy Office. Incorporating insights from the wider body of Lunacy Office case files, this chapter builds an initial picture of how and why this branch of mental health law was used: usually, as a solution to specific and very practical problems, in which social welfare and not medical treatment was at stake. Miss Alexander's situation was highly unusual because of the lack of family or institutional involvement. Those around her might recognise her as vulnerable and in need of care, but this was not very widely understood as a problem for the law or the state to address. The fact the Lunacy Office *did* hear about Miss Alexander can be attributed, speculatively, to some matters of chance: her neighbour's family ties and extreme political views. Although this particular confluence of coincidences may have been unusual, it acts as a signpost to contextual factors that made Miss Alexander's experience possible and relatively unobjectionable to her contemporaries. Such features shaped more typical Lunacy Office encounters as well.

Miss Alexander's situation appears additionally unusual because it was an argument, not a sudden financial or health crisis, that prompted contact with the Lunacy Office. This application for the appointment of a receiver, the subject of chapter 3, generated *another* argument. Miss Alexander opposed the application on the basis that she was perfectly capable of looking after herself. This was rare, but the very fact of a disagreement shines a light on the ways in which mental capacity was evaluated, described, and interpreted, and by whom. Ideas about mental deficiency played an important role, but so too did ideas about Miss Alexander's living situation and vulnerability. Importantly, the treatment of medical evidence in her case suggests that there was little space for 'medicalism' within this branch of mental health law. Reviewing wider law and practice around mental capacity, I argue that this remained the case until at least the 1950s. The indeterminacy of the law is particularly evident here, with many possible outcomes to the case – and several possible readings of Miss Alexander's own views and situation, as well.

Finally, chapter 4 considers the kind of care that Miss Alexander received in the years that followed. Her nurse-companion, Miss Wortt, plays an important role, not only as her primary caregiver, but as the dominant voice within the archive. Miss Wortt's care was emotional and material, private and public, and she herself became the object of caring interventions from the Official Solicitor in later years, highlighting some of the many blurred boundaries that a focus on care can introduce. Care included supervision and control in the home: mental health law was not only concerned with involuntary confinement and medical treatment, and supervision in the community was not confined to people falling under the purview of the Mental Deficiency Acts. The kinds of care envisaged and provided by the Lunacy Office and by its official receivers indicate a broader view of the responsibilities of the state than had been the case decades earlier, and a reliance on the unpaid caring work of women. Recognition that this care included significant elements of control, with scope for harm, also brings back to the foreground some of the interpretive difficulties surrounding Miss Alexander, and the role of imagination and my own emotional investment in the process of piecing together her story.

In the course of researching this book, I came to care very much about Miss Alexander – and Miss Wortt, as well. This made me defensive of their capabilities at times, and also very ready to see a largely happy outcome to what seemed at first to be a sad story. Others who played a role remained consistently much more elusive (and sometimes, I admit, much less likeable). These personal perspectives and reactions are made explicit at times, sitting alongside and every so often contrasting with the views of historical actors. This account, like all historical writing, is made up of such interactions between past and present.[68] A keen awareness of the insecurity of much of my knowledge of Miss Alexander has also prompted me to highlight the role of imagination and uncertainty, in both legal and historical work. Rather than trying to establish exactly what happened or whether Miss Alexander was 're-ally' incapable – whether the events of 1939 were a correct application of the law, or an appropriate restriction of her rights and freedoms – I have thought about the creativity that lay behind these events; the people, structural forces, and coincidences that shaped them; and the possibilities that their archival traces present.[69] Miss Alexander's unusual story, and the surprising role played in it by the Lunacy Office, were clues that fortunately proved too tempting to ignore.

I

❀

ORIGINS

In the summer of 1939, the paths of Miss Beatrice Alexander and the Lunacy
Office crossed. This was an unlikely encounter in many respects. Firstly, the
work of the Lunacy Office had supposedly petered out decades earlier, after
the Lunacy Act of 1890 rendered its inquisitions and subsequent interventions
in the affairs of 'lunatics' and 'idiots' obsolete. Secondly, Miss Alexander was
an unlikely candidate for proceedings concerning 'lunatics' and 'idiots', since
she did not seem to be either. She was categorically 'not mental', as several
doctors reportedly confirmed, and was 'well read & clever & can talk well on
many subjects'.[1] Yet when their paths did cross, the assistant master of the
Lunacy Office issued an order confirming that Miss Alexander was incapable
of managing her affairs, and appointing the Official Solicitor to act in all
financial matters on her behalf. Clearly the office *was* still active, and Miss
Alexander *did* somehow fall within its remit.

Any attempt to make sense of these facts requires some insight into both
the Lunacy Office and Miss Alexander. This chapter therefore provides a kind
of pre-history for each. It begins with a detailed introduction to the Lunacy
Office, the nature of its work, and the statutory framework within which it
operated. It describes the transformations that took place before and especially
after the Lunacy Act of 1890, and suggests why the Lunacy Office was busier
than ever by the 1930s. This disentangles some of the complexities around
capacity law in the twentieth century, for the benefit of historians who may
be less familiar with the legal processes concerned and legal experts unfamiliar
with the history. The chapter then turns to Miss Alexander. It explains how
she came to be living in the Old Rectory in the 1930s as a woman of private
means, and why some aspects of her situation could become a source of concern to those around her, and perhaps to Miss Alexander herself.

This account of Miss Alexander is contextualised with reference to her working life, her personality and personal relationships, and the wider landscape of matters of 'mental welfare' in the first half of the twentieth century. The very different attitudes displayed towards Miss Alexander and the family that eventually came to live with her, the Humphries, prompt reflection on the different ways in which mental health law could be implemented to limit individual freedoms, and the complex interplay of care and control. Much less clear are the details of Miss Alexander's past life and present circumstances in the 1930s, including her relationships with those around her and her own wishes and feelings. Sparse archival foundations give hints, and imaginative interpretation has to do the rest.

INTRODUCING THE LUNACY OFFICE

In the early years of the twentieth century, senior lawyer Henry Studdy Theobald unsuccessfully applied for the position of Solicitor to the Board of Revenue. As he recalled years later in his memoir, he was told at the time that something better was coming his way. This better offer 'turned out to be a Mastership in Lunacy to take the place of Ambrose who had become incapacitated'.[2] 'Ambrose' was William Ambrose, an elderly barrister who was one of the two sitting Masters in Lunacy, and Theobald was unusually well equipped to take his place. Theobald had qualified in law thirty years earlier and had acquired considerable knowledge of what was then called 'lunacy law' through his civil service work. He had drafted many of the rules that governed lunacy practice, and had contributed significantly to the major lunacy law reforms of the late nineteenth century. He was, as one of his distant successors has remarked, well aware of his own brilliance and not afraid to note the failings of others.[3] By the time the mastership was offered to him, Theobald recounted, the role had become 'sufficiently endowed to be worth having but not so important as to make the incompetence of the holder a public scandal'. For those in the know, the Lunacy Office had become something of a joke. Ambrose and his fellow elderly Master, Thomas Fischer, were in Theobald's view so inept that the situation 'would have been ludicrous if it had not been tragic. Their work was, in fact, carried on by one or two competent clerks and the office was in a lamentable condition'.[4]

This depiction of an insignificant department, in which a few clerks could keep business ticking over and for which fundamental disfunction mattered little, fits comfortably with existing accounts of the law surrounding mental capacity. As mentioned in the previous chapter, the Lunacy Act of 1890 is often understood to mark the beginning of the end for the Lunacy Office. Lunacy inquisitions were effectively rendered obsolete, and so presumably the office responsible for this work went into terminal decline in the early twentieth century. In fact, Theobald's account of his time there, alongside information in contemporary legal textbooks, administrative files, and the case records of the office itself present a rather different view. This view is essentially one of rapid expansion and a degree of professionalisation, bringing the terms of the Lunacy Act firmly into action in the twentieth century. Notwithstanding Theobald's tendency towards immodesty, this is a more accurate picture of the Lunacy Office in the twentieth century than the narrative of terminal decline. It also accounts for the position and role of the office in 1939, when it received its first letter about Miss Alexander.

The Lunacy Office was a rather ancient institution. Its powers dated back at least as far as a royal prerogative first committed to writing in the thirteenth century, which confirmed the monarch's authority over the persons and property of 'idiots' and 'lunatics'. By the sixteenth century, this power was becoming less and less about 'the king's rights over the lands and bodies of idiots and lunatics', and more about 'his obligation to protect them', or more specifically, to protect their families' estates and inheritance, which were at risk of being dispersed, squandered, or stolen.[5] Predictably, in this context, only individuals and families with something substantial to bequeath, misplace, squander, or inherit ever came into contact with the royal prerogative in action.

The monarch's obligations in this line were eventually delegated to the Lord Chancellor and, from the mid-seventeenth century, were carried out by the Court of Chancery via a lengthy procedure rife with curious terminology. In brief, any interested party could petition the court for a Commission in Lunacy, which would prompt an event called an inquisition to determine whether the person named in the petition was indeed a lunatic or idiot. A jury would hear the evidence for and against, and would then make its decision. For those who were found to be lunatic or idiot, the judge would order the appointment of a 'committee of the estate' or a 'committee of the person'. A committee was often a family member. If tasked with the 'estate', the committee had control

over property and business affairs, while a committee of the person was responsible for personal care and welfare. Although a committee of the estate
managed day-to-day finances and real property, the court itself held any cash
or investments belonging to the so-called lunatic or idiot. Exactly how effective
the Court of Chancery was in terms of actually protecting the personal and
financial interests of those under its care in the late seventeenth and eighteenth
centuries has been the source of some debate, but overall the picture is not an
impressive one.[6] Significant theft and corruption seem to have combined with
the vast costs and delays for which the Chancery Court later became infamous.

This branch of lunacy law, much like the better known laws dealing with
asylums, underwent significant reform in the nineteenth century. Responsibility for exercising the royal prerogative was removed from the Court of
Chancery in 1842 and placed under the control of two senior barristers, who
eventually came to be known as the Masters in Lunacy. The Lord Chancellor
retained ultimate authority over their Lunacy Office, although with ever less
direct involvement as the decades went by. Juries at lunacy inquisitions became
optional, fees were reduced, and some new elements of oversight and care
were introduced. Notably, these included the creation in 1833 of the position
of LCV, which remained very much in existence for the next 150 years. There
were to be three such visitors at any time: two doctors and one barrister, all
of suitably lengthy experience. It was their duty to visit on a regular basis those
who had been found lunatic or idiot by inquisition, making sure that they
were properly cared for, that the appropriate sums of money were being spent
on their wellbeing, and that their committees of the estate or person were still
necessary. Idiocy was understood to be permanent and unchanging, but in
the case of lunacy, recovery was always theoretically possible. LCVs were to
keep an eye out for its signs.[7]

Such visits were particularly important for the significant proportion of
those found by inquisition to be lunatic or idiot who lived at home, in the
care of family, friends, or paid staff. Lunacy inquisitions were entirely separate
from the law and procedure surrounding committal to a madhouse or asylum.
Many of those found lunatic or idiot at inquisition did not live in institutions,
and most of those admitted to institutions never came under the purview of
the Masters in Lunacy at all. But, as asylums grew in number and size over
the course of the nineteenth century, additional legal reforms were introduced
to provide access to (or protection of) the property of those living in asylums,

by adding to the powers of the Lunacy Office. The Lunacy Regulation Act of 1862 allowed for an asylum patient's property to be made available to fund the patient's maintenance, by paying it over to a relative or other responsible person with instructions as to how it should be spent. The person taking responsibility for this money was known as a 'receiver'. This process neatly avoided the whole business of a Commission in Lunacy and inquisition to establish lunacy: the fact of being lawfully detained in an asylum meant that the person's inability to manage their own property was taken as read. The role of the receiver was a significant one, in terms of later events: Miss Alexander's encounter with the Lunacy Office in 1939 saw the Official Solicitor appointed to act as *her* receiver.

Miss Alexander did not live in an asylum or mental hospital, though. One further legal reform was necessary first, before it would be possible to appoint a receiver for someone like her, who lived at home without any constraints on her movements. This reform came with the Lunacy Acts Amendment Act in 1889 and the consolidating Lunacy Act of 1890, drafted by someone with the mastership of the Lunacy Office in his future: Henry Studdy Theobald. The 1890 Act directed that a receiver could be appointed for anyone at all, and not just those in asylums. Section 116(d) of the Act empowered the judge and Masters in Lunacy to appoint a receiver for any person as long as they were convinced that the person was incapable of managing their affairs 'by reason of infirmity caused by disease or age'.[8] The main aim of this subsection, according to Theobald, was to provide for the protection of those 'wealthy men who, though perfectly sane, had attained such extreme old age, that they could not safely manage their own affairs'.[9] These people could not be found lunatic or idiot at inquisition because they were neither lunatics nor idiots, nor were they usually resident in institutions, meaning that a receiver had not previously been possible.[10] This seemingly small adjustment to the law – with a specific and small set of beneficiaries in mind – had a disproportionate (and wholly unplanned) effect on the Lunacy Office. It also paved the way for its interactions nearly fifty years later with Miss Alexander.

The advantages of requesting a receiver, rather than petitioning for a Commission in Lunacy, undertaking a lunacy inquisition, and then having a committee of the estate appointed instead, were numerous. For one, it was a lot faster. Receivership decisions could usually be made based simply on the papers submitted to the Lunacy Office, without any need for evidence to be given in person. This also reduced the likelihood of unwelcome publicity: lunacy inquisitions were sometimes covered in very great detail in newspapers, with large crowds attending.[11] Fees for receiverships were also substantially lower, both at the time of the application and afterwards. As has been well documented elsewhere, the wider availability of receiverships after 1890 brought about, in effect, the demise of the costly and long-winded Commission in Lunacy.[12]

What is much less well appreciated is the truly remarkable popularity of receiverships in the years that followed, and the resultant growth of the Lunacy Office. In 1919, at the time of a wide-ranging review of the office's function, its staff comprised nineteen clerks and a handful of senior figures including the two Masters. By 1934, staff numbers had jumped to about eighty and were increased again that year by a further 50 per cent, to 120. This small army spilled out of its allocated rooms at the Royal Courts of Justice and struggled to keep on top of its burgeoning workload. Its responsibilities were financially significant, since the value of the property belonging to those found incapable, for which many thousands of individual receivers and ultimately the office itself were responsible, was estimated to be worth no less than eighty million pounds in the mid-1930s – very approximately four billion pounds today.[13]

Such a fortune was the result of rapidly escalating numbers of receivers being appointed for escalating numbers of incapable people, far outstripping the number of inquisitions in the previous century. During the 1870s, there had usually been a little over a thousand persons found lunatic or idiot at inquisition and with committees of the person or estate in place at any time. Evidence gathered by Akihito Suzuki suggests that this decade saw the number of Commissions in Lunacy reach their peak. In the aftermath of the Lunacy Act of 1890, numbers of committees of the person or estate tailed off to barely a few hundred.[14] Meanwhile, by 1905 the Lunacy Office was responsible for well over three thousand receiverships, rising to over five thousand in the early 1920s.[15] The 1920s and 1930s then saw the sharpest increase, with the total number of people with receivers peaking in the late 1940s at just over 30,000 – a figure that would be reached again towards the end of the century.[16]

The cause of this increase, and particularly the dramatic rise in the interwar years, prompted some contemporary speculation. Common consensus at the time was that a good portion of the increase was down to a gradual spread of awareness amongst solicitors, bank managers, doctors, local welfare officers, and the general public that the affairs of a person of doubtful capacity should not be ignored or left in the hands of unofficial helpers, and that the receivership process provided an alternative to the costly old inquisition.[17] Other explanations, with the benefit of slightly more hindsight, cited 'social changes resulting in redistribution of wealth' and the 'stress of economic conditions during recent years'.[18] In other words, more people were coming to the attention of the Lunacy Office because more of the population had assets that might need protecting, and because more people were suffering from mental infirmity as a result of the economic turbulence of the 1930s and then the war years.

Such discussions about caseload also touched upon the wider context of mental illness, and its prevalence and diagnosis. In the late twentieth century, similar discussions tended to assume an absolute increase in the number of people unable to manage their affairs thanks to medical advances sustaining life after severe injury or illness, and an ageing population at growing risk of dementia.[19] There are examples of this thinking in the early twentieth century too: one leading textbook referred to the 'increasing number of persons under mental disability' as a matter of fact, and commentary from the 1930s also observed that receiverships were lasting longer as people with receivers lived longer.[20] These earlier commentators were also sensitive to the idea that perceptions of mental illness or defect might be changing. The Mental Deficiency Acts of 1913 and 1927 and Mental Treatment Act of 1930 were said to have added 'a considerable number' to the office's workload.[21] None of these Acts were directly concerned with the operation of the Lunacy Office: their impact was down to the fact that they brought larger numbers of people to the attention of various medical and welfare authorities, and implicitly expanded the parameters of mental abnormality. These Acts addressed forms of mental defect that were not as severe as 'idiocy' and mental disorders that were less debilitating than 'lunacy', providing new routes for supervision, care, and treatment. In this context, the statutory requirement for there to be 'infirmity caused by disease or age' before a receiver was appointed could be interpreted rather more widely than its nineteenth-century drafters had intended.

This growth in receiverships brought with it a changing demographic of Lunacy Office clients, or 'patients', as they were always called. In the mid-nineteenth century, as Suzuki has observed, lunacy inquisitions concerned almost exclusively the very wealthy. This was sustained in later years too: one expert witness giving evidence to the 1877 Select Committee on Lunacy Law reported that 'a good many' of those found to be lunatic or idiot at inquisition received an annual income of £3,000 or more (equivalent to something like £200,000 today).[22] The rich continued to be well represented in the twentieth century, with the Lunacy Office consistently engaged in managing large houses and country estates, five- and six-figure inheritances, and sometimes much more income than could possibly be spent.[23]

Miss Alexander, on the other hand, was comfortable but not exactly wealthy. Much more modest estates such as hers came to dominate the work of the Lunacy Office over the first half of the twentieth century. Between 1900 and 1906, the office was involved in the affairs of about 600 people whose total annual income was less than £20, or about £1,500 a year in today's money.[24] The number of lower-value estates then rose as the overall caseload increased, and in the 1920s a Personal Application Division was set up within the office to handle applications for receivers made directly by private individuals instead of solicitors. This division was generally used where the cost of instructing a solicitor to make the application was disproportionate, relative to the value of the property to be managed. Within five years, up to half of all applications to the Lunacy Office came through the Personal Application Division, and the vast majority of these concerned very small estates indeed.[25] There are signs that this trend continued: by 1975, one memo recorded that fully 80 per cent of the cases brought to the Court of Protection (as the Lunacy Office had become in 1947) involved an annual income under £1,000.[26] To appoint a receiver to manage a person's property and affairs did require there to be *some* property to be managed, but not necessarily a great deal.

There is one last element of the expansion of the Lunacy Office to mention here, which has particular importance for Miss Alexander: the role of the Official Solicitor. Once described as 'an obscure figure in the ancient machinery of English justice', the job of Official Solicitor was not a glamorous one.[27] It had evolved as a result of the perceived need for children, lunatics, and the impoverished who became embroiled in legal proceedings in the Chancery Court to have some form of legal representation. By the twentieth century, the Official Solicitor was called upon to act in a variety of circumstances in which an independent lawyer or guardian of last resort was required. One such circumstance was where a person was thought to be incapable of managing their affairs, but no family member or other interested party was available to take action on their behalf. When such cases came to the attention of the Lunacy Office, the Master in Lunacy could instruct the Official Solicitor to make an application for his (always *his*, until 2019) own appointment as the incapable person's receiver.[28]

There could be understandable confusion about the distinction between the offices of the Official Solicitor and the Master in Lunacy.[29] The Master in Lunacy (and his senior assistants) made determinations of incapacity, appointed receivers, gave them instructions, dealt with their queries, and generally oversaw their activities, particularly by means of annual accounts to show how the incapable person's property was being managed. The Official Solicitor could be appointed as a receiver, and would then manage the incapable person's property with the aid of his staff, paying bills, preparing annual accounts, and ultimately answering to the Master in Lunacy. In practice, both offices were in correspondence with families, doctors, and carers for various reasons, and would correspond frequently with one another as well. The confusion about which office did what was compounded when, in the early 1930s, the Official Solicitor expanded his staff to include two 'visitors', analogous to the LCVs, who were still hard at work visiting those under the auspices of the Lunacy Office. These new Official Solicitor visitors began travelling the country, calling in to see all those for whom the Official Solicitor had been instructed to act as receiver. They reported back on matters of health, welfare, and general wellbeing, and suggested whether the Official Solicitor could or should do anything differently in his management of the case. One such person was Miss Alexander.

INTRODUCING MISS ALEXANDER

In the early years of the twentieth century, just around the time that Theobald was being offered the mastership in lunacy, Beatrice Alexander left home and moved to London. Exactly what prompted this move is hard to say. It was probably not an urgent need to find paying work: she was by this point already in her late twenties, the eldest daughter of a large, respectable, and reasonably financially secure farming family. Her father, Dennis, leased and managed several farms in Long Stratton, Norfolk, aided by his six sons, his wife, and his two daughters, as well as occasional employees. He served on the parish and county councils, cofounded the local agricultural show (at which his family frequently excelled), and was a much-admired figure in the community.[30] Miss Alexander's mother, Ruth, won prizes for her eggs, her butter, and the 'big boned turkeys from her celebrated pens', and both daughters initially followed in these footsteps.[31] 'In the class for two pounds of fresh butter, slightly salted, Miss Helen Alexander, of the Home Farm, Long Stratton, took first prize', I read in a 1902 edition of the *Norfolk News*, but 'her sister, Miss Beatrice, took second. Both their samples were excellent'.[32] Already invested in Miss Beatrice Alexander's fortunes, I was pleased to see that the positions were reversed four years later, after she had taken lessons at 'dairy class under the [Norfolk] Education Committee', and she went home with first prize.[33]

Farms, family, home-churned butter: it sounds idyllic – at least to someone like me, who has not spent much time up close and personal with cows. Perhaps Miss Alexander was less than charmed by the hard work of running a farmhouse; perhaps she sought new experiences and broader horizons beyond the village where she had grown up. In later years she was consistently fond of the countryside and reminisced warmly about farming life, but the realities of rural living for her as a young woman may have been less enjoyable – especially if marriage to a local farmer, the path followed by her younger sister, did not appeal.[34] If I had a little more than these few newspaper reports, then I might be able to stitch something together about ambition and aspiration, or about a woman who did not quite fit into rural Norfolk life, or even some tension between parent and daughter, or between siblings, or a heartbreak or scandal to push her out of her home town. The possibilities are almost endless; more melodramatic options are appealing, but no more likely for that.

There are no photographs of Miss Alexander in the many files about her, and no descriptions of her as a young woman anywhere in the available archives. In her retirement and in the years after being found incapable, she was characterised as rather reserved and shy, reluctant to meet new people, unsettled by change, and sometimes hesitant to express her own wishes. More than once, her nurse-companion described her as 'gentle'. She was said to be intelligent, well read, good conversational company, and extremely keen on billiards, gardening, and – after seeing her first one in 1955 – the television. She was always pleasant, well mannered, and 'likes to have everything very nice'.[35] With the domestic skills acquired in the Norfolk farmhouse of her youth, and her appreciation for quiet consistency and 'niceness', she may have been rather well suited to the role of housekeeper for a small urban household. She found this household in Queen Anne's Gate, an area of London close to Buckingham Palace and Westminster Abbey, in the home of Dr John Norton.

This may or may not have been Miss Alexander's first and only job outside of her childhood home, and she may or may not have arrived at a rather difficult time for the Norton family. Details, such as the exact year of her arrival in London, are thin on the ground. Her employer, Dr Norton, left a larger paper trail for this period thanks to his professional and somewhat unhappy personal life. The son of a Somerset carpenter, John Norton had done well for himself. He qualified as a doctor in 1889, took an additional diploma in public health, and developed a steady and successful, if not exactly glamorous, medical practice in London which included many years as a police surgeon.[36] He married twenty-two-year-old Mabel Nunn in 1898 and their son, Richard, was born the following year, but the marriage did not last. In 1909, Dr Norton was one of fewer than 600 people who successfully initiated 'expensive and complex' divorce proceedings.[37]

The adversarial nature of these proceedings meant that accusations and blame were compulsory, but there are signs that *Norton v Norton* was genuinely acrimonious. In what was read by some as a blackmail attempt, a man with whom Mrs Norton had allegedly had an affair encouraged her to 'beard the doctor with all the facts of the case, and try to get him to agree to an amicable separation on the threat of exposure'. Dr Norton, meanwhile, described in florid detail his wife's drug addiction, infidelity, and ongoing ill health, alleging that she was 'highly neurotic and hysterical'. Mrs Norton then responded by saying that her husband had 'treated her with unkindness and cruelty' for years, encouraging their young son to do likewise and causing her health to worsen. She also alleged at least one instance of physical violence. In court, this seems to have met with little sympathy. Although Dr Norton was instructed to make a financial contribution towards his wife's care in a nursing home for three months, the judge remarked rather cruelly that Mrs Norton's ill health was 'chiefly due to her own fault'.[38] The fact of the divorce remained somewhat shameful: Dr Norton described himself on the 1911 census as a widower, although his ex-wife was alive and perhaps well, or at least better than she had been, in the town of Exmouth.

Miss Alexander may already have been working for the Norton household in the midst of the divorce. Servants were mentioned in the divorce proceedings as sources of information, but they were not named. It is also possible – and perhaps more likely – that Miss Alexander was hired after the divorce was finalised, to give the household a fresh start and to take over its management once Mrs Norton's absence became permanent. Exactly how the vacancy for a housekeeper became known to her is impossible to say. Although Dr Norton had no obvious connection to Norfolk, such a connection may have existed. Miss Alexander could well have been employed as a result of personal contacts and pre-existing relationships: historian Lucy Delap has found that many women working in service 'found their first few jobs through their mother's intervention', or through other family or neighbourhood contacts.[39] At some stage, there certainly developed close ties between Dr Norton and the Alexander family. Mrs Ruth Alexander handcrafted a rug for Dr Norton, still in his possession at the end of his life, and one of Miss Alexander's brothers and his wife were occasional visitors to the Norton household in London. Dr Norton in turn left a substantial gift in his will to Miss Alexander's younger sister, Helen, suggesting strong affectionate bonds.[40] It seems likely that some kind of personal relationship between the families predated Miss Alexander's employment, prompted her move to London, and was sustained and enhanced by her position as Dr Norton's housekeeper as the years went by.

During Miss Alexander's years in London, the Norton household was a small one. Dr Norton kept a maid and a cook as well as a housekeeper, but his young son, Richard, was sent away to boarding school in Abingdon and then Brighton after the divorce, and did not always return to London during the holidays.[41] Daily life in London was no doubt governed to some extent by Dr Norton's professional schedule and commitments, but the good doctor's style of household management is a blank: little is known about interactions between male employers and their servants 'since it stimulated less social commentary' than women's struggles to assert domestic authority during the early twentieth century.[42] Miss Alexander's working life was unlikely to have borne much resemblance to the better-documented work of housekeepers in large country houses; experiences of domestic service in the twentieth century were very diverse.[43] Being a housekeeper, especially in an urban setting like London, could be a route other than marriage to greater freedom for women. Miss Alexander may have been one of those who, in historian Leonore Davidoff's words, 'found their horizons widened by their experience of service, by having witnessed new ways of living, by having been introduced to new tastes, new forms of beauty in the furnishing, decorations, flowers and gardens of the houses where they worked'.[44] Their London home was probably not especially grand and beautiful, but Miss Alexander undoubtedly fell in love with Dr Norton's house and garden in the Dorset village of Chilfrome, to which they moved after his retirement. To what extent this home reflected Dr Norton's temperament and tastes, or Miss Alexander's, or an evolving combination of the two, is a matter of speculation.

So, too, is the extent of any disruption to Miss Alexander's employment and daily life caused by the outbreak of war in 1914. What *is* clear is that Miss Alexander and Dr Norton shared heavy personal losses. Dennis Alexander, the second youngest of Miss Alexander's brothers, died at sea in 1915, aged only 18. Kenneth Alexander died in the Battle of the Somme the following year, and Frank Alexander died of tuberculosis the year after that. Frank had been serving with the 13th Battalion of the Australian Infantry when he fell ill, having emigrated down under before the war, but was the only one of the three brothers to be buried back in Long Stratton. Did Miss Alexander return to Norfolk for funerals and memorials? I hope so. She still spoke often about her lost brothers many decades later, and treasured keepsakes from them. Her own family tragedies were soon followed by the death of Richard Norton, who had left school for a cadetship at the Royal Military College and joined the 9th Battalion Norfolk Regiment in 1917. He died in action 'in the field. France or Belgium', two months before the armistice in November 1918, aged nineteen.[45] Dr Norton commemorated his only son with a memorial in the churchyard next to the house where he spent his retirement, shown in figure 1.1. Like Miss Alexander, he kept reminders of lost loved ones around him, with several paintings of Richard and his former wife hanging in his home.

This home was the Old Rectory, in Chilfrome. Dr Norton and Miss Alexander moved there in 1924, around the time that Dr Norton turned 60 and probably to mark his retirement from medical practice. The house had only very recently ceased to serve as the rectory proper, in 1923, when the benefices of Chilfrome and neighbouring village Cattistock were amalgamated. Described by its ecclesiastical sellers as a 'residence of quite moderate size', the property included a stable, garage, cowshed, 'pleasure grounds', kitchen garden, and meadows, plus a 'large detached cottage' in the grounds as well.[46] There are

Figure 1.1 Holy Trinity Church and churchyard in Chilfrome, Dorset, in August 2010.
The Old Rectory is just visible in the background.

no pictures of the house from this time, but photographs from the mid-1960s, one of which is shown in figure 1.2, show a substantial ivy-covered building surrounded by mature trees and large gardens. The cottage in the grounds was soon occupied by John and Mary Humphries, a younger married couple who were employed as gardener and cook respectively.

The village of Chilfrome was a small community of around a hundred residents. Many worked in dairy farming, making it a (welcome?) return to familiar territory for Miss Alexander. It was not a village of labourers, though: far from it. Near neighbours at the Old Rectory included a justice of the peace, a retired vice admiral, and an oil executive. The retired doctor was in good company, but there are the smallest hints that Dr Norton was not wholly absorbed and accepted into village life. The first indication of this is an absence of evidence. The local paper, always keen to report on the activities of councils, churches, societies, and local notables, does not mention him or his death at

Figure 1.2 The Old Rectory in 1965.

all, save for one brief note the year of his arrival.[47] Of course, in his retirement he may have preferred a quiet life without much civic engagement. Equally, his declining health may have prevented many activities of note. Or, as a relative newcomer to the district, Dr Norton may simply not have been sufficiently involved or well known in local life to merit a journalistic mention.

There is, though, a more direct intimation of disapproval recorded within Miss Alexander's Lunacy Office files, from an anonymous source. This source was most likely Dr Norton's own doctor, who played an important role in later events. The source reportedly said that 'Dr Norton was unfortunately inclined to drink and died from its effects, and he had influenced [Miss Alexander] to do the same thing'.[48] This comment appears as an aside, in the context of considering the characteristics of a suitable nurse-companion for Miss Alexander, and it is tantalising. It hints at a degree of community disapproval towards the goings-on at the Old Rectory, and perhaps regarding not only Dr Norton's habits in drink, but also the relationship between Dr Norton and his household staff.

The degree of intimacy between Dr Norton and Miss Alexander is an open question. After his death, Miss Alexander reportedly described Dr Norton as her 'dear doctor' or 'her beloved Dr', and treasured an amethyst necklace that he had once given to her. She also had a burial plot reserved next to his. Those around her half-jokingly described him as 'her (God) Dr Norton': his position in her memories was exalted indeed.[49] The two lived together for twenty-five years, and her happy memories along with his unusual generosity to her in his will indicate that they were close. Dr Norton's will, made in 1928, left his entire estate to Miss Alexander for her lifetime benefit. She received all of his household goods outright, and was free to continue living in the Old Rectory for as long as she wished. She was also to receive a steady income from his investments, worth about £8 a week in the late 1930s: more than she was likely to have earned as a housekeeper, and enough to provide for a comfortable retirement. It was perhaps not entirely surprising that Dr Norton would make Miss Alexander the primary beneficiary of his estate, given her many years of service and his own lack of immediate family.[50] It was also not unusual for employers to deliver some form of pension to current or retired staff in their wills, albeit not usually on this scale.

And yet, it was really very generous. An administrative memorandum from the 1950s describes Dr Norton as Miss Alexander's 'Husband' – a slip of the pen by a clerk who knew them only in the abstract, or a reflection of something that was widely acknowledged but not usually committed to paper? The inaccessibility of divorce was the most common cause of cohabitation in the early twentieth century. With no such legal impediment, is it not unlikely that Dr Norton and Miss Alexander would have lived as husband and wife without obtaining the social and legal clarity of the marriage ceremony?[51] Is a romance improbable? They could simply have been an employer and employee who viewed each other affectionately after many years in each other's company. Dr Norton, fifteen years her senior, may have adopted a paternal role towards Miss Alexander that included a sense of responsibility towards her, which took the shape of long-term financial support. (Perhaps he always knowingly underpaid her, and finally felt a squeeze of guilt as he made his will. He did not exit his marriage covered in glory, after all.) I suspect that Miss Alexander was not 'just' a housekeeper: I suspect that they were close friends of a sort, for whom the employer-housekeeper designation was a convenient shorthand. I suspect that this was a mutually beneficial relationship that included elements of financial support, domestic care, and companionship: a relationship that slips past the narrow categories of official documents. Suspicions abound.

Of course, Dr Norton and Miss Alexander's relationship could have in-cluded all of these elements, at different times and in various combinations. For one version of this story, it doesn't matter in the slightest: all that matters is that Miss Alexander came into some independent wealth when Dr Norton died. Their relationship has little direct impact upon the events surrounding Miss Alexander's legal incapacity, but it still matters to me because Dr Norton clearly mattered to Miss Alexander. The little that I know about their rela-tionship, and indeed about her twenty-five years as his housekeeper and the years before that, is a salutary reminder of just how much is unknowable, and how much of her life remains untold in this account of it.

Their relationship may also have shaped events following Dr Norton's death in 1934, after ten years at the Old Rectory. Miss Alexander was fifty-six years old, and suddenly alone. If Dr Norton had not been fully embraced by the local community – whether because of his drinking habits, his health, or his own preference for a more private retirement – then what was Miss Alexan-der's status in this place? As highlighted by Davidoff in her work on domestic service, marriage, and gender, Miss Alexander's whole life 'from material sup-port to human surroundings' had relied upon Dr Norton for a quarter of a century, whether in the role of employee or quasi-wife (or something in be-tween or distinct from both). His death was a momentous rupture.[52] Miss Alexander found herself without close friends at the very moment that her life was turned upside down.

Except, of course, she was not *entirely* without friends. The gardener and the cook, John Humphries and his wife, Mary, were still there in the cottage in the grounds, and were more than willing to remain in post and in residence. They had already been working there for ten or so years; presumably their work was good enough, and it was not beyond Miss Alexander's new means to employ them with the money she received from Dr Norton's investments. Certainly, given the size of the house and grounds, she would need some help. Who better than those she already knew, and who had known the Old Rectory with Dr Norton? If Mr and Mrs Humphries stayed, she would have some fa-miliar faces nearby, with whom she shared memories of her beloved doctor. It would avoid the potentially difficult business of trying to hire new help, which was not at all easy in a rural spot with no large number of prospective servants, particularly for someone like Miss Alexander who was anxious about meeting new people and wary of change. All in all, the decision to maintain the status quo after Dr Norton's death was wholly understandable.

Miss Alexander was not unaware that this arrangement might bring problems. The Midland Bank had been appointed as executor and trustee of Dr Norton's estate, and representatives of the bank came to meet with her at the Old Rectory straight after Dr Norton's funeral. Their recollection of that meeting was that Miss Alexander 'feared that John Humphries and Mrs M A Humphries his wife (who had been Dr Norton's Cook) would get the better of her unless their position was made perfectly clear'.[53] It sounds as though she wanted help around the house and garden and perhaps also some companionship, but foresaw that her relationship with Mr and Mrs Humphries could become complicated. Miss Alexander must have known the Humphries well from their decade of living and working together: she may have recognised the potential for personality clashes. It is also easy to imagine that the shift in social terms, from all three being employed by Dr Norton, to Miss Alexander in her new position of affluence employing the others, could be an awkward one to navigate. Miss Alexander may have recognised her potential isolation in the village, without close friends or family to whom she could turn for advice or support, as she adjusted to this new phase of her life.

Various retrospective accounts from bank employees of their meetings with Miss Alexander are the only intimation that after Dr Norton's death she was 'not entirely normal'.[54] It is not clear what exactly anyone meant by this, and it was expressed only with hindsight, after Miss Alexander had come under the purview of the Lunacy Office and been found incapable of managing her own affairs. Miss Alexander's deviation from normality was certainly not enough to merit consultation with such a thing as a doctor in 1934. The Midland Bank did make contact with her sister, Helen, back in Norfolk, to ask whether a family member could come to live with her. Helen, now Mrs Baldry, replied in the negative. Copies of this exchange do not survive to show how the question was asked and answered, but Helen Baldry's husband and brothers were all farmers with interests quite literally rooted in the land many hundreds of miles away. Her children were still at school, too young to relocate in order to become companions to a distant aunt. The practical difficulties facing any of the Norfolk family moving to Dorset to take up a nebulous role as minder or companion were considerable. It may also have seemed a strange and unnecessary request, if Miss Alexander's family had not previously thought of her as in any way 'not entirely normal'.

After nearly three decades of geographical separation, it is not clear how well the Alexander family members still knew one another. Miss Alexander was the only surviving sibling who lived at a distance. The rest of the Alexander clan remained in and around Long Stratton. Geographical distance may have encouraged other kinds of distance, particularly after the deaths of their parents in 1927 and 1933. The lives of the siblings may simply have diverged, amidst the everyday worries and demands of spouses, children, and work.

In the years following Dr Norton's death, Miss Alexander lost touch with her family completely. She and her siblings stopped corresponding, which was, so Helen Baldry thought, down to a rather callous lack of interest on her sister's part.[55] Alternative readings, with the benefit of hindsight, might see it as evidence of Mr and Mrs Humphries's increasing involvement in Miss Alexander's life, which may have included some desire to isolate her from her family. It could also have been a symptom of Miss Alexander's deteriorating wellbeing, if indeed such a deterioration took place. In any case, this estrangement from her large Norfolk family shaped later impressions of Miss Alexander as highly vulnerable, as chapter 3 explains in more detail, and it was why the Official Solicitor rather than her next of kin had to act as her receiver.

One account of events leading up to the summoning of the Lunacy Office was given by Dr Humphrey Meigh Stephenson, physician and possible friend to the late Dr Norton, and likely anonymous source on matters of drink at the Old Rectory. Stephenson lived in the next village over with his wife and children, and was to become a significant figure in Miss Alexander's affairs. He later explained that he had 'attended Dr Norton during his last illness and that he [Dr Norton] had requested him to keep an eye on the welfare of Miss Alexander'. Stephenson agreed to do so, and fulfilled this promise by paying a visit to the Old Rectory about once a month after Dr Norton's death. He quickly became unhappy with what he saw there. Although Mr and Mrs Humphries had been permitted to stay on at the cottage on the strict understanding that they were Miss Alexander's employees, neither this hierarchy nor the separate living arrangements proved durable.[56]

Over the course of a few years, Mrs Humphries came to occupy the main house with Miss Alexander. Stephenson observed that her husband seemed to live there too, more often than not, and at various times they were joined by up to three of their adult children, an elderly parent, and several infant grandchildren. None of the Humphries family seemed to have any other source of income beyond their wages from Miss Alexander, Stephenson noted with displeasure, and the arrangements for this seemed to have fallen into disarray. Miss Alexander was seen in threadbare clothes, and some of the furniture that she had inherited from her dear doctor disappeared from the Old Rectory and reappeared in other homes around the neighbourhood, sold for ready cash. Eventually, Miss Alexander was rarely seen at all on her own, without one of the Humphries by her side, even when withdrawing money from her own bank account – which she began to do regularly and to the greatest possible extent. The implication was clear: Mr and Mrs Humphries had taken over the Old Rectory and Miss Alexander with it, for their own gain.

RESPONDING TO MENTAL WEAKNESS

The Humphries family were not well regarded by local authority figures. During their fact-finding missions to Dorset in 1939, representatives of the Lunacy Office and Official Solicitor gathered information on the family from the local vicar's wife, police constable, and neighbours of the Old Rectory. If anyone did have anything positive to say, it was not recorded. The police knew of nothing concrete, but had heard 'various stories of drinking'.[57] (Stories told by Dr Stephenson, I wonder?) The Humphries were known by more than stories to the Dorset Voluntary Association for Mental Welfare (DVAMW). Mental welfare associations such as this were branches of a Central Association, formed in 1913 in response to the Mental Deficiency Act of that year. As historian Jonathan Toms has put it, these 'local voluntary organizations could appoint themselves experts in surveying the local population and assessing their mental competence'.[58] Such self-appointed expert-volunteers for the DVAMW undertook enquiries into and supervision of 'defectives' in their area, and two of the younger Humphries had been the object of such enquiries in the past. Although they had not been found 'defective', the DVAMW's secretary, Miss Stevenson, maintained that at least one was 'just on the borderline'.[59]

In reporting this, Miss Stevenson was not just providing diagnostic information. She set about painting a rich picture of a family and a lifestyle of which she thoroughly disapproved. The young Miss Humphries was not simply on the borderline of mental defect; she was, as Miss Stevenson put it, an 'undesirable girl who has one illegitimate child by a gipsy' and another on the way. She was 'a thief & drinks like her family'.[60] Connecting the 'mental calibre' of the Humphries family members to their moral fibre, Miss Stevenson reproduced a model of mental defect that had come to prominence in the first few decades of the twentieth century. At this time, anxiety about mental defect had strongly associated feeble-mindedness with assorted social problems including the degeneracy of the 'race', illegitimacy, criminality, and drunkenness. The sexual behaviour of so-called feeble-minded women was a particular worry, and there is some evidence of strong support in Dorset for eugenic measures including the sterilisation of those deemed mentally defective.[61] With references to borderline mental defect, children born out of wedlock and fathered by a 'gipsy', plus family habits of thieving and drinking, Miss Stevenson's comments bundle together all of these concerns admirably clearly, and show their persistence in mental deficiency work in the community at the end of the 1930s. Such comments also strongly implied that the actions of the Humphries family must be malicious, bordering on criminal, and their words could not be trusted.

Miss Alexander, on the other hand, was seen very differently. While the Humphries family was thoroughly disreputable, she was their pitiable prey. Despite also being 'not entirely normal' in some estimations, and despite those fleeting rumours of bad household habits in alcohol, she was at no time described in the same terms as the Humphries, as a case of borderline mental deficiency with drunkenness and general bad conduct. The language describing Miss Alexander is compassionate and sympathetic, if sometimes also patronising or reflecting frustration at her role of 'willing victim'.[62] If she drank, it was only because Dr Norton (and then Mr and Mrs Humphries) had led her astray. While Mrs Humphries was described as 'coarse' or 'slattenly [*sic*] and blousy', Miss Alexander was 'a pleasant little lady' leading a 'wretched' existence and in need of 'friendly care'. The Humphries family embodied a raft of social ills; Miss Alexander was a 'poor soul' and 'unfortunate lady' in a 'deplorable' situation. The Humphries family needed to be put in their place while she needed help, even though she said quite the opposite.[63]

Such contrasting views of the Humphries and Miss Alexander were bolstered by a range of considerations, including matters of money and social class. Although Miss Alexander did not own the Old Rectory outright, her right to occupy it for life coupled with her comfortable income had brought her considerable independence. If she wanted to be idle (or drunk) she could afford it; the same could not be said of the Humphries. More to the point, her comfortable retirement had been funded by the late Dr Norton, in recognition of her contribution to and status in his life. She had been his housekeeper, a cut above the position of cook or gardener. The Humphries did not have this status; they had not lived in the Old Rectory with the good doctor; they had received nothing in his will. By living in the Old Rectory and spending Dr Norton's money, the family looked as though they were interfering with his wishes. Miss Alexander had received the late doctor's blessing to live a comfortable, financially independent life, and in so doing she had acquired some of his social standing. Mr and Mrs Humphries had not.

Perhaps just as important was the fact that Miss Alexander had not previously been associated in any official way with mental or moral defect. This is not to say that her state of mind necessarily changed on or around the time of Dr Norton's death. Rather, she had lived for many years exactly as was expected and desired, working in a domestic setting and showing herself able and willing to look after herself. Her mental weakness, if any had previously existed, did not lead her towards disruptive social deviance. As her neighbours saw it, Miss Alexander's unhappy situation by 1939 was a little bit to do with her own weakness of mind or excessively gentle character – she *had* allowed the Humphries family to move in to the Old Rectory and take advantage of her, after all. But it was a lot more to do with extrinsic forces that had changed her circumstances and brought her low, leaving her alone and vulnerable to Mr and Mrs Humphries's machinations. Sympathy towards Miss Alexander reflected perceptions of a kind of mental weakness that was very much worsened, if not wholly created, by her environment. Although there was probably little awareness of the exact nature or implications of capacity law within the community around the Old Rectory, this community's willingness to engage with the Lunacy Office and the Official Solicitor suggests a firm belief that Miss Alexander needed help – perhaps even that a woman like her had a right to some form of protection from the state.

In contrast, claims of borderline mental defect within the Humphries family, with criminality and drunkenness permeating the whole family, insinuated a very different problem. Historian Mathew Thomson has argued that new laws and policies surrounding mental defect in the first half of the twentieth century reflected an acknowledgement of some element of state responsibility towards those classed as mentally defective, but this responsibility was shouldered primarily because of anxiety about their socially disruptive potential, and not because of any right they had to care and assistance.[64] Investigations into mental defect within the Humphries family, and subsequent hostile commentary concerning their dealings with Miss Alexander, reflect this kind of motivation for intervention. In the end, it was Miss Alexander and not any member of the Humphries family who came under permanent supervision and control, but this was enabled by different legal structures that addressed mental deficiency only indirectly. Concern about mental weakness and choices about how to implement mental health law (and which laws to use) could play out in very different ways.

In deciding what to do, those around Miss Alexander had to interpret her decisions and her relationship with the Humphries family. The common conclusion was that she was so weak and timid that she could not stand up to them. The Humphries family were deemed disreputable, greedy, and cruel, and had taken advantage of her, intimidating Miss Alexander to such an extent that her decisions – to let them move in to the Old Rectory, to allow the extended family to live there too, to give them money beyond wages – were made in fear and did not really reflect her true wishes. These seem like logical explanations for the events at the Old Rectory, or, from the perspectives of Miss Alexander and Mr and Mrs Humphries, 'rational strategies for social negotiation', as historian Shannon McSheffrey has put it.[65]

My own interpretation is different, but then again, it serves a different purpose: it aims to present these individuals in more rounded terms, and to suggest a wider range of possibilities behind the events at the Old Rectory. Events and actions might have been, in McSheffrey's words, 'motivated by unreason or emotion, or by a different kind of self-interest' that does not seem rational or logical at first glance.[66] Emotion must have played a role in Miss Alexander's decisions. A form of unreason is also not out of the question, whether fleeting or more long-lasting. Did Dr Norton ask his own doctor to keep an eye on her because he knew very well that she would not cope as the head of a household on her own? Or because he perceived some deterioration in her capabilities, as they both aged, that caused him concern? Or, did Dr Norton's death leave her distraught and disturbed, unable to think clearly about her present and future?[67] Did she retain the services of Mr and Mrs Humphries out of a sense of loyalty and friendship, a reluctance to rock the boat, a fear of angering them, a dread of being alone, a belief that they would help and look after her, or a desire to recreate happier times? Did she want the Midland Bank to tell the Humphries quite clearly that they were her employees, not her equals, because she foresaw the difficulties associated with her changing role, because she relished the new powers that her inheritance had given her over them, because she disliked or feared them, or because the bank staff suggested it? Or was she under the impression that to remove them from her life would be morally wrong, or practically impossible? Did she welcome their advice and trust them absolutely with her money? Was she confused, overwhelmed, heartbroken? Was she unable to identify exactly what she wanted to do, let alone how to express or enact it?

All of these options are plausible. I think they all had some part to play. I also think that Mr and Mrs Humphries are not so easily condemned. Like Stephenson, they claimed that they had promised Dr Norton to look after his housekeeper after his death; unlike Stephenson, they lived alongside Miss Alexander and may have come to realise that she should not be alone in the Old Rectory, or that she needed help and encouragement with everyday tasks like going to the bank.[68] Their involvement with her may, at the very least, have begun as a genuine desire to provide care and companionship – even if the quality of their relationship with her changed as time went by. But as the spectre of the Lunacy Office began to loom over Miss Alexander's future in 1939, there was no space for any such uncertainty or plurality. Almost exactly four years after Dr Norton's death, Miss Alexander would be found incapable of managing her affairs under the terms of section 116(d) of the Lunacy Act of 1890, 'by reason of infirmity caused by disease or age'. For this to be possible, her decisions to live with the Humphries family and to share her wealth with them had to become the product of an infirm mind. Decisive steps to intervene required a clear picture of vulnerability, but legal interpretations of her situation, her decisions, and her state of mind, like their historical counterparts, had to be built on uncertain ground.

2

❀

TURNING TO THE COURTS

Miss Alexander's situation was brought to the attention of the Lunacy Office in April 1939 by Dr Humphrey Stephenson. Having promised the late Dr Norton to 'keep an eye' on Miss Alexander, Stephenson was true to his word and visited the Old Rectory regularly. Over time, he became increasingly worried about Miss Alexander's living conditions there, her relationship with Mr and Mrs Humphries, and their behaviour towards her. He remonstrated with the household, but to no avail. He found himself in a difficult position. He clearly disliked the Humphries and thought that they were behaving very badly, but there was nothing exactly criminal going on, so it was hardly a matter for the police. It was not his house, and not his place to give them orders. As for Miss Alexander, she was entitled to make her own decisions, even if they struck him as unwise or even contrary to her own best interests. Ultimately, the question that presented itself was whether he could do anything to 'rescue' Miss Alexander, even though she was a 'willing victim' who did not seem to want to rescue herself.[1]

The Lunacy Office emerged as one possible answer. As the previous chapter described, it was experiencing a boom-time during the 1930s, with numbers of applications for its interventions rising year on year. It was bigger and better known than ever before, aided by rising numbers of people with bank accounts, pensions, insurance policies, and other assets that they might become incapable of managing. Even so, Miss Alexander's circumstances were notably different from those of most of its 'patients', and this chapter begins by reflecting on these more typical cases against which Miss Alexander's stands out in sharp relief. It outlines what kinds of people usually made applications to the Lunacy Office and why, highlighting the importance of family members and, to a lesser extent, people acting in a professional capacity. The contrast between Miss Alexander's case and its less exceptional counterparts draws useful attention to the contours of the more typical Lunacy Office case.

The fact that Miss Alexander *did* come to the attention of the Lunacy Office, despite her atypical circumstances, was entirely down to Dr Stephenson himself. He is the only general practitioner within the archived case files to initiate receivership proceedings, and the only non-family member to do so in a personal rather than professional capacity. He was unusual in several further respects, each of which may have informed his decisions and the subsequent direction of Miss Alexander's life: he had a family connection to the Lunacy Office, his youngest son was 'mentally defective', and he was a member of the British Union of Fascists (BUF). Delving into this final aspect of Stephenson's life involves dwelling on dislike and its consequences, and it becomes particularly obvious that this account is made up of both past actors and events, and present feelings and views.[2]

This chapter concludes with a look at one final unusual aspect of Miss Alexander's case: the immediate cause of the application to the Lunacy Office. There was no marked deterioration in Miss Alexander's health and no sudden change in her mental state, nor were there any urgent financial matters that required attention. There was an inheritance causing problems of a sort, albeit not the same kind of problems that generated the family antagonisms seen in nineteenth-century lunacy inquisitions. The disagreement that prompted this unusual application to the Lunacy Office was of another kind altogether.

LUNACY OFFICE APPLICANTS

How did people usually come to the attention of the Lunacy Office? In his study of Commissions in Lunacy in the nineteenth century, Akihito Suzuki locates requests for this kind of legal intervention firmly in the hands of the family members of alleged lunatics,[3] and families certainly remained prominent as applicants for receivers throughout the twentieth century. Parents, spouses, children, siblings, nieces, and nephews were all very frequently involved in sending preliminary enquiries to the Lunacy Office and then filling out the paperwork to complete an application. Understandably, the applicant was usually the nearest relative in terms of both geography and relationship, who had the opportunity to observe their family member's mental state and was sufficiently well informed to know that there might be property or assets that required attention.

Some examples from Lunacy Office case files help to flesh out this picture. Parents, spouses, and adult children were the most regular applicants to the Lunacy Office, although nieces and nephews, siblings, and uncles and aunts were also commonplace, usually making an appearance when there was no closer family. When the immediate next of kin was untraceable, living abroad, unwilling to get involved, or unwell, more distant relations might step in. Edith Phillips's father filled out the application for his daughter's receivership instead of her husband, for the very practical reason that nobody had seen or heard from Mr Edith Phillips for several years. Similarly, Doris Perry was separated from her husband and had been so for some time, so it was her young daughter who first wrote to the Lunacy Office with concerns about her mother.[4] Esther Cohen's sons were living in New York when she was admitted to the private mental hospital Chiswick House in 1920, and so it was her brother, a London-based barrister, who applied to the Lunacy Office for a receiver.[5]

Of Clara Bathurst's seven nieces and nephews, the one who submitted an application to the Court of Protection was the nephew who had lived closest to her in recent years, who had moved in to her home for a time to keep her company after she was widowed, and who always hosted her at Christmas. He had previously held a power of attorney for her, and was well aware that there were debts and other financial matters that needed attention as her health began to fail.[6] Similarly, of Mary Ross's two adult sons, the one who eventually wrote to the Lunacy Office was Percy, who had been living closer to her home than his brother and had moved in with her as she began to struggle to manage on her own.[7]

Miss Alexander's geographical distance from her family and her increasing estrangement from them following Dr Norton's death therefore removed one very common route by which people came to the attention of the Lunacy Office. That said, the twentieth century also saw much greater engagement in the process of appointing receivers amongst those acting in a professional capacity of some kind. Such professionals would generally make every effort to trace family first of all, but if this yielded nothing then they made applications to the Lunacy Office themselves, as a representative of their employer. This growing involvement of professional applicants may have been thanks to growing attention amongst a range of welfare professionals to matters of the mind. It must also have been connected to more widespread awareness of the business of the Lunacy Office, the (relatively) cheap and quick receivership process, the purpose of mental capacity law, and the need for formal steps to safeguard (and access) the money of the mentally infirm.

The earliest example within the twentieth-century archives of an application to the Lunacy Office from someone acting in their professional capacity is from 1912. Andrew Down had been admitted to the London County Asylum in Hanwell the year before, as a person of unsound mind. He had no known relatives, and in addition to an annuity from the government of New Zealand, he had several hundred pounds in savings to his name. A representative of the London County Council, which was responsible for the Hanwell Asylum, wrote to the Lunacy Office and successfully requested that the Official Solicitor be appointed as Mr Down's receiver. The Official Solicitor would then be able to pay a regular sum to Hanwell Asylum from Mr Down's income, to cover the cost of his care. A similar sequence of events played out at the Essex County Asylum, home to Ann Nightingale, and the Suffolk District Asylum, where Emma Brothers had lived for many years. In both cases, a clerk on behalf of the local poor law Board of Guardians contacted the Lunacy Office to request the appointment of a receiver for their patient and then some form of payment from their patient's assets, either immediately or in the future.[8]

After the Local Government Act of 1929 and its restructuring of health and welfare services, different personnel within the machinery of welfare began to appear as applicants in Lunacy Office records instead of these clerks for poor law Boards of Guardians.[9] 'Public Assistance', the successor to the poor law, became the responsibility of local government and so county council and county borough council officers became involved in Lunacy Office applications from the 1930s onwards. West Sussex County Council applied to the Lunacy Office in 1936 regarding Constance Parker, a patient in Graylingwell Hospital there, and a representative of Surrey County Council wrote to the Lunacy Office about Elizabeth Hoskins, an elderly patient at Frimley and Camberley District Hospital. In both cases, as with the poor law Boards of Guardians before them, the council's primary objective was to obtain some form of payment from these patients' property, for services rendered.

Even when it appeared at first glance that a local council took action because of concerns about financial abuse, the underlying motivation was still to secure payment for council services. Middlesex County Council wrote to the Lunacy Office in 1940 to express their concerns about Henry Millar, a voluntary patient since 1934 at Shenley Mental Hospital. His adult children were accused of dealing improperly with their father's assets, transferring his house and bank accounts into their own names without his knowledge or consent. A council officer noted that Mr Millar had once been very wealthy, but now had nothing to his name and was costing the ratepayers no less than £344 a year. The officer sought to have a receiver appointed, who would then investigate whether these past transactions had been valid. Unluckily for the council, Mr Millar was found to have been perfectly able to make his own decisions in recent years and must therefore have freely agreed to his children taking ownership of his house and money. His receiver, the Official Solicitor, could only conclude that the council should have acted much sooner to prevent Mr Millar from dissipating his estate before becoming mentally incapable.[10]

Central government might also take action on rare occasions, when a person's apparent incapacity intruded on government activities. This was particularly common with war pensions, since a not insignificant number of those found incapable over the middle decades of the twentieth century had served in the First or Second World War. One such person, Ernest Jones, had been hospitalised since 1917 and was in receipt of a pension awarded 'in respect of unsoundness of mind, attributable to or aggravated by service in the war'. Faced with a need to make arrangements for his pension to be used to cover the cost of his residence in hospital, and in the absence of any known family to deal with these matters, the Ministry of Pensions wrote to the Lunacy Office directly in 1934 to initiate its involvement in Mr Jones's affairs.[11]

In later decades, applications concerning those without known family were more likely to come directly from those working in healthcare and social welfare, although many were still a part of the machinery of local government.[12] Social workers, welfare officers, and medical officers of health all became involved in receivership applications from the 1940s onwards. The area welfare officer advised a firm of solicitors acting for Bertha Knock's landlord to contact the Court of Protection in 1954, since Miss Knock had been hospitalised and it seemed likely that she was no longer capable of dealing with her rental payments.[13] The geriatric almoner at the Whittington Hospital applied for a receiver for her patient, Annie Gilliam, who was being transferred into a nursing home in 1961, and it was Mrs Rigby, assistant social worker at Winwick Hospital near Warrington who alerted the Court of Protection to a troubling situation concerning their patient, eighty-year-old Mary Walmsley, whose nephew was suspected of dealing inappropriately with her money. The Swansea medical officer of health made contact in 1968 about Edith Rees, who was newly resident in a nursing home in his district, and a social worker from Brighton made the application for a receiver for hospital patient Beatrice Grant in 1973.[14]

This shift in the identity of applicants to the Lunacy Office, from poor law Boards of Guardians to local (or occasionally central) government welfare departments and then to public health and social workers, mirrors the shifting structures of public social care in England over these years. Such care became increasingly professionalised, and increasingly closely associated with health-care rather than relief from poverty. It also hints at changing motivations behind those receivership applications. Prior to the more substantial welfare state established in the late 1940s, those who had no means to pay for hospital or other residential care came under the aegis of poor law or charitable services, and then local government services. When these bodies discovered that someone in their care did in fact have some income or property, it was very much in their interests to secure it. Even when such assets were minimal and were required for their owner's immediate personal use, Boards of Guardians and local authorities could and did request in their applications to the Lunacy Office that they benefit from a charge over this property, so that their costs for providing care could potentially be reimbursed at a later date.[15] With the arrival of centrally funded medical treatment under the National Health Service Act of 1946, the question of recouping fees for hospital care was largely removed. A few years later, the National Assistance Act revised the terms under which councils provided residential accommodation for those in need of other types of care, with the result that fees were means tested and charging orders were no longer granted to local authorities, as a rule.[16]

One major incentive for intervening in the property of those in hospitals or nursing homes was thus removed. Applications for receivers from the 1950s onwards from medical and social care workers very rarely generated any economic benefit to the organisations that employed them, which must be why it fell to staff directly involved in welfare, rather than the keepers of council or institutional purse strings, to initiate these applications.

The willingness of social care professionals to initiate legal proceedings on behalf of their clients is open to a number of interpretations. For one, the larger welfare state that emerged after the Second World War may have encouraged a belief that it should be the role of welfare workers, broadly defined, to concern themselves with wellbeing in a wide sense – including the protection of someone's money, home, and belongings. Hospital and health care workers may also have become more aware of the potential for financial harm to befall vulnerable people, or were perhaps better able to perceive vulnerability to such harms. The involvement of this cohort may also suggest an ever-widening circle of professions with some awareness of the law and procedure surrounding mental capacity, much as Lunacy Office officials had speculated in the 1930s.

This latter point is borne out by signs that local solicitors as well as health-care workers were increasingly aware of the role of the Lunacy Office, and sometimes took it upon themselves to make contact when they were concerned about a client's capacity and property. Former headmistress Ellen Quigley had suffered a breakdown in 1928 and was admitted to Peckham House, a private hospital in South London; Mr Potter, a solicitor who had acted for her in the past, swiftly applied to the Lunacy Office for the Official Solicitor to be appointed as her receiver to take care of her home and possessions.[17] The solicitor dealing with the estate of Basil Evans's late mother got in touch with the Lunacy Office to request that a receiver be appointed for Mr Evans, since he seemed unable to manage his inheritance independently and his remaining family either lived overseas or apparently showed no interest.[18] The situation was similar for Sir Roland Gwynne, whose health had been declining for some time and who was admitted to the Berrow Nursing and Convalescent Home in Eastbourne in the mid-1960s. The solicitors dealing with a Gwynne family trust initiated receivership proceedings once they felt confident that Sir Roland was no longer able to make decisions about the trust himself.[19]

Notably, there are no examples in the archives of applications initiated by bank managers or bank clerks. These were the only people who retrospectively reported professional concerns about Miss Alexander's situation, and would have been well placed to alert the Lunacy Office. According to Lunacy Office staff, after all, by the mid-1930s 'the functions of the department are becoming more widely known to Banks, Insurance Companies, Trustees, and others'.[20] Miss Alexander had opened a new bank account in 1937 after inheriting a sum of money from her late father, and saw branch manager Mr H. P.

Trueman and his chief clerk A. G. Sage regularly thereafter, until the account was empty and the inheritance spent. Messrs Trueman and Sage later reported their dissatisfaction with the influence that an unidentified man and woman, the man 'of gardener class', seemed to wield over Miss Alexander when she visited the bank. They took steps to separate Miss Alexander from her companions in order to speak to her privately, but the idea of alerting the Lunacy Office did not occur to them.[21] Nor did it occur to the Midland Bank staff dealing with Dr Norton's will trust, despite Miss Alexander's apparent concerns during their meeting about her ability to remain independent of Mr and Mrs Humphries. Whether because of a lack of knowledge of the Lunacy Office, or a perception that mental incapacity in its legal sense could only apply to those in mental hospitals or nursing homes, none of these bank employees took any further action.

The idea that legal incapacity would only be found amongst those in institutions was not wholly misplaced. All of the above examples of applications to the Lunacy Office by those acting in a professional capacity shared one important feature: those whose mental capacity was in doubt were all in 'mental hospitals', as asylums were coming to be called, or nursing homes. Although the Lunacy Office had nothing to do with most people in asylums, hospitals, or other places for residential care, a great many of those with receivers in place *were* institutionalised. Comprehensive data is lacking, but the archives are indicative. Prior to the Mental Health Act of 1959, fully 80 per cent of the archived Lunacy Office and Official Solicitor case files concerned those who had been 'certified' and involuntarily detained as persons of unsound mind.[22] Of the remaining 20 per cent, about half were in a hospital or nursing home as a voluntary patient. Some spent the best part of a lifetime in these institutions, entering in their twenties or thirties with diagnoses of delusional insanity, mania, epilepsy, melancholia, or mental defect and remaining there for decades, usually until they died. A smaller but not insignificant group were hospitalised for their final years only, with terms such as 'senility', 'confusional insanity', and 'dementia' next to their names. A handful were eventually discharged from mental hospitals as 'recovered' or 'improved', although this often took a matter of years rather than months. Discharge from hospital would prompt enquiry from the Lunacy Office into whether the person was still incapable, or whether they could be 'restored to their property', as the terminology went.[23] Perhaps surprisingly, some of those who 'recovered' preferred to leave their finances in the hands of a receiver, cheerfully receiving annual visits from the Lord Chancellor's official visitors to their home and tolerating the fees that the Lunacy Office took.[24]

The high prevalence of institutionalisation amongst those found incapable was something new for the twentieth century. In the past, those subject to Commissions in Lunacy had only occasionally been confined in asylums.[25] At first glance, this nineteenth-century picture may seem surprising: it was the golden age of the asylum, after all. But Commissions in Lunacy tended to involve the very wealthy, for whom paid care at home was possible and often preferred. As the Lunacy Office increasingly became involved in the affairs of those of much more modest means in the twentieth century, this began to change. For many of those grappling with severe physical or mental infirmities, and their families, home care was simply unaffordable and an institution was the only option.

Nevertheless, care in the community was still very common throughout the twentieth century. As Peter Bartlett and David Wright have suggested, 'care outside the walls of the asylum remained the primary response of industrial societies to the problem of the mentally disordered from 1750 to the present day'. This was often provided by family members, sometimes with an element of paid help where means allowed.[26] It is telling, therefore, that those in institutions came to dominate the work of the Lunacy Office to such an extent. It suggests that knowledge of the Lunacy Office remained somewhat limited, and only those interacting in some way with mental hospitals, nursing homes, lawyers, or welfare officers would become aware of it. For many of those who could have been found incapable of managing their own affairs, perhaps even the majority, they received care at home from their family in terms of material and financial support, and the issue of mental capacity and lunacy law simply never came up. Some may have been under the guardianship and supervision for which the Mental Deficiency Acts provided, but the majority were probably not. The notion that those receiving care in the home might be vulnerable to harm, and particularly financial abuse, was only very gradually beginning to arise.

Within the archives, only about 10 per cent of those found incapable were, like Miss Alexander, living in their own homes. This small cohort included a good number receiving round-the-clock care and supervision, organised and sometimes provided directly by family members.[27] As chapter 4 discusses in

more detail, engaged and involved family members were central to the provision of care, but this brief overview of applications to the Lunacy Office indicates that close family was also important when it came to making contact
with the Lunacy Office – especially for those who were not in hospitals or
other institutions, and would therefore escape much official attention. Of the
small number of those found incapable who were not hospitalised, it was a
family member who initiated proceedings with the Lunacy Office each and
every time – *except* when it came to Miss Alexander.

Miss Alexander lived independently in the beautiful Old Rectory. With no
institutional fees to be paid, no institutional staff members paying attention
to her state of mind or personal affairs, and no institutionalisation to send a
strong message to all and sundry that she might not be able to fend for herself,
she was much less likely to prompt thoughts of the Lunacy Office in those
she met. For the Lunacy Office, Miss Alexander's circumstances were not run
of the mill. Nevertheless, they were not inconceivable; they did not prompt
any particular comment or surprise, as far as the archival records show, and
Stephenson's request for help was certainly not dismissed out of hand. Sitting
somewhere near the margins of Lunacy Office work, Miss Alexander's case
gives a sign of the full extent of mental capacity law in 1939. The Lunacy Office
was sufficiently accessible and well known, and took a broad enough view of
its potential 'patients', that anyone at all could, in theory, approach it about
anyone at all.

UNDERSTANDING DR STEPHENSON

Although the Lunacy Office was by 1939 very much open to all, it was still rare
for someone like Stephenson, acting in a personal capacity, to make contact
about a friend or neighbour rather than a close family member. Part of the
explanation for Stephenson's actions was the geographical and emotional distance that had grown between Miss Alexander and her own family in Norfolk,
meaning that her legal next of kin were not in a position to do anything.
Perhaps even more significant, by way of explanation, was a quirk of fate:
Stephenson happened to be related to a very senior figure at the Lunacy Office.

This relationship was not close, as far as it appears on a family tree: in 1901,
Stephenson's cousin Henry Daukes had married Gladys Poyser, the older

sister of Arthur Hampden Ronald Wastell Poyser (known as Ronald). Many years later, long after Henry Daukes's death, Ronald Poyser became Master of the Lunacy Office – and at the time of Dr Norton's death and Stephenson's worries about the situation at the Old Rectory, he was already an assistant master: a very senior role. Stephenson was therefore a cousin-in-law of a Lunacy Office assistant master. It sounds tenuous. Would Stephenson necessarily have known the nature of his cousin's wife's brother's job? A closer examination suggests that the answer may have been yes. He and cousin Henry had both been partly raised by their wealthy grandfather after being orphaned as children, and were only three years apart in age, so they probably knew each other very well in their youth. What's more, shortly after his marriage to Gladys Poyser, Henry himself joined the Lunacy Office as a clerk, very possibly drawing on the networks that came with his new in-laws. As a young man, then, Stephenson would have had some knowledge of this office from his own immediate family, as well a connection to the Poyser family.

In fact, the Poyser family connections with the Lunacy Office were numerous. Gladys Daukes, née Poyser, and her siblings may have remembered going to stay as children with their elderly great-aunt Isabella, who had been the subject of a lunacy inquisition in the late nineteenth century. Their mother, Isabella's niece, was Isabella's 'committee'.[28] It is just about possible that this family interaction with the Lunacy Office was how Gladys's older sister Ida met her husband-to-be, Gerald Mills, who had joined the Lunacy Office as a clerk in 1895 and married Ida in 1900. Mills could well have been one of the handful of 'competent clerks' of the early twentieth century who were mentioned by Master Henry Studdy Theobald and quoted in the previous chapter, since Mills's career at the office was long and successful.[29] He rose to the position of assistant master a few years before his brother-in-law Ronald Poyser achieved the same distinction, and the two co-authored several editions of the leading textbook on Lunacy Office practice in the 1920s and 1930s.[30] Lunacy law was very much the family business. The Daukes-Stephenson-Poyser families must have stayed in touch to some degree: by 1940, Stephenson was described as a 'personal friend' of Assistant Master Poyser.[31]

So it was that when Stephenson was faced with Miss Alexander's unhappy situation in the Old Rectory in 1939, he was rather more aware of the existence of the Lunacy Office than the average member of the public – or even the average country doctor. Although he insisted in his correspondence that he had no specific knowledge of the law or the powers of the office, he did at least have some idea of the nature of its business. He may have discussed his concerns with these experts in law and lunacy in his extended family network, gauging their reactions and soliciting their advice – it could even have been Assistant Master Poyser himself who suggested the involvement of his office, after hearing Stephenson's woes. And it could not hurt that Stephenson was able to address his letter directly and personally to one of the Lunacy Office's most senior figures, increasing its chances of meeting serious and sustained attention.[32] Although there is no sign that Poyser took any direct personal interest in the case once Lunacy Office enquiries had begun, he passed Stephenson's letter on to his colleagues within a day or two, and with orders for urgent action. It was probably treated a little more carefully than most: a memorandum to one of the Official Solicitor's visitors from 1940 made special mention of the personal connection, an observation that must have lingered in the minds of all whose desk it crossed.[33] Anyone at all could contact the Lunacy Office about anyone at all, but the fact that Miss Alexander's circumstances were not typical – along with the happy coincidence of Stephenson's family connections – suggests that friends and neighbours around the country were not rushing in huge numbers to send testimonials about their eccentric acquaintances to the Royal Courts of Justice.

There is a further aspect of Stephenson's family life that may be relevant. According to the 1939 register of civilians in England and Wales, compiled in anticipation of wartime needs, Stephenson's second son (also named Humphrey) was 'defective'. The Stephensons therefore had some personal experience of mental infirmity, although it is unclear what exactly this experience involved. Unlike his siblings, who are easier to trace, Humphrey junior is mostly a mystery.[34] He was living at home with his parents in September 1939 when the register was collated, aged about twenty-four, but he was no longer with them after the war. He may have been with his parents only temporarily in 1939, thanks to the large-scale evacuations and upheaval taking place around the country. Many hospitals and institutions were emptied at around this time, in anticipation of war casualties filling their beds, and so perhaps he returned home for a while and went back to institutional care once the initial turmoil was over. In the 1950s, he appears in a telephone book as a resident of Vine Farm in Brownshill, Gloucestershire: local history suggests that this farm was part of a Catholic community that offered care for priests and others with mental illnesses, and that at one time, Vine Farm housed 'a group of mentally retarded young men' who provided 'manpower' to keep the farm running for the benefit of the patients.[35] It is very possible that Humphrey was one such young man. Notably, Stephenson left nothing to Humphrey in his will under any circumstance, requesting instead that his daughter 'does what she can to look after my son'.[36] Humphrey was not to be trusted with his own money. It seems likely, then, that Stephenson had cause to learn about different manifestations of mental weakness, to reflect on the harm that might come to those affected, and perhaps even to find out about legal measures available to protect and control them.

There is one final striking feature of Stephenson's personal biography that may be relevant, although this requires even more speculative work. Around the time of Dr Norton's death in 1934, Stephenson and his wife, Gladys, enrolled as members of the BUF. This was not quite so shocking as it first appears: fascism enjoyed pockets of popularity in the 1930s not only in urban centres such as East London, where a BUF presence culminating in the 'Battle of Cable Street' is fairly well known, but also in rural areas such as Dorset. Here and in other predominantly agricultural regions of England, BUF leader Oswald Mosley 'tapped into the traditional conservativism of a farming community which had been suffering from apparently intractable economic problems since the end of the [First World] war'.[37] Gladys Stephenson was a particularly enthusiastic and active member, becoming BUF women's district leader in 1938.[38] Mrs Stephenson may have been the driving force behind their membership, but both remained loyal for decades. Unlike many of those who joined in 1934, the year during which BUF membership peaked, the Stephensons kept up their membership throughout the 1930s and beyond.[39] Dr Stephenson was one of around eight hundred BUF members to be arrested and interred, after the organisation was banned under Defence Regulation 18B in 1939. As the Dorset BUF district leader Robert Saunders later recalled, this was no small matter: Stephenson 'was getting on in life and found conditions [in prison] very hard'. Nevertheless, the Stephensons remained firm supporters of Mosley and fascism even after the end of the war.[40]

What does this say about Stephenson's approach to Miss Alexander? At first glance, perhaps not much. In policy terms, the BUF showed no particular interest in matters of mental health law or mental impairment at all. The party paid attention to health only insofar as the BUF claimed that they would revive the nation by creating the conditions for healthy minds in healthy bodies, and would encourage all citizens to see the protection of their health as their responsibility to the nation.[41] This was not so very far from the broader policy mood in the early decades of the twentieth century. There was no explicit BUF policy regarding those who were, like some of the Humphries family, said to be on the borderline of mental defect and leading lives that appeared dissolute, even quasi-criminal. Nor was anything said about those who were, like Miss Alexander and perhaps Humphrey junior, potentially incapable by reason of illness or age of living independently and looking after themselves. Social policy questions of care and control were not the BUF's main interest. Although Stephenson's steadfast commitment to the BUF and Mosley before, during, and after the Second World War suggests a strong belief in the group's goals, there was nothing within BUF policies that directly addressed the kind of situation that he encountered at the Old Rectory.

Yet, Dr Stephenson's commitment to the BUF might nonetheless be suggestive of his views of mental impairment or mental 'weakness', individual rights, and state intervention. In broad terms, fascism was characterised by an 'obsession with the moral, physical and racial degeneracy afflicting Western societies'.[42] This prompted racism, anti-Semitism, and exclusionary forms of nationalism, clear traces of which can be found in Mrs Stephenson's correspondence with BUF district leader Robert Saunders.[43] It also prompted high anxiety about mental defect, which was seen as both sign and cause of this national or racial degeneration. Although eugenic thought was far from the only driver of mental deficiency policy in the early twentieth century, legislation to enable the detention, segregation, or close supervision of those deemed 'mentally defective' was said to be in the interests of 'stemming the increasing tide of degeneracy'.[44] As indicated in the previous chapter, a view of 'mentally defective' people as biologically different and therefore unable to behave as responsible citizens permitted them to be treated in law and policy in a way that seems to be at odds with the liberal reforms of the era. The Mental Deficiency Act of 1913 was not primarily motivated by fascist thought, but it was certainly informed by similar concerns about 'regulating the boundaries of responsible citizenship'.[45]

This is not to say that the Mental Deficiency Acts, or the mental hygiene movement, which shared some similar aims, or indeed the Lunacy Office itself, were intrinsically or overwhelmingly fascist. Stephenson himself was 'not willing to act so as to split a Conservative vote', according to his BUF membership card, indicating his primary political allegiance when election time rolled around.[46] All it means is that there was ample room for those sympathetic to fascist ideas and those who supported state intervention and surveillance of those with mental infirmities to become fellow travellers. It also means that the Stephensons may have looked with particular hostility at the Humphries family, seeing their behaviour as degenerate and their association with 'gipsies' as threatening to the 'race' or nation. The Stephensons may have been more comfortable than most with the idea of state interventions to control and supervise those they saw as mentally weak, such as Miss Alexander.

The Stephensons' involvement with the BUF means something else, too: it means that I began to dislike them. Only three of the twelve files about Miss Alexander were open for public inspection when I began my research, and the disclosure that Stephenson had been arrested and imprisoned for his BUF membership was casually mentioned in a letter to the Official Solicitor in the last of these three files. It was the finale, the big reveal: Stephenson was a died-in-the-wool fascist. No wonder, I thought. No wonder he saw no good at all in the Humphries family; no wonder he so eagerly wanted this intrusion into Miss Alexander's home and private life; no wonder she protested. Here was the answer. Even his friends and patients had begun to keep their distance: Mrs Stephenson had reported that some in the local community would not accept their views.[47] Wasn't Miss Alexander quite right to reject his interference? As a fascist, didn't Stephenson hold individual rights and freedoms in supreme disregard? Wasn't he disgusted by weakness, and intolerant of any hint of disability or difference? Wasn't this a terrible thing that he had done, calling in the heavy hand of the law to declare Miss Alexander incapable just because he disapproved of how she chose to live?

Many months later, the remaining files about Miss Alexander became available to read. I could unravel some of the long-term consequences of Stephenson's actions, discussed in depth in chapter 4. My certainty wavered – had it been such a terrible thing, after all? – but antipathy towards the Stephensons remains and has consequences. Would I have noticed the patronising tone of Stephenson's remarks about Miss Alexander without it? Would I have identified prejudice towards the Humphries family, rather than justifiable anger towards a family that was exploiting someone? (Would I have judged less harshly the novel that Stephenson published in 1927, in

which a naïve young man murders a blackmailer but escapes from prison –
at great, great, great length – and is eventually, implausibly, pardoned once
his admirable personal qualities are recognised?[48]) Have I read too much
into Stephenson's political allegiance simply because it provoked me, ignoring alternative matters of potential significance such as his religious faith?
Or, have I ended up over-compensating for my dislike, trying too hard to
see positive outcomes to his actions?

With these questions lurking in the background, Stephenson's view of Miss
Alexander and the Lunacy Office begins to develop a hazy outline. Given his
son's impairment, Stephenson may have been particularly attentive to signs
of mental infirmity, and particularly sensitive to the possibilities for the abuse
or exploitation of those affected. Unlike his son, Miss Alexander had no family
on hand to help her. She was not mentally defective under the terms of the
Mental Deficiency Act, leaving her beyond the official purview of the DVAMW.
The Stephensons thoroughly disapproved of the Humphries family and of
the situation at the Old Rectory, seeing idleness, alcohol, and children born
to unmarried parents as signs of decaying standards and degenerate people.
If Miss Alexander were mentally weak and therefore unable to exercise her
freedoms in any meaningful sense, this placed her beyond the scope of ordinary citizenship; following the principles of mental deficiency policy and BUF
faith in the corporate state, Stephenson may have been more willing than
most to believe that an organ of the state such as the Lunacy Office might
hold the answer to this problem. And, of course, he happened to know that
such an institution existed. The particular combination of Stephenson's politics, personal connections, and experience of mental impairment meant that
he was unusually likely to act as he did.

Miss Alexander may have been gentle and timid, but I am sure that she was
not oblivious to the world around her. I envision her tolerating Stephenson
while he came to the Old Rectory as Dr Norton's medical attendant, delivering
remedies, recommendations (to stop the heavy drinking, to stop fraternising
with the staff), and end-of-life care, but not necessarily liking him. News of
his BUF membership drifted through the village, whispered in sometimes hostile tones, eventually reaching her ears from the lips of Mr or Mrs Humphries,
no doubt. His insistent regular visits after Dr Norton's death became a trial,
during which nothing, ever, was to his satisfaction. He summoned up the
ghost of Dr Norton to ask whether 'this' – this state of affairs – was what the

good doctor would have wanted; he looked in horror at any sign of drinking or fun; he insulted her friend Mrs Humphries behind her back (and eventually to her face). Miss Alexander may not have been entirely happy, but she might also have been very much tired of him. Eventually, in April 1939, matters came to a head.

REQUESTING A RECEIVER

Stephenson's decision to write to the Lunacy Office was prompted by an 'altercation' at the Old Rectory. He had been worried for some time about the behaviour of the Humphries family towards Miss Alexander, and had not concealed his dissatisfaction during his regular trips to the Old Rectory. Finally, his remonstrations went too far and he was told during one heated exchange that 'Miss Alexander did not wish him to make any more monthly visits'.[49] Stephenson did not believe for a moment that this was her genuine wish, but what could he do to honour his promise to the late Dr Norton if he were barred from seeing her? Miss Alexander seemed to be at the mercy of Mr and Mrs Humphries, unable or unwilling to extricate herself from their control. Following this final confrontation, Stephenson was prepared for more drastic action.

As this sequence of events suggests, there was no sudden change in Miss Alexander's mental state or living situation that prompted his letter to the Lunacy Office. This was unusual. A good proportion of applications for receivers were provoked by an evident deterioration in health that finally resulted in hospital or nursing home admission. Mrs Emily D'Aguilar had been 'in a bad state of health' for a while, but her situation changed substantially when she was admitted to hospital in early 1919 as a person of unsound mind, and her cousin made the application for a receiver shortly thereafter. Similarly for Mrs Esther Cohen, it was her arrival at Chiswick House Asylum in 1920 that prompted her brother to write to the Lunacy Office.[50] Mrs Florence Kendall had reportedly been 'abnormal' for 'some few years' but had deteriorated considerably in the months leading up to her admittance to the Scalebor Park Mental Hospital in 1932 as a voluntary patient. It was this hospitalisation that led her husband to request that he be appointed as her receiver. Reverend Verner White had been showing signs of 'senile decay' for a while, to the extent that his sister Emily White 'had for the last three or four years been taking care of the patient and looking after his finances'. As he deteriorated further and required nursing home care – for which payment would be necessary – she wrote to the Lunacy Office to put this status quo on a more official footing.[51]

For those whose mental state appeared to deteriorate suddenly rather than gradually, receivership applications could be equally swift where there were urgent financial matters to address. Robert Gladstone's solicitors, for example, contacted the Lunacy Office only seven days after their client's breakdown in September 1939, for the pressing reason that Mr Gladstone's staff salaries had to be paid and there were other business dealings, including some that he had undertaken when perhaps not wholly well, which were in need of rapid attention to untangle.[52] Wealthy businessman Herbert Roberts had been paying his grandson's school fees and supporting various family members prior to suffering a series of strokes in 1937, and his family contacted the Lunacy Office with haste because these personal payments and other aspects of Mr Roberts' 'private affairs' needed to continue, even during his serious illness.[53]

The proximate cause of an application to the Lunacy Office was just as often a change in personal circumstances that demanded some financial reorganisation, rather than a change in health. This was also quite different from Miss Alexander's situation. For Miss Mary Barnes, it was the advancing age and increasing frailty of her uncle and aunt, who had looked after her since childhood but struggled to cope as they both approached the age of eighty. Miss Barnes was said to require 'much attention' in the form of help with washing, dressing, and more or less constant oversight. Her family, who were barely making ends meet, contacted the Lunacy Office in 1931 in the hope that a receiver could be appointed and could then use Miss Barnes's modest personal assets to pay for such help.[54] Historians Bartlett and Wright have suggested that economic factors must have regularly informed family decisions concerning the hospitalisation of those who needed a great deal of supervision and care,[55] and this was clearly the case for the Barnes family. They were 'anxious not to put the Patient into an Institution but their means are very straightened', making it all but impossible for anyone of working age to stay at home to look after her without dipping into Miss Barnes's own money.

Pressing financial difficulties of this kind encouraged many families to turn to the Lunacy Office. For the Kendall family mentioned above, Mrs Florence

Kendall's hospitalisation coincided with her husband experiencing some 'unfortunate difficulties in his partnership business', with the result that he could not pay her hospital fees in full. Had he been in a more comfortable financial position, it seems unlikely that he would have needed to access his wife's small savings account and so would not have needed to become her receiver.[56] Similarly, Mrs Emily Mathews contacted the office in 1928, two years after her husband, Charles, had been detained in hospital as a person of unsound mind, because she could no longer afford the premiums on their joint life policy with the Prudential. Mrs Mathews asked to be appointed as her husband's receiver so that the policy could be surrendered, easing the burden on her small income and releasing the capital to her and her husband.[57]

Financial strain was itself mentioned in some of the literature and commentary surrounding the Lunacy Office as the cause of mental infirmity, rendering people unable to manage the property and affairs that caused them grief. 'Economic mishaps' had a centuries-old place within both medical and lay lists of the causes of mental breakdown.[58] The Master of the Lunacy Office during the economically turbulent 1930s, Henry Methold, agreed that financial stress was not infrequently a cause of the mental strain and collapse that resulted in applications to his office: he said that many were 'driven insane from losses in business' and came to the attention of his office 'loaded with debt'.[59] The idea of a relationship between prevailing economic conditions and applications for receivers is strengthened by the fact that the number of receiverships rose once again in the 1970s, just as unemployment rates and severe inflation began to take their toll.

Miss Alexander's situation was therefore unusual, in that neither her health nor her finances had changed immediately before the approach to the Lunacy Office. Nevertheless, her financial position *had* definitely changed quite substantially five years earlier in the form of her inheritance from Dr Norton, and this she shared with many others who encountered the Lunacy Office. An inheritance was a regular prompt for receivership applications. Joseph Higgins had served in the Royal Lancashire Regiment during the First World War and was, in November 1915, certified as a person of unsound mind at Napsbury War Hospital. A few years later, his sister Sarah Makin wrote to the Lunacy Office to request a receivership, prompted by the recent death of an aunt in the United States and a small inheritance due to her brother as a result.[60] An even longer period had elapsed after the initial signs of debility before an application was made for Miss Annie Alpass, who had suffered a head injury in her youth and been 'mentally deficient' since then. When Miss Alpass was about sixty-four years old, in 1927, an application for a receiver was made by one of her sisters following the death of a brother and an inheritance from him due to Miss Alpass. The same pattern played out later in the century as well: Mr Gladstone Whitehouse's brother Thomas applied to the Court of Protection in 1951 concerning an inheritance of £66 now payable to Gladstone, who had been detained in hospital since at least 1924.[61] And for Miss Jean Carr and Mr Arthur Short, applications from their mothers came on the occasion of their twenty-first birthdays: both young people stood to take possession of an inheritance from their deceased fathers as soon as they attained their majority.[62]

In one sense, this is a continuation of the pattern of nineteenth-century Commissions in Lunacy, which were often used to protect family property and inheritances. Several important things had changed, though. Firstly, the sums of money at stake were often quite small. Rather than vast family trusts or country estates, the twentieth-century inheritances that prompted contact with the Lunacy Office were frequently modest cash sums, such as Mrs Kendall's bank account balance of £156, or Mr Whitehouse's £66. The latter was enough to provide him with a weekly allowance for 'extra comforts' in the form of cigarettes, sweets, and occasional items of clothing. When he died in 1958, the hospital had £12 left to put towards his funeral costs.[63] Secondly, receivership applications in the twentieth century were usually prompted by someone coming into an inheritance that required some administration, rather than a fear on the part of family members that their own future inheritances were being squandered. Commissions in Lunacy in the nineteenth century had often been provoked by 'family feuds' in which family wealth – and future inheritances – were at stake; family disputes rarely seem to have prompted contact with the Lunacy Office in the twentieth century.[64]

This does not necessarily mean that family disagreements over money and property were actually any less common. Suzuki has suggested that the particular social and legal context of the nineteenth century may have encouraged their appearance within the sphere of the lunacy inquisition, in particular.[65] But, the apparent absence of family disputes as a prompt for receivership applications in the twentieth century might be more of a question of perception. Historical insight is inevitably shaped by the very different archives available for the two centuries, and also by the different legal processes involved. Lunacy inquisitions were, at least until the mid-nineteenth century, jury trials in which witnesses for opposing parties gave evidence, and lawyers elicited and presented competing versions of the facts. This adversarial event was then reported in newspapers, which provide the primary source base. Such procedures and reportage often placed a spotlight on family disagreements, with members of a family contradicting one another in their evidence and tales of family breakdown and conflict providing good newspaper copy.

In contrast, receivership applications were usually decided on the basis of written evidence alone. This was delivered by means of affidavits that followed a predictable form of words or, from the 1920s onwards, by completing pre-printed forms. These papers offered little space and even less encouragement to give lurid details of family disagreements. In writing, within the constraints of a template, there was barely any opportunity to let slip a sign of simmering hostilities. Occasional hints about such disputes appear instead as marginalia or brief file notes jotted down by Lunacy Office staff, easily missed amongst the pages of official statements and financial records. These annotations hint at conversations or correspondence that did not become part of the official file, in which Lunacy Office staff learned much more about family dynamics than standardised documents could contain. Within Miss Alice Dowdy's file, a laconic note observed that 'it would appear that there is a family dissension in this case', the 'primary cause' of which was one of her sisters. No further information was provided. 'You will observe that there is a history of family differences', recorded a similar scrawled note in Miss Ann Taylor's file, several decades later.[66]

Adding to these material restrictions that limited the airing of family tensions was the fact that in the twentieth century, successful receivership applications were very rarely contested. This meant that only one perspective – the view of the applicant – was put forward and recorded. The Lunacy Office does not seem to have kept any record of applications that it received and then rejected, whether as a result of valid objections raised by family members or for any other reason. This makes it hard to tell whether receivership applications really were very rarely the subject of any kind of disagreement. Did a formal objection, perhaps coming from another family member who strongly disagreed with the proposed course of action, usually mean that the application was rejected and left no archival trace? It is possible. However, the fact that the business of dealing with disputed and unsuccessful applications is not mentioned anywhere, despite several accounts of Lunacy Office duties that go to great lengths to emphasise its very heavy workload and weighty responsibilities, suggests that they were probably not a very frequent occurrence.[67]

Occasional disagreements over receivership applications that *were* eventually successful demonstrate just how much family animosity could emerge within the files as soon as the Lunacy Office found itself arbitrating between different points of view. Two of George Mower's three sons presented just such a situation in 1966, after Mr Mower senior had been admitted to hospital with dementia. They were at loggerheads over their father's care and, of course, his finances. Accusations of neglect and self-interest flew back and forth, accompanied by comments on character and statements from Mr Mower's milkman and a former work colleague and friend. Mr Mower himself also weighed in. A third (estranged) son was induced to comment from his home in Australia, and wrote sharply that both of his brothers were 'persuaded and possibly inspired by thoughts of gain'.[68] Clearly, applications for the appointment of a receiver could still be a battleground for warring families. More often than not, though, legal procedure in the twentieth century successfully muted family disputes, treating them as incidental to the matter in hand.

In essence, the twentieth-century archive of receivership applications contains relatively little disagreement, whereas competing viewpoints are central to the inquisitions of the nineteenth century. The application concerning Miss Alexander is one of barely a handful within the archives in which, as with Mr Mower, a formal objection was raised to the appointment of a receiver. Mr Mower's sons disagreed over which of them should be his receiver, but the objection from Miss Alexander was of a more fundamental nature, connecting it firmly to its nineteenth-century precursors. Miss Alexander's solicitor argued, quite simply, that his client was perfectly capable of managing her own affairs. Was she?

3

❀

FOUND INCAPABLE

Quirks of fate may have contributed significantly to the fact that Miss Alexander came to the attention of the Lunacy Office, but there were other forces at work too. These became evident as her case moved through the Lunacy Office systems. Miss Alexander was an unusual person for the office to consider: she had not been 'certified' as a person of unsound mind or detained as mentally defective, nor was she in a hospital or nursing home as a voluntary patient. She was not receiving nursing care in her own home, nor had she suffered any significant episodes of ill health in recent times. She did not need help with everyday tasks like getting dressed, nor were there any reports of the growing confusion and forgetfulness that was sometimes associated with advanced age.[1] Miss Alexander presented none of the signs that usually provided clear confirmation of the presence of mental infirmity, of the kind that would prevent her from looking after herself.

With this in mind, this chapter considers the central issue that faced the Lunacy Office upon receipt of an application for the appointment of a receiver: was this person incapable of managing their own property and affairs? Here, the unusual qualities of Miss Alexander's situation are especially helpful. They prompted people to get involved and to generate paperwork, leaving traces of everyday assumptions and practices – even as those assumptions and practices were disrupted by the twists and turns of the case. Unusual events also demand explanation: what contexts or circumstances enabled them to take place? Miss Alexander's case signposts some possible features of mental capacity law and society in the mid-twentieth century that made her situation possible, and would affect more typical Lunacy Office matters as well.

Accounts of the dominance of 'medicalism' within mental health law over this period suggest that mental capacity was a question for psychiatrists to answer, and so this chapter begins by looking at medical evidence. The Lunacy Office's informant, Humphrey Stephenson, was a medical doctor and his correspondence implied that Miss Alexander was mentally deficient in some way, but he was no expert and did not offer a formal expert opinion. Medical statements about Miss Alexander remained notably absent until the application for a receiver was opposed. This relaxed approach to medical evidence suggests that medical expertise occupied a much less significant position in practice than might be expected. Assessing mental capacity in the early to mid-twentieth century was not so much a question of identifying illness, as of identifying social difficulties or vulnerabilities. These difficulties were understood to be intelligible to any reliable man, and, on the whole, were slightly more readily found amongst women. Incapacity to manage one's affairs was not seen as something tricky to identify, and was rarely the subject of legal dispute. Only in the 1950s did the first intimations appear that it was perhaps not so easy after all.

This analysis builds upon Peter Bartlett's work on judicial responses to insanity, which has described the emerging centrality of delusions to determinations of mental incapacity over the course of the nineteenth century. A focus upon delusions as evidence of incapacity was then gradually replaced during the twentieth century by attention to reasoning ability and intellect.[2] Events surrounding Miss Alexander and the eventual determination that she was indeed incapable of managing her own affairs do not contradict this trend. Instead, they point towards additional considerations at work within this strand of mental health law as it was used in practice, including attention to a person's specific living situation and vulnerability to harm.

The decision that Miss Alexander was indeed incapable of managing her affairs and the resultant instructions about what should be done implied that specific facts were true, and advocated for a particular way of seeing things. Different facts and perspectives were possible. The events that occured required creative decision-making, even rule bending, and an element of chance, all of which illustrates the 'indeterminacy of law' – something often overshadowed by impressions of the law as consistent, authoritative, self-contained, and unambiguous.[3] The same is true of historical writing, and this account is one version among many. This version responds to contemporary concerns about the proper role of medical expertise within mental health law, the role of the Court of Protection, and the views and feelings of those considered incapable. It also reflects my own imaginative horizons and willingness to speculate, in the interests of making sense of something that was at first quite baffling to me: Why on earth was Miss Alexander found incapable?

EVALUATING MISS ALEXANDER

According to the Lunacy Act of 1890, a receiver could be appointed for Miss Alexander as long as a judge or Master in Lunacy was convinced that she was incapable of managing her property and affairs 'by reason of infirmity caused by disease or age'. Exactly what constituted 'infirmity', 'disease', or indeed 'age' was left open to interpretation. 'Disease' in particular, noted the textbook co-authored in the 1930s by none other than Assistant Master Ronald Poyser, could be a broad field as far as the Lunacy Office was concerned.[4]

Dr Stephenson set out his view of Miss Alexander in careful but clear terms. In his first letter to the Lunacy Office, shown in figure 3.1, he claimed emphatically that her 'trouble is weakness of character chiefly' and that she was 'without character and without courage'.[5] Alongside these references to a rather nebulous lack of character, he asserted that she was 'definitely subnormal mentally' and 'of low mentality', as any mental expert would easily see. Stephenson was no 'mental expert' and was unwilling or unable to offer anything more definitive in his own letter. Nevertheless, these terms skirted around the edge of a diagnosis, pointing towards mental defect, or at least 'feeble-mindedness', but leaving it open for an official expert to come to their own preferred conclusion.

'Subnormality' was associated with 'mental deficiency', a well-established medico-legal term by 1939. The Mental Deficiency Act of 1913 had described four types or 'grades' of defective person: idiot, imbecile, feeble-minded, and moral imbecile. A diagnosis of any kind of mental defect in accordance with this Act could result in institutionalisation, or the appointment of a guardian and regular supervision in the home. These interventions were quite separate to the workings of the Lunacy Office, but after 1913 the office did begin to process receivership applications for people described in medical statements as 'defective within the meaning of the Mental Deficiency Act'. These were always a minority of all applications: only about fifteen appear within the available Lunacy Office and Official Solicitor archives.[6] It is likely that alternative arrangements were usually made to take care of the property of those considered

Maiden Newton,
Borset.

A doctor Norton died in this district about five years ago and left
nearly £800 a year and a house to his old housekeeper. The Trustees
for the capital are the Westminster Bank and the name and address of the
housekeeper is

            Miss Alexander
              Chilfrome,
                Cattistock, Dorchester

P.S. Do not communicate with this lady by letter. I have reason to
     believe her letters are opened.

     Miss Alexander is definitely subnormal mentally, without character
and without courage.

     Her gardener and his wife - people called Humphries have taken
possession of her and her money and are spending it on themselves.
They have sold a large part of her furniture, nominally in her name
but really for their benefit. Two daughters, two illegitimate
children of one of the daughters and an old grandmother are among those
who live on this unfortunate Miss Alexander.

     About a year ago they (nominally of course Miss Alexander) bought
a car and introduced their son into the house as a chauffeur. They are
continually going for jaunts in this car, hardly ever taking Miss Alexander
with them. She is dressed in dingy old clothes because she cant afford
new ones. They are both frequently drunk and the unfortunate lady is
terrified of them.

     Miss Alexander's trouble is weakness of character chiefly. Still
she is of low mentality and I do not think your mental expert would have
any doubt after interviewing her that she was quite unable to manage her
own affairs. Do something and soon if you possibly can. The position
of this poor weak lady is really deplorable.

                    Always Yrs

                    Humphrey

Note: I need hardly say that Humphries - the gardener - has done little
or no work as a gardener for some years. The first thing your
representative will note when he arrives is that the garden is a tangle
of dandelions and nettles.

                    H.

Figure 3.1 The surviving copy of Humphrey Stephenson's first letter to the
Lunacy Office. The signature – 'Always Yrs, Humphrey' – provided the first clue that
he knew someone at the Lunacy Office in a personal capacity.

mentally defective, either through informal mechanisms or guardianships, or by reorganising family finances during their childhood, without recourse to the Lunacy Office. Nevertheless, the Lunacy Office and the doctors preparing statements for its benefit clearly recognised that mental defect as defined in law was likely to indicate a lack of mental capacity.

The small number of applications to the Lunacy Office mentioning 'mental defect' or 'imbecility' give a picture of highly variable capabilities and difficulties. Mr William Sims was said to be unable to read, write, answer any questions, keep himself clean, tell his age or name, or 'appreciate any remarks that are made to him', and neither Blanche Parrish nor Leslie Trounson could wash or dress themselves or communicate verbally or in writing at all. Others could look after their own daily needs and communicate without too much trouble, but had not shown themselves able to learn about money: this was particularly significant evidence for the Lunacy Office that they would not be able to manage their own property and affairs. As their doctor acknowledged, William Sims's brother Arthur could read and write a little, and knew that 'twelve pence make a shilling and that there are twenty shillings in a pound', but his arithmetic was unreliable and he had 'never heard of investment, per cent, interest' or 'having a stamp or receipt' after paying a bill.[7] These were apparently all necessary skills for looking after his own modest income.

An additional or alternative symptom of mental defect, and one that was of particular concern when it came to capacity to manage property and affairs, was a lack of independent thought. It was here that Annie Alpass and Thomas Scotney, both classed as defective within the meaning of the Mental Deficiency Act, were found wanting: Miss Alpass because she appeared 'not capable of forming her own opinions, but will do what she is told by anyone', and Mr Scotney for being childish and 'devoid of initiative', 'requiring instruction in all things'.[8] This sounds a little like the weakness of character described by Stephenson, causing Miss Alexander to fall under the influence of the Humphries family and leaving her without the ability to concoct, express, or pursue her own ideas and wishes. Notably, though, Stephenson's account of Miss Alexander avoided mention of her educability or conversational abilities, two additional aspects that were often mentioned in descriptions of people called mentally defective – probably because she was, according to later accounts, highly literate, perfectly 'normal to talk to', and indeed a good conversational companion, all attributes that were unlikely to help Stephenson's case.[9] In what he said and did not say, Stephenson nudged the Lunacy Office towards the idea of mental defect of some kind.

Stephenson's commentary as a medical man, with the added weight of his status as a friend and relation of Assistant Master Poyser, was enough to prompt the Lunacy Office to take action. The office requested an urgent 'special visit' to the Old Rectory by one of the Lord Chancellor's medical visitors, to report on whether Miss Alexander seemed to be incapable and in need of a receiver.[10] As had been the case when the role of LCV was first created in 1833, two doctors and one barrister held the position in the 1930s. In May 1939, Hubert Meysey-Thompson was one of these three, and duly set off for Dorset.

It was probably from Meysey-Thompson himself that Miss Alexander first learned of the Lunacy Office's interest in her situation. His arrival at the Old Rectory on 11 May 1939 was startling, not least because it was unannounced. Stephenson, abruptly banished from the Old Rectory after that final 'altercation', was unlikely to have kept the household updated about his conversations and correspondence with Assistant Master Poyser. Nor would the office of the LCVs necessarily have written to give notice of their representative's arrival: they would do so for regular visits to those already under the auspices of the Lunacy Office, to make sure that the person being visited would be available, but in this case Stephenson had cautioned against making contact with the household in writing: Miss Alexander's post was probably opened by Mr and Mrs Humphries. In light of his portrait of the situation at the Old Rectory, there was good reason to suspect that Mr and Mrs Humphries might prevent any official from seeing Miss Alexander by simply taking her away from the house, given the chance. And Dorset was no easy destination for any of the London-based visitors: popping back the following day was not an option. The best solution was to catch the household unawares.

Meysey-Thompson's unexpected appearance on the doorstep of the Old Rectory left no doubt that this was a serious business. He cut an imposing figure. Born into a family of lawyers, peers, and politicians, he had been privately educated before being called to the bar in August 1904. His legal career had been interrupted by a period serving as an officer during the First World War, but then continued with reasonable success. He had been appointed as an LCV in 1928, so he had over ten years' experience.[11] Just a few years before his trip to the Old Rectory, he had been energetically criticised by one of the more financially straightened households he visited on a regular basis in Toot-

ing, South London, for 'swaggering around in a large car' and making the subject of his visit 'discontented' with her own very modest living circumstances.[12]
His swagger may have been overstated, but Meysey-Thompson's family background, education, profession, and affluence all marked him out as a man of
influence and elevated socio-economic status. Whether he came to Dorset in
his large car or more modestly as many others did, by train, his arrival at the
Old Rectory must have been daunting.

Even if he successfully remembered to dodge the outdated terminology of
'lunacy', the purpose of his visit no doubt caused consternation too. Meysey-
Thompson's report for the Lunacy Office was brief, but hints that the visit
was not a comfortable one. He provided some highly critical comment concerning the Humphries family, closely echoing Stephenson's account. 'The
present position', Meysey-Thompson wrote, was that Miss Alexander lived in
the Old Rectory 'with the Humphries[,] their two daughters, the two illegitimate children of one daughter and their son who acts as chauffeur to a car
apparently bought with Miss Alexander's money'. Rather than any kind of
regular wage, the whole family seemed to live on Miss Alexander's income.
Meysey-Thompson was 'not favourably impressed by Mrs Humphries[,] a
coarse looking woman with the appearance of a heavy drinker. She was by
turns truculent and cringing and tried to stop me talking to Miss Alexander
alone'. As for Miss Alexander and the all-important question of her capacity
to manage her own property and affairs, Meysey-Thompson came to a definite
conclusion. 'Miss Alexander is a plesant [*sic*] little lady but she was entirely
under Mrs. Humphries' influence. Her memory for dates is very vague and
she could not give me any clear account of how her money is spent'.[13] To his
mind, the situation very definitely called for the appointment of a receiver.

Bearing in mind Meysey-Thompson's unexpected and intimidating presence, Miss Alexander can perhaps be forgiven for being 'vague'. By all accounts,
she was often uncertain and anxious around strangers, even in the best of circumstances, which these were not. Imagine her alarm, following the knock
at the door and the appearance of a fancy London lawyer, talking about lord
chancellors and laws and masters and whether she was in her right mind. Mrs
Humphries's behaviour can also be explained by nerves, whether for the dubious reason that she realised the urgent need to conceal some aspects of Miss
Alexander's situation from their surprise guest, or simply because these kinds
of intrusions into her domestic situation from the great and the good generally

boded ill. No doubt she remembered recent evaluations of her children by the DVAMW, with a view to declaring them mentally defective and perhaps even removing them to some distant institution – the nearest colony for mental defectives being over fifty miles away at the Royal Western Counties Institution in Devon.[14]

Not unexpectedly, in light of this past experience, Miss Alexander was soon under the impression that the involvement of the Lunacy Office would mean her own removal to an asylum. Officials later suspected that this was a malicious piece of misinformation told to her by Mr or Mrs Humphries to encourage her to resist Lunacy Office intervention.[15] It seems just as possible to me that it was the result of a genuine misunderstanding. Receiverships were nowhere near as commonplace as hospitalisation, after all: everyone knew about mental hospitals, but making sense of the Lunacy Office and mental capacity law was another matter altogether. Fear of being taken away from her much-loved home of fifteen years and deposited in a strange and frightening hospital may have dawned on Miss Alexander while she was being quizzed by a stranger about her annual income, her weekly expenditure, and just how long it had been since her dear Dr Norton had died. It was not a fear that Mr and Mrs Humphries could or would assuage. The reactions that Meysey-Thompson reported certainly could correspond with Stephenson's portrayal of Mrs Humphries as a devious and controlling drunkard and Miss Alexander as mentally feeble – a portrait that must have influenced this eminent visitor's perceptions from the outset – but there are other possible explanations, too.

Despite the fact that the Lunacy Office had expressly requested a report from a medical visitor, Meysey-Thompson was no doctor. He may have been sent to Dorset in error, as there certainly were occasional miscommunications between the Lunacy Office and the office of the LCVs.[16] It is also very possible that he made the journey for want of any alternative, because there was no medical visitor available. The number of LCVs had not changed in over a century, despite the very dramatic increase in cases overseen by the Lunacy Office. By the late 1930s, their workload was heavy. Desperate pleas a few years earlier for the appointment of an additional LCV had been rejected, and over the six months leading up to March 1939, the three visitors had undertaken no fewer than 680 visits: a rate of more than one per day per visitor, seven days a week, covering collectively a distance in excess of 20,000 miles.[17] When the request to visit the Old Rectory was submitted to the LCVS' office, one of the two medical visitors had only been in post for six months, and the other was unwell and absent for an extended period – apparently as a result of overwork.[18] Thanks to Assistant Master Poyser's personal connection to the applicant, there was also a sense of urgency surrounding Miss Alexander's situation, perhaps encouraging officials in both offices to overlook irregularities and technicalities in the interests of speed.

Human error, outdated staffing structures, visitor illness, a need for haste: any combination of these generated less than ideal circumstances for progressing the case in line with proper procedure. Although Meysey-Thompson as a lawyer could not provide medical evidence, he gave an absolutely decisive answer to the question he was asked. 'In my view', he wrote in his report, 'she is not fit to manage her own affairs'.[19] The fact that this was not the statement of a medical expert did prompt a moment's pause at the Official Solicitor's office, where the receivership application was compiled. Could the application proceed without medical evidence? A telephone call to the Lunacy Office ended with confirmation that 'the Master's Department would accept the Lord Chancellor's Visitor's Report as sufficient medical evidence'.[20] In other words, the Lunacy Office would accept a barrister's report as an expert medical opinion.

Here, it seems, are examples of the kind of 'agency, creativity, and chance' that socio-legal scholars have identified as influential within legal decision-making, as people respond to the situation before them.[21] This was a bit of creative paperwork in the hands of one or two clerks, very probably influenced by staffing problems with the LCVS and the fact that this case had been initiated by a friend of one of the masters and was to be treated with urgency. Yet, these particular demonstrations of agency, creativity, and chance were not only prompted by specific circumstances and individual decisions, but also enabled by particular ways of seeing mental capacity and the role of the state.

For one, determining mental capacity was not seen as something that really required expert medical evidence. The role of the medical expert in legal decisions about mental state had evolved significantly since the early nineteenth century, gradually becoming much more common in both criminal and civil contexts thanks to changes within medicine and law.[22] For the administration of mental capacity law, the Lunacy Act and Rules of 1890 and 1892 confirmed this trend and stated that medical expertise was vital: all applications for a receiver had to be accompanied by affidavits from two doctors giving their views of the person's ability to manage their own affairs.[23] By 1920, though, this requirement had been modified for lower-value cases, in which the person alleged to be incapable had less than £700 to their name or an annual income of under £50. Presumably to reduce the costs of the application, only one medical certificate or statement was required in such cases.[24] This reduction then spread to *all* receivership applications by 1927. For those who were detained involuntarily as mentally defective or lunatic, the requirement for any medical evidence beyond the fact of their detention quietly dropped away entirely within another decade. No reason was given within the textbooks and practitioners' guidance, but the fact of a person's detention was presumably proof enough of incapacity. Procedural rules specified that one medical statement remained essential for anyone not so detained, a minority of all cases.[25]

Amidst the rapidly growing case load and more involved case management undertaken by the Lunacy Office during the 1920s and 1930s, medical evidence apparently presented itself as one administrative burden that could be largely set aside. The unusual events in Miss Alexander's case are signs of the full extent of this, in practice. Even for someone like Miss Alexander, who was not in hospital and whose income was just about substantial enough to pay for doctors' appointments and certificates, an expert medical statement was nothing but a formality that could be fudged. Expert evidence carried so little weight in the minds of the decision makers that in a pinch, its absence could be glossed over.

A willingness to proceed without any formal medical statement or certificate of involuntary detention at all was unusual. Statements from mental experts abound in the archived files, even for those detained in mental hospitals for whom they had become technically redundant. Such statements were usually concise, simply confirming a person's illness and poor prospects of recovery, sometimes with a sentence or two to elaborate upon their condition. Symptoms commonly included 'incoherence' of speech, confusion for time or place, memory loss, delusions or hallucinations, and incontinence or 'dirty habits'. For those under regular medical care or confinement in an institution, an official medical statement was an easy formality to fulfil.

The absence of a medical statement in Miss Alexander's case is anomalous but extremely revealing, especially when placed alongside the declining weight given to medical evidence in official guidelines and practice notes. It points towards several important features of incapacity proceedings. The first is that these proceedings were less to do with disease or disorder, which might require medical insight to identify and define, and much more to do with how successfully or otherwise the person functioned in the world, or their social competence. For all those detained in institutions, their functional difficulties had already been made manifest in the very fact of their detention, and wherever such people had property or business affairs that required attention, the Lunacy Office considered itself authorised to intervene. For anyone else, the central question was not a matter of medical insight but common sense: anyone of irreproachable social competence and some experience of the world could answer it.

Historical scholarship on family law has pointed out the significance of a shared social background between judges and lawyers, leading to shared beliefs that informed legal argument and decision-making.[26] All those involved in evaluating Miss Alexander shared the same social background – and to a surprising extent, as already indicated, even the same social and family circles.[27] Their shared idea of what it meant to be capable of managing one's own affairs was that of a professional, masculine elite. The lack of written judgements within the Lunacy Office meant that interpretations of 'incapable to manage property and affairs' rarely had to be articulated, but some traces can be pieced together from the files about Miss Alexander. Stephenson made his own views plain in a statement lightly disguised as a question. 'Is not the keeping of five servants and a motor car on £8 a week evidence of inability to manage her affairs on the part of this lady[?]' he wrote. Miss Alexander was 'completely dominated' by the Humphries, who were obviously disreputable and would not be trusted by any sensible person.[28] To him, Miss Alexander's behaviour was self-evident financial incompetence: she had proved herself unable to manage her own money in a responsible manner. Her weak character prevented her from refusing Mr and Mrs Humphries anything, and she had been blind to their obvious ulterior motives. Meysey-Thompson's report echoed Stephenson's portrait of the situation at the Old Rectory, that Mrs Humphries was very obviously an undesirable character and Miss Alexander had entirely failed to keep control of her home and affairs. The willingness of senior staff at the Lunacy Office to proceed on this basis suggests that such opinions were persuasive.

Although no other archived file features quite such clear breaches of protocol, there are traces of shared views and assumptions elsewhere that help to build a fuller picture. Miss Jean Carr, a wealthy young heiress, gathered together the paperwork and medical evidence in 1936 to set aside the receivership that had been in place for her since her twenty-first birthday. The Master demurred and asked for the opinion of LCV Dr Raw. Dr Raw, who had once been a member of the Liverpool Eugenics Society, was equivocal.[29] The two men discussed Miss Carr at length until they agreed that 'it w[oul]d be better to let the Receivership remain in force'. Their concern was that Miss Carr showed a lack of confidence and 'no initiative', and if the receivership were to be set aside, it 'might have disastrous results if she ever got into the hands of dishonest persons'. Miss Carr was disheartened, but tried again a few years later with the same result. Once again, the evidence from her own doctor about her recovery and mental abilities could not outweigh official anxiety about the £40,000 that Miss Carr stood to control and the danger of some future unscrupulous suitor or husband accessing her fortune. Lunacy Office discussions were not about her diagnosis (which remained somewhat opaque), or her mental state (which was rarely mentioned), but her wealth and her lack of self-confidence and social experience, which might make her easy prey.[30] As with Miss Alexander, concerns circled around a lack of confidence and courage, making both women too easily influenced by others to be able to exercise their own freedoms meaningfully.

For Mrs Emily Waite, who had been found incapable in 1931 on the basis of 'alcoholic excess' or 'dypsomania', the Lunacy Office showed itself willing to sidestep the requirement for 'definite medical evidence of the Patient's continued inability to manage her affairs'. This evidence would have been required to replace the existing receiver, Mrs Waite's daughter Mrs Churchill, whose seven unhappy years in the role had taken their toll. 'I do not seem to be able to keep my mother happy & safe from taking alcohol', she despaired. Presented with information about Mrs Waite's relapses and their consequences, the Lunacy Office was keen to keep the receivership in place to prevent Mrs Waite from having access to her own money to spend on alcohol – even if this meant avoiding the question of whether she was, in medical eyes, actually incapable of managing her property and affairs. The Lunacy Office persuaded the reluctant Mrs Churchill to remain as receiver so that the question could be avoided altogether. She stayed in post until her mother's death a few years later.[31] As with Miss Alexander, for Mrs Waite, past evidence of poor choices outweighed the need for medical expertise or insight. For Mrs Waite, her compulsion to drink prevented her from exercising self-determination; for Miss Alexander, it was her timidity: in both cases, the decisions that they made as a result were seen as harmful to their own best interests.

These were, like Miss Alexander, women who were judged unable to look after their own financial and personal interests adequately. It seems very possible that it was easier for the men who evaluated their capabilities to see women, rather than their fellow men, as being in need of the kind of intervention offered by the Lunacy Office. There is no fudging of medical evidence requirements where potentially incapable men were concerned; no refusals to remove a receivership in the face of expert opinion to the contrary. For a man's property and affairs to be handed over to another, there had to be very significant infirmity. There is in the archives only one example of a man whose affairs were placed in the hands of a receiver in spite of what was described as very 'thin' evidence – that of Arthur Short. More substantial evidence was sought out, and Mr Short was eventually said to have 'mental and moral defect'. Coming from one of the medical LCVs, this assertion was sufficient for the appointment of a receiver, although the visitors who saw him in subsequent years were less certain that the receivership was necessary. Meysey-Thompson, for one, described Mr Short in florid terms as 'loquacious, grandiloquent and aggrieved', but thought that he was probably capable of managing his affairs and might even benefit from being given the chance to do so. Although Mr Short later spent four years in a mental hospital – four more than any of the women mentioned above – he was given back control of his property as soon as he requested it.[32]

These were all somewhat unusual Lunacy Office cases that tested the boundaries of mental capacity law. Together, they suggest that those boundaries could be pushed a little further for women than for men. In the eyes of the men of the Lunacy Office, women were just a bit more likely to be incapable of managing their own affairs, more likely to appear vulnerable to harm or exploitation, and more likely to need help. Their difficulties arose from their inability to make good decisions: they could not judge the characters of others accurately, appreciate their own limitations, or resist temptation or domination, whether emanating from alcohol or stronger-willed people. Particularly in the absence of fathers or husbands, these weaknesses of character put their money, and by extension their homes and health, at great risk. The rights of single women to make seemingly bad decisions; the needs of men to receive help and support: even at the very edge of Lunacy Office work, these did not quite fit.

At times, the women themselves reportedly agreed that they were ill-suited to their responsibilities. Mrs Waite had initially been keen for her daughter to take control of her money as a temporary measure, to allow her to remain free from alcohol for a period of two years to break the habit. Miss Carr agreed – albeit in conversation with various officials, who may themselves have taken advantage of her lack of self-confidence to press their own views on her – that she was without much life experience and would prefer for the bulk of her fortune to be safely out of her hands. A little while after the Official Solicitor had been appointed as her receiver, Miss Alexander also agreed, in private conversation with one of the official visitors, that 'she was terrified of the Humphries' and desperately wanted someone else to take action to make them leave the Old Rectory. As long as she did not have to be around them after they had been told to go, she wanted them gone.[33] She repeated this to Stephenson, so he said, only to write to him almost immediately afterwards to change her mind:

> I shall be making my own arrangements, & as you have made enough trouble for me already I shall not put up with any more interference from any one … Please do not think I have been influenced in writing this letter, as I am not ill & I am quite capable of looking after my correspondence.[34]

This letter, shown in full in figure 3.2, was dismissed by both Stephenson and various officials as a fiction, probably dictated by Mr and Mrs Humphries and not indicative of Miss Alexander's true wishes. Miss Carr's frustrations with her receivership were considered to be symptomatic of her strained relationship with her mother and brother, who acted as her receivers, and not a true reflection of her views. Mrs Waite's desire to be restored to her property after some five years was simply seen by the Lunacy Office as ill-advised, symptomatic of her inability to recognise her own weakness. Such interpretations may have contained some elements of truth, but it is striking that these women's opinions were only taken seriously when they tallied with the views of the men determining their fate.

CONTESTING INCAPACITY

Miss Alexander's experiences highlight a second feature of Lunacy Office cases: disagreements over what it meant to be 'incapable of managing one's affairs' were rare. All interested parties, including next of kin and the allegedly incapable person, had to be notified of a proposed receivership and were invited to raise any objections.[35] As mentioned in the previous chapter, applications that were ultimately *un*successful presumably generated more of these objections than successful ones but have left no archival trace, making the true scale of opposition difficult to assess. The idiosyncrasies of Miss Alexander's case shed some oblique light on this gap: surely, if anyone at the Lunacy Office had anticipated an objection to the appointment of a receiver for Miss Alexander, they would not have casually confirmed that a short report from a lawyer – even one with the exalted position and experience of LCV – would suffice as 'medical evidence'. Surely, if opposition were at all conceivable, there would have been closer attention to the evidence required. Surely the absence of medical evidence was a shortcoming that even the most cursory opposition to the receivership would spotlight?

In the event, that is exactly what happened. A hearing was scheduled for 26 June 1939 to determine whether Miss Alexander was incapable, and if so, the next steps. Instead of being able to confirm quickly and easily that the Official Solicitor was appointed as Miss Alexander's receiver, the assistant master handling the case was met by a solicitor from Messrs Bell, Broderick, and Gray, who had been instructed to oppose the application on behalf of Miss Alexander. The assistant master was presented with a sworn statement from a Dr Margaret Vivian of Bournemouth that Miss Alexander was 'of sound mind and quite capable of managing her affairs'. 'Although her reactions were somewhat slow', Dr Vivian acknowledged, 'she answered in a perfectly intelligent manner questions which I put to her concerning her life and the management of her money'. Furthermore, she 'appeared to me to be quite capable of appreciating the value of money and the importance of paying her accounts

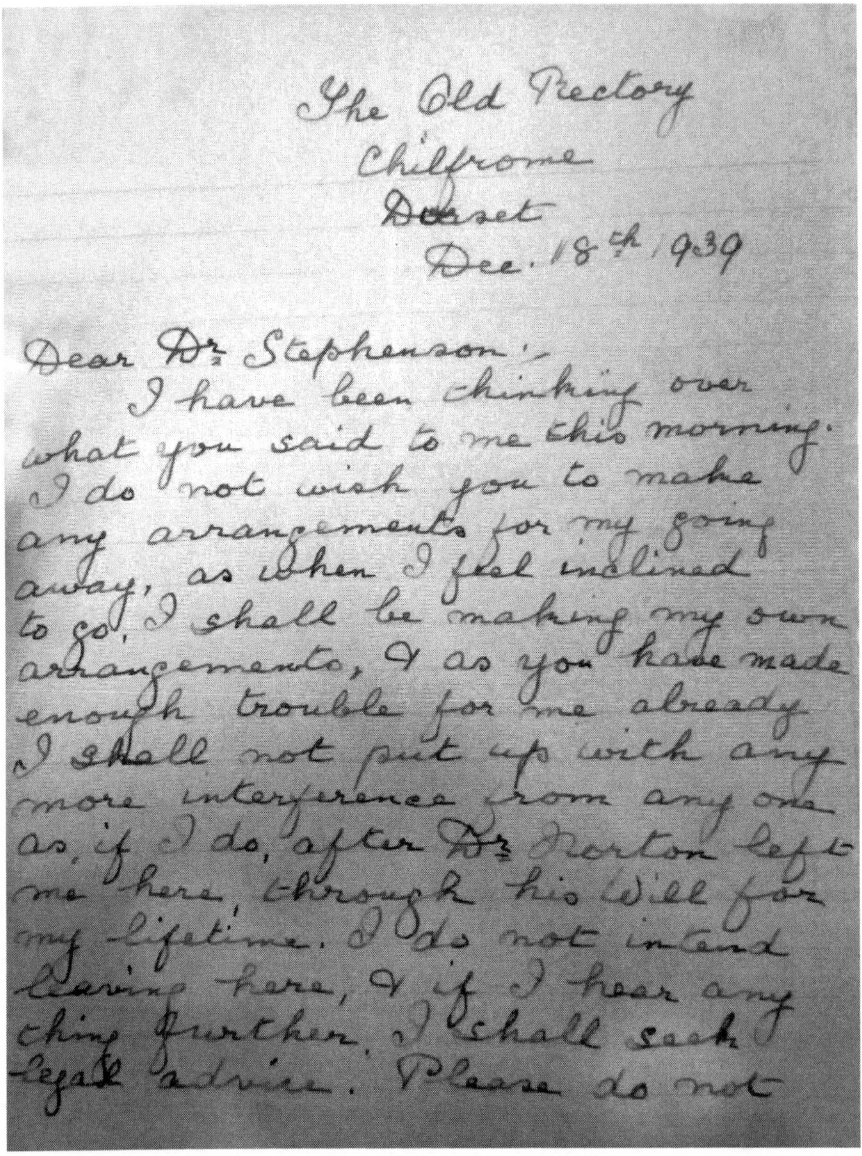

The Old Rectory
Chilfrome
~~Dorset~~
Dec. 18th 1939

Dear Dr. Stephenson,
I have been thinking over
what you said to me this morning.
I do not wish you to make
any arrangements for my going
away, as when I feel inclined
to go, I shall be making my own
arrangements, & as you have made
enough trouble for me already
I shall not put up with any
more interference from any one
as, if I do, after Dr Norton left
me here, through his Will for
my lifetime. I do not intend
leaving here, & if I hear any
thing further, I shall seek
~~legal~~ advice. Please do not

Figure 3.2 Above and opposite: Miss Alexander's two-page letter to Dr Stephenson, asking that he stop interfering.

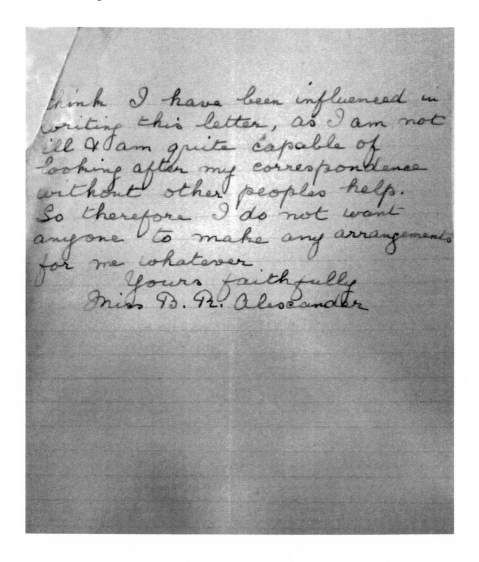

...think I have been influenced in writing this letter, as I am not ill & I am quite capable of looking after my correspondence without other peoples help. So therefore I do not want anyone to make any arrangements for me whatever.

Yours faithfully

Miss B. M. Alexander

regularly'. Dr Vivian was 'strongly of the opinion that under no circumstances could it be said with fairness that she is incapable of managing her own life'.[36] In light of this unequivocal sworn statement from a doctor, and the fact that there was a distinct lack of medical evidence from the other side, the hearing had to be adjourned.

Miss Alexander is the only person within the archives whose mental capacity was itself the subject of dispute from the very outset. There are examples of objections to specific receivers or financial proposals: Mrs Emily Willard wrote to object to the appointment of her niece Ellen, and her doctor initially wrote to dispute her incapacity, but as soon as it became clear that Mrs Willard was quite content for a different niece to act as her receiver, all objections fell away.[37] Mr William Kilbey wrote from Broadmoor to object that 'I have never given consent for [my brother-in-law] S H Johnson to hold any money of mine'. 'In my opinion this matter of my property is not being dealt with fairly', he concluded.[38] Others got in touch many years after being found incapable to argue that the finding was unjust. For Mr Thomas Cook, the fact that his wife had taken control of his finances as his receiver was just as galling as the fact of his long-term detention as a person of unsound mind at the Warneford, a private mental hospital in Oxford. 'Infamous, unjust, nefarious, baffling all the powers of language to fully denounce it', he fumed.[39] The Lunacy Office dutifully responded to such objections, sometimes in consultation with family members and the person's doctor, but these complaints had no impact whatsoever upon determinations of mental capacity itself.

There is no sign of concern amongst doctors, lawyers, Lunacy Office officials, the broader legal system and civil service, or the press about the operation of the Lunacy Office/Court of Protection and its methods of determining capacity until the very end of the century. In 1992, Master of the Court of Protection Mrs Macfarlane confirmed that when it came to defining mental capacity, 'from our point of view, it doesn't seem to give rise to many problems'.[40] Recent research suggests that the same applies today insofar as capacity to manage property and affairs rather than personal welfare is concerned, with almost no decisions under this heading becoming contentious.[41] The lack of controversy surrounding determinations of incapacity also helps to explain why the continued existence of the Lunacy Office has gone largely unnoticed by historians and legal scholars alike. Not unrelated is the fact that it was not a court of record, meaning that its judgements were not recorded or reported for the benefit of the legal profession. Only if a decision were formally appealed was there a chance of it appearing in any legal report, and this was very rare. During the first six decades of the twentieth century, a handful of Lunacy Office decisions were appealed and reported. These dealt with issues such as the exact powers that a receiver or Master in Lunacy had, or how the fees charged by the Lunacy Office should be calculated, and not the question of capacity itself. The latter remained uncontroversial and unchallenged.[42]

The paucity of reported judgements meant that there was no judicial determination of the meaning of 'incapable of managing property and affairs' until 2002, in marked contrast with other areas of mental capacity law.[43] A test for capacity to make a will, for example, had been set down in 1870.[44] Within the medieval and early modern wardship system that later evolved into the lunacy inquisition, there had also been a 'test' for competence that 'covered the three basic areas' of 'perception, cognition, and memory', but as time went by it did not gain formal recognition in statute or case law.[45] The absence of any such formal test for capacity to manage property and affairs may have left applicants, doctors, families, and officials all somewhat freer to apply their own approaches and understandings.

Mental capacity as determined by the Lunacy Office could therefore be particularly susceptible to individual interpretation, creative thinking, and the dominant concerns of decision makers. The circumstances surrounding Miss Alexander's case suggest that decision makers were rarely challenged, and since formal appeals and press attention were both vanishingly rare, Lunacy Office decision makers did not have to explain themselves to much of a wider world at all. Their audience was limited to those with whom they had direct dealings: those found incapable (or not, as the case may be), and their receivers and families. For as long as they remained unchallenged by lawyers, doctors, appeal judges, patients, or the press, these decision makers could cultivate their own views of mental capacity in something approaching isolation. It is likely that those at the helm of the Lunacy Office had a great deal of influence over its model of capacity, and so it becomes important that Master Poyser felt strongly that it should be understood as a 'welfare state service', financially supported by state funding and available to all who needed it.[46]

Although its decisions were not publicly reported, they were still part of a conversation and a negotiation of sorts. By deciding that Miss Alexander was incapable, the Lunacy Office held that any person (and particularly a single woman) of means might deserve or require help from the state, if they seemed unable to protect their own finances and wellbeing. This implicitly advocated for the role of the state in providing such legal protection and, as the next chapter discusses in more detail, in facilitating more quotidian forms of care and support, not only through the Lunacy Office but also through the Official Solicitor. This message was negotiated and expressed in their dealings with all those interested in Miss Alexander: Dr and Mrs Stephenson, Miss Stevenson of the DVAMW, Mr and Mrs Humphries, the neighbours in Chilfrome, Miss Wortt the nurse-companion, Miss Alexander's Norfolk family, and Miss Alexander herself. The willingness of the Lunacy Office, Official Solicitor, LCVs, and most of this wider community to accept that Miss Alexander was incapable and in need of legal intervention reflected some element of support for a larger state that might involve itself in such situations, with barely a whiff of mental infirmity as might be defined by doctors.

The position began to change from the 1950s. Dissatisfaction concerning other branches of mental health law began to surface, taking their clearest shape in the National Council for Civil Liberty's highly critical 1951 report on those 'certified as mental defectives', and the Royal Commission on the Law Relating to Mental Illness and Mental Deficiency that sat from 1954 to 1957.[47] For all that the Court of Protection still failed to grab headlines (or much interest from royal commissions), a handful of people appealed its decisions concerning their incapacity as well. The outcomes of these appeals provided much more specific directions about how mental capacity should be evaluated, and in so doing, increased the role of medical expertise. In a case known as *re EAKM*, the appeal judge found that, although the person in question did still experience significant delusions regarding various family members, these did not affect her ability to manage her own property and affairs, and she should therefore be restored to her property.[48] This contradicted the initial decision from the Court of Protection and set down an important legal precedent. Delusions, or indeed any other symptom of mental illness or weakness on its own, would not be enough to render a person incapable. This reflected the approach adopted much earlier within other branches of capacity law, that illness had to actually affect a person's decision in order to render the decision invalid.[49] Mental infirmity did not necessarily mean mental incapacity. The Court of Protection had been slow to catch up, having operated without challenge for so long and become very ready to take a much more expansive approach.

The appeal judgement in *re EAKM* pre-empted by a few years the view of the Royal Commission on the Law relating to Mental Illness and Mental Deficiency, which recommended in 1957 that there should be no assumption that any patient in a mental hospital was necessarily incapable of managing their affairs.[50] Although this royal commission said little else about the Court of Protection and mainly focused on admission to hospital and treatment, its comments reflected a growing desire to reduce legal involvement in matters of mental illness. Some resistance to the reach of the Court of Protection began to emerge, and mental capacity could no longer be treated as quite so self-evident. It seems unlikely that Miss Alexander would have been found incapable twenty years later, amidst this subtle disquiet about legal intrusion – even though she did remain under the auspices of the Court of Protection for another twelve years, until 1969.

In other ways, perceptions of Miss Alexander's incapacity reflected habits within mental capacity law that had been around for a long time and showed little sign of changing. In 1961, the case of *re CAF* confirmed something that had long been recognised in practice: a person's capacity to make decisions should not be considered in the abstract, but in relation to their specific circumstances. The decision in *re CAF* indicated that someone with more complicated decisions to make would need to show a higher degree of mental capacity (or a lower level of impairment), in order to continue managing their own affairs, than someone facing less difficult decisions.[51] This approach is aligned with what is known today as a functional model of capacity, in which a person's capacity to make decisions will vary depending on the particular questions facing them.[52]

A similar principle was at work in Miss Alexander's case – and earlier cases, too. Her mental capacity was at no point considered as an abstract, objective proposition; it was always described in relation to the situation in which she found herself. Importantly, this was not only a matter of the complexity of her affairs, but also encompassed her broader social situation. The Humphries family were living off her income and in her house. This was the focus of discussion not only because it provided evidence of her social and functional failure, as described above, but also because it created a challenging situation for her to manage. She had to decide whether to allow Mr and Mrs Humphries to continue to live there, and whether to make a change to the financial arrangements between them: these were important decisions, but for Miss Alexander, seemingly impossible ones.

Such attention to specific living situations was not unique to Miss Alexander, for all that it played no part in the majority of determinations of incapacity in which the person in question lived in a hospital. Where allegedly incapable persons lived more independently, their personal circumstances – including the kinds of decisions that might arise for them – had to be considered. For

Miss Carr, the young heiress, her mental capacity was considered in light of her vast fortune and also her somewhat strained relationship with her family, leaving her potentially isolated and easy prey. For Mrs Willard, who had expressed strong views about which of her nieces should act as her receiver in 1931, there was concern that she lived alone and had previously supported rather outré causes such as the 'anti-vivisection cult', bringing her into unsupervised contact with those who might be unfettered by social norms (such as those permitting vivisection) and might take advantage of her 'generous disposition'.[53] Capacity was not inherent within these people, but conceptualised in relation to their specific circumstances and potential decisions.

In recent years, socio-legal scholars have criticised the idea of mental capacity as something that a person either has or lacks, independently of extrinsic factors such as their living situation or the people around them. This draws on theories of vulnerability, highlighting that the notion of an objective state of mental incapacity flowing from mental infirmity ignores 'the broader structural factors that render us [all] vulnerable' to harm or coercion, irrespective of physical or mental impairment.[54] Views of incapacity as objectively present alongside mental illness can be found in the mid-twentieth-century Lunacy Office, in its easy acceptance that all those taking up long-term residence in hospitals or nursing homes must be lacking capacity – that their illness had produced an inherent incapacity, no matter what kinds of decisions faced them. Miss Alexander's case highlights that this was not the only view of incapacity, though. Vulnerability was not a part of Lunacy Office or medical vocabulary in the mid-twentieth century; nevertheless, Miss Alexander and other women whose cases tested Lunacy Office boundaries left signs that the office was alert to circumstances that might place people at risk of financial harm, albeit only certain kinds of circumstances, and certain kinds of people.

THE FINAL DECISION

Dr Rotherham, one of the two medically qualified LCVs in post in 1939, finally went to see Miss Alexander in early July. No copy of his report survives. I can say that medical visitors did not always support applications for receivers, because I have found one example in which an LCV does not do so: in the early 1920s, Dr Nathan Raw visited Mrs Maria Wilson, a woman in her eighties whose son alleged that she was incapable as a result of 'the influence exercised over [her] by one Minas Krikorian, an Armenian Secretary in her employ'. This had some similarities with Miss Alexander's situation, in that the alleged incapacity was evidenced by susceptibility to the unwelcome influence of others. After visiting Mrs Wilson, though, Dr Raw's report 'was unfavourable to the application which was dismissed'. In other words, he found Mrs Wilson to be perfectly capable of responding appropriately to Krikorian's influence and looking after her own interests.[55] Dr Rotherham, by contrast, did not hesitate at the Old Rectory – or did not hesitate much, at least. As soon as the Lunacy Office had his report, a new hearing was scheduled for Miss Alexander's case.

The final determination was made by Assistant Master Keely in his office at the Royal Courts of Justice, on 24 July 1939. Notably, this was still considered a straightforward case: it fell to Master Henry Methold to deal with anything complex, while the two Assistant Masters Keely and Poyser divided up the rest between themselves. Also present in the room was the Official Solicitor's representative Mr Graves, and perhaps also a clerk to assist Keely – although clerks were in short supply.[56] Assistant Master Keely had read over the written submissions in advance. A draft of the Order that would give formal standing to his decision and instructions had already been prepared. This decision, a momentous one for Miss Alexander's future, was issued quietly and quickly. The hearing did not last long. Miss Alexander was at home in Dorset: she would never meet anyone from the Lunacy Office at all.

Was Miss Alexander even aware that it was happening? She must have suffered through Dr Rotherham's visit with considerable anxiety, feeling that her home, her way of living, her mind, and her every word were being scrutinised by a stranger yet again. Did she hope that these visits would bring change of some kind, and that they might reduce the role of Mr and Mrs Humphries in her life, or did she see the dreaded mental hospital as the only outcome if she was found wanting? Did she wish that all this trouble would just go away, and did she decide to stop engaging with it with that wish in mind? The Lunacy Office was obliged to notify her solicitors of the second hearing, but did this news definitely find its way to Miss Alexander? Did she appreciate its implications? Did she want to lodge another objection? Did her solicitors advise against a battle with more compelling evidence from a Lord Chancellor's doctor, or was the household unable to keep up its fight in the face of relatively fast-moving legal complexities – because of a lack of means, a lack of will, or an equally insurmountable lack of familiarity with deadlines and procedures? Were there disagreements amongst all those at the Old Rectory about next steps, preventing any kind of decisive action? Did these strange legal proceedings in London simply fade from view amidst everyday trials and tribulations: minor illnesses, accidents, celebrations, arguments, outings, family announcements (Mr and Mrs Humphries's daughter was pregnant again), money worries (Miss Alexander's accounts were overdrawn), even war worries (there were air raid exercises over Dorset, warning of what was about to come)?[57] I can imagine a household in turmoil after Stephenson's banishment, Meysey-Thompson's visit, and the first flush of legal events, but as the summer dragged on and the Lunacy Office pressed forward with another hearing, the picture fades.

Assistant Master Keely's Order confirmed that Miss Alexander was incapable of managing her affairs by reason of mental infirmity, and appointed the Official Solicitor to act as her receiver. It directed the Official Solicitor to spend up to but not exceeding Miss Alexander's income on 'her maintenance and for providing her with such extra comforts as she can enjoy', a piece of standard wording. Less typically, it also directed the Official Solicitor to make all necessary enquiries to establish the exact extent of her fortune, and to investigate and report back concerning her family, 'the existing arrangements for the care and maintenance of the Patient and as to whether any alteration in such arrangements is necessary or desirable', and whether any person had undertaken any 'dealings' with Miss Alexander's property since 1 January 1939 – the notional date upon which her mental incapacity had begun.[58]

Although she became incapable in law, uncertainty remains. Was Miss Alexander really terrorised and bullied by Mr and Mrs Humphries and living in misery, unable for some reason connected to her mental state to speak up for herself or to take action? Or, was this version of events a rather melodramatic account of a domestic arrangement that the men (and some women) who peered in on life at the Old Rectory did not like? In other words, to what extent was she 'really' incapable of looking after her own affairs?

Miss Alexander's own version of events is often ventriloquised through others. Very possibly her letter to Dr Stephenson asking him to stop interfering *was* dictated to her, but very possibly she did also resent his interference after years of being told by him that she should behave differently. Having criticised the Lunacy Office for dismissing the views of its 'patients' when they failed to tally with its own preferences, I am reluctant to dismiss this letter entirely. Elsewhere, Miss Alexander expressed contradictory views. To the Official Solicitor's visitor Mr Reginald Winder, Miss Alexander reportedly expressed delight at the prospect of a 'holiday' away from the Old Rectory, so that the Humphries family could be removed in her absence. Then one month later she 'wept so much & there was such a scene' at the prospect of her beginning this holiday, that the attempt was abandoned. Miss Alexander, so it was said, wanted to remain at home to celebrate young Miss Humphries's wedding the following day.[59] Criticisms of Mr and Mrs Humphries that were later attributed to Miss Alexander did not extend to their children and grandchildren, whom she had known since birth or early childhood. She was a gentle person; she did not like to make waves; and she may have loved these young people very much. Being abruptly told to miss a family wedding: her tears are easy to understand.

When she did finally leave the Old Rectory temporarily, in January 1940, Miss Alexander was described as 'very happy and delighted'. She reportedly characterised her years with the Humphries family as 'terrible'. Mr Humphries, in particular, had 'frightened and bullied her'.[60] 'She said that this was the first time for years that anybody had been kind to her', according to Mr Winder, for whom this meant a very satisfactory conclusion to his rather unusual (and protracted) job of work in Dorset. He did not mention whether Miss Alexander was missing any of the Humphries family, or her beautiful home, or whether it had been made clear to her that she no longer had control over her money and her future.

My speculations emphasise how much remains unknowable, even while official reports sound final and complete. Miss Alexander's case shows the extent to which legal decisions rely on creativity and chance, and hints at the disorder lurking behind every seemingly secure judgement. Disorder lurks behind every orderly historical account too; this particular account finds one way for Miss Alexander's surprising experiences to make sense. It was possible for Miss Alexander to be incapable in law of making her own decisions, even though her 'disease' required no medical insight or treatment, and her 'infirmity' did not prevent her from living in her own home and community. This generated a pressing question for her receiver, the Official Solicitor. What kind of care did this sort of person need?

4

§

PROVIDING CARE

After the hearing at which Miss Alexander's incapacity to manage her affairs was confirmed, the Official Solicitor's office began to piece together a picture of her financial and personal circumstances. This was delayed thanks to the '[i]nternational situation developing as it did', with the country declaring war on Germany and the evacuation of most Lunacy Office and Official Solicitor personnel out of central London to Cambridge.[1] The Official Solicitor's visitor Mr Winder finally undertook a fact-finding mission to Dorset in November 1939, and letters then flew back and forth between Cambridge and Dorset to make plans. In early January 1940, Mr Winder was at last able to return to Dorset to put these plans in motion. After some tumultuous scenes at the Old Rectory, he drove Miss Alexander to the home of her new nurse-companion, Kate Wortt, in the nearby town of Corfe Mullen, and a few months later the two women returned together to the Old Rectory. Here they remained for the next twenty-five years, with Miss Wortt diligently reporting to the Official Solicitor on a regular basis about her work providing companionship, supervision, support, advice, and care.

Being found incapable therefore introduced a consistent element of care and external control into Miss Alexander's life. This chapter builds on historical work that has drawn attention to the 'pluralistic landscape of care' for mental illness, and for older people as well, in which family care, institutional care, and other formal and informal services all co-existed.[2] Research on the implementation of the Mental Deficiency Acts in particular has drawn attention to the importance of care and supervision in the community, rather than in institutions.[3] The role of mental capacity law in delivering care and control in the community is little known, having been very much overshadowed by attention to legal processes addressing hospitalisation. Miss Alexander's experience suggests that the broader context highlighted by work on mental deficiency, in which policies and laws responding to mental weakness or a 'lack of character' could lead to significant and long-lasting interventions in the home, had much broader ramifications. At the same time, close scrutiny of this involvement in community care is also suggestive of the low profile and status of care work in the home, even when it became the responsibility of the state.

Nurse-companion Miss Wortt came to occupy a central place in Miss Alexander's life. She is also one of the most important people in the archival records about Miss Alexander: her regular letters to the Official Solicitor begin in late 1939 and continue until shortly after Miss Alexander's death three decades later, in 1969. It is therefore mostly through Miss Wortt's eyes that Miss Alexander's life after being found incapable takes shape. Miss Wortt's role and presence brings to the foreground questions about care as paid employment, personal imperative, and social responsibility. Legal scholar Lydia Hayes has argued that paid care in the home is often unhelpfully conceptualised as something very different from care in institutional settings, because its supposedly private and intimate qualities make it appear highly individualised and rooted in personal relationships. In fact, as she proposes, homecare workers 'carry public priorities, public duties and public policy into domestic environments'.[4] The personal relationship between Miss Alexander and Miss Wortt was undoubtedly very important to both women, but Miss Wortt's work was one small part of a larger system of care governed by capacity law and policy. Importantly, recognition of this draws attention to the operation of capacity law itself as a form of care.[5]

Miss Wortt's role and her letters also highlight the relationship between care on one hand, and constraint or control on the other. Histories of medico-legal interventions such as involuntary detention in asylums rarely depict constraints or controls over patients as caring, or in a positive light, while historically informed work on nursing has highlighted that care can very easily co-exist with harm.[6] The care provided to Miss Alexander entailed a great deal of control, and considerable scope for harm. Miss Wortt controlled Miss Alexander's money, supervised her everyday activities, and also spoke on her behalf to the civil servants who had ultimate control over her future. These forms of control, which flowed from the Lunacy Office to the Official Solicitor to Miss Wortt and were a significant infringement of Miss Alexander's rights, were an integral part of the care provided to those seen as vulnerable and in-capable of managing their own affairs. Insight into the interplay between care and control in the administration of mental capacity law is informed here by work on assisted decision-making in the first decades of the twenty-first cen-tury, which has begun to suggest new ways of conceptualising care, control, and capacity itself.[7]

For Miss Alexander the care provided by the Lunacy Office seems to have had largely positive outcomes, but, as always, uncertainty lingers. I rely a great deal on Miss Wortt's letters but know little else about her, and less still about Miss Alexander's own experiences or views during these years. Past actors and events collide once again with present concerns and feelings: I came to like and admire Miss Wortt, and to have my own hopes for her future with Miss Alexander. This emotional investment may have prompted my own at-tempt to provide a kind of care, by paying close attention to the ladies of the Old Rectory, but such care is also entangled with control. After all, this story follows the contours that piqued my interest and ultimately persuaded me, in the hope that they will persuade others and at the expense of that which interested me less. This chapter closes by probing some of the difficulties of interpreting – and delivering – care and control.

CARE IN THE HOME

To establish what kind of care Miss Alexander needed, the Official Solicitor's representative Mr Winder canvassed local views. He consulted the vicar's wife, the secretary of the local mental welfare association, the DVAMW, the local police constable, and of course, Dr Stephenson, who had brought Miss Alexander to the attention of the Lunacy Office in the first place. Mr Winder was persuaded by their shared perspective: the Humphries family had to be removed immediately, and someone else must be found to help look after the Old Rectory and Miss Alexander. The initial picture that Stephenson had painted, of a disreputable family taking disgraceful advantage of a weak and pitiful woman, was apparently recognised and endorsed by all those with whom Mr Winder consulted – and in the end, by Mr Winder himself. Assistant Master Keely of the Lunacy Office gave his approval to the proposal to evict the Humphries with all possible haste, and to find a more suitable person to live with and look after Miss Alexander. Mr Winder subsequently received a £10 Post Office warrant from the Official Solicitor, and 'carte blanche' to do whatever was necessary to achieve this.[8]

Receivers often had quite a bit of work to do as soon as they were appointed – not least because, as discussed in chapter 2, their appointment was often prompted by financial issues that needed attention. Lunacy Office masters could usually give specific directions at the outset, having been provided with a full account of these issues. Mr Robert Gladstone's interim receiver, for one, was instructed to start making fixed monthly payments to Mr Gladstone's current and former wives and to carry on the running of Mr Gladstone's business, a preparatory school – a task made much easier by the receiver's status as the school's accountant.[9] But Miss Alexander's receiver was not the only one to return to the Lunacy Office fairly swiftly, seeking approval for further steps to disentangle difficulties. Mr Michael Golodetz's receivers corresponded at length with the office about making changes to the partnership agreement for the family business, 'to arrange matters as to the best tax advantage of [Mr Golodetz's] partners as well as of other members of the family'.[10] Facing problems of a different sort, Mrs Alice Froud's niece and receiver liaised closely with the Lunacy Office to pursue and then settle on Mrs Froud's behalf a legal dispute over the late Mr Froud's will.[11] The dispute was a very personal one, and emotions ran high. Such matters could be complex, requiring time and careful negotiation to resolve. Miss Alexander's experience is particularly distinctive only because of the detail and sense of drama with which it was reported.

Disagreement regarding the Official Solicitor's plan of action for Miss Alexander came, very understandably, from the Humphries family, whose home and employment was threatened, and in a much less assertive manner, from Miss Alexander herself. Miss Alexander was very probably fearful of being taken to a mental hospital and anxious not to upset Mr and Mrs Humphries; it is also possible that she was fond of some (if not all) of the family and unhappy at the prospect of living alone. But, once she had been taken away from Mr and Mrs Humphries, and it was clear that her long-term future lay back in her own home and with a companion, her objections seemed to disappear entirely.

Dealing with the Humphries family, on the other hand, was awkward and protracted. As he told his employer on the telephone from Dorset, fresh from the excitement of an extraordinary workday, Mr Winder 'had received considerable opposition and abuse' from Mr and Mrs Humphries upon telling them that they had to leave the Old Rectory: 'in fact he was threatened by Mrs Humphreys [sic] with a frying pan'.[12] (I have to assume that this ambush with kitchenware was a professional first for Mr Winder, for all that it is recounted in the deadpan tone of officialdom.) Mrs Humphries maintained that she and her husband had solemnly promised the late Dr Norton to look after Miss Alexander, while her son penned a letter to beg that his parents be permitted to remain in what had been their home for fifteen years. 'After all', wrote the newly minted Private Humphries from his barracks on the south coast, 'I am helping to protect this country, and why should my mother and father be turned out into the cold'?[13]

Such pleas fell on deaf ears. Mr and Mrs Humphries were threatened with eviction through the courts, and finally left the Old Rectory a few months later, in spring 1940. 'The patient is very happy now that the Humphries have left', wrote Official Solicitor's visitor Mrs Lucy Winder in June 1940, 'and she has no longer the fear of meeting them'.[14] Always a fleeting archival presence, written in by men and women who thoroughly disapproved of them, the family vanish from the records and from Miss Alexander's life.

As to who should replace them, Miss Stevenson of the DVAMW had been able to recommend Kate Wortt, an ex-nurse in her mid-fifties who was 'strong-minded but kindly, in fact just the person required'. Miss Wortt was running a wool shop in nearby Bournemouth, but was keen to return to nursing. Her previous experience included care of a 'mental patient' of 'a mild type', and a career in her youth as a children's nanny.[15] Presumably, given the ominous mutterings of drink at the Old Rectory, Miss Wortt was also not known to indulge in alcohol herself. She was prepared to move to the Old Rectory to live, and had no dependants to complicate matters. Mr Winder met with her and found her to be an extremely suitable person. After serving notice on the Humphries and facing down the frying pan in January 1940, he drove Miss Alexander to Miss Wortt's bungalow in Corfe Mullen, a temporary refuge until such time as Mr and Mrs Humphries were gone from the Old Rectory and both women could return to Chilfrome together.[16]

In the short term, Miss Alexander's material living conditions and wellbeing were considerably enhanced by Miss Wortt's care. Miss Alexander reported that she was pleased to be 'allowed' a hot water bottle in bed on cold nights, and Mr Winder found that she had 'improved wonderfully' after only a few days in Corfe Mullen.[17] Miss Wortt purchased for her a new coat, dressing gown, nightdress, and stockings, and organised a home visit from a dentist, a general check-up with the local doctor, and, with the doctor's agreement, ordered in a supply of Guinness, fortified wine, and 'Veganine tablets' to build up her frail charge's strength.[18] However, as far as Miss Wortt could see, the 'real cure' for Miss Alexander's nervousness and indifferent health was the Old Rectory itself, the house and gardens that Miss Alexander loved so much, and she advocated for a speedy return.

When they finally moved back to the Old Rectory in April 1940, Miss Wortt 'worked valiantly to get the house in order and really has done wonders', according to official visitor Mrs Winder. Miss Wortt's work included dealing with a flea infestation throughout the house, bringing the large gardens under control with the aid of a local gardener, getting the kitchen and bathroom into working order, and equipping the premises with all necessary home comforts, linens, and crockery – most of which had reportedly disappeared during Mr and Mrs Humphries's final months there. Miss Alexander, like the house, was transformed by Miss Wortt's efforts. No longer cowering and fearful around visitors, she was 'lying in a deck chair in the garden' when Mrs Winder arrived in June 1940, 'reading, and when the evening comes she generally plays croquet. I understand she is eating and sleeping well', Mrs Winder added, 'and certainly Miss Wortt gives her every care and attention and they seem to get on excellently'.[19]

Until both Miss Wortt and Miss Alexander struggled with illness in the 1960s, when they were in their seventies and eighties respectively, there was little discussion of medical care. Certainly, in Miss Wortt's eyes, Miss Alexander did not need medical treatment for the unspecified mental infirmity that rendered her incapable of managing her own property and affairs. She was 'very highly strung & nervous', but this did not require medical intervention – particularly since any such intervention would most likely have to involve a mental hospital. Voluntary treatment had become more widely available since the Mental Treatment Act of 1930, but clinics for outpatient treatment for mental illness were still relatively few and far between and were mostly 'under the auspices of the local mental hospitals':[20] an unappealing prospect. As the true cost of running the Old Rectory (and the limitations of Dr Norton's estate) became more apparent in the summer of 1940, the Official Solicitor very tentatively suggested that Miss Alexander might consider living elsewhere, such as a hospital – where the vast majority of people for whom the Official Solicitor acted as receiver could be found. This was quickly shot down. 'I feel most of all, Miss Alexander's health would suffer greatly', Miss Wortt responded. 'I am sure she would never consent', and it would be absolutely impossible to hospitalise her against her will since she was not at all 'certifiable'.[21] Following this unequivocal statement, institutional care was not mentioned again for over twenty years, until the prospect of a nursing home with round-the-clock staff to meet Miss Alexander's increasing needs had to be faced.

To remain at home, those found incapable of managing their own affairs usually had to have highly engaged family members on hand who would either organise paid care or provide it themselves. The latter was the only option for those whose means were limited. Lunacy Office records note with sympathy the financial hardship that providing full-time care could cause, but many family members did care for their relatives at home nonetheless, sometimes for long periods and at considerable personal expense.[22] When there was more money available, long-term live-in companions like Miss Wortt were not unusual. Miss Eileen Beresford had already been living with Miss Thomas, a companion employed by her family, for six years when she was found legally incapable in 1922, and this arrangement with Miss Thomas continued until Miss Beresford's death eighteen years later.[23] Similarly, John Brocklehurst's daily care was entrusted to a Miss Tullett, who had looked after him since his childhood in the 1930s and remained with him for at least twenty-five years and possibly very much longer.[24] For those without willing and interested family members to organise or provide care in the home, whether or not they required medical treatment, institutionalisation was usually the only solution.[25] The Official Solicitor and Miss Wortt stepped in to compensate for Miss Alexander's distant family and very limited fortune, but for others found incapable, there was no guarantee of such diligent attention.

As scholars of care in the twenty-first century have pointed out, where medical and social care are firmly separated, those who need help with everyday tasks but cannot afford to pay for such help often find themselves 'injected' into the health care system. Social care thus becomes a subdivision of medical services, and the non-medical aspects of care are sidelined.[26] There are signs that the same was true for Miss Alexander and others found incapable, in the interwar years. In 1939 to 1940, all agreed that Miss Alexander needed care in the form of companionship and an element of supervision rather than medical treatment, but this required money. Miss Alexander's income from Dr Norton's will trust was barely enough to meet the costs of running the Old Rectory, leaving almost nothing to pay for care; only the industrious efforts of the Official Solicitor and the unpaid work of Miss Wortt made it possible. This effort to keep Miss Alexander in her home, often in quite trying circumstances, was undoubtedly part and parcel of the care that the Lunacy Office, her receiver, and her companion provided. Attention could therefore focus on 'the non-medical aspects of care' for Miss Alexander at home.

Hints across the archives suggest the kind of daily care that Miss Wortt provided, which was considerable in its range and extent. Notes and passing references suggest that Miss Wortt slept in the same room as Miss Alexander for at least a few years, brought her breakfast in bed, prepared her food and encouraged her to eat well, organised appointments for her, and sometimes provided physical assistance when accidents or bursts of acute illness impaired her mobility.[27] She took responsibility for the problems of lodgers, home repairs, and generally making ends meet, and also urged Miss Alexander to meet new people, in some cases building friendships that would last many years.[28] Miss Wortt did not spend a night away from Miss Alexander for twenty years, with the exception of a few brief stays in hospital – and during those stays, Miss Wortt took it upon herself to ensure that Miss Alexander was not alone at the Old Rectory. Even after suffering a serious haemorrhage and fall in the winter of 1960 to 1961, Miss Wortt was joined in her convalescence at the seaside by Miss Alexander, since there was no one else available to take Miss Wortt's place at the Old Rectory.[29] In 1962, as Miss Alexander became increasingly frail and forgetful, Miss Wortt observed that her charge was 'now at the stage where I can't leave her alone' at all, meaning that she was providing constant supervision.[30] This continued for three years, until Miss Alexander entered a nursing home. Although the exact nature of Miss Wortt's work was only mentioned in passing over the years, it was far from insignificant.

The smallness of the hints about Miss Wortt's activities reflects the longstanding invisibility of much care work.[31] Taking place within the home, such work entailed forms of labour that were little valued, and indeed, could barely be perceived as 'real work' of any kind. As sociologists of care in the twenty-first century have argued, work such as 'making a cup of tea, having a chat, taking time to make people feel good about themselves' is rarely noticed and counted as work, while the intimate and private setting of the home brings with it 'reductive and isolating assumptions' about what caregiving means and who should provide it.[32] This is echoed throughout the surviving Lunacy Office and Official Solicitor records, in which very little is said about the care work carried out by companions and carers of all stripes. Although Miss Alexander's home had become the locus of public policy intervention, with the appointment of the Official Solicitor as her receiver and the organisation of a full-time live-in companion, the work actually carried out by this companion was of minimal official interest. As long as there were no complaints – and a balanced budget – both the Official Solicitor and Lunacy Office did not have to think too hard about it.

Admittedly, the primary role of these departments was to manage the finances of those found incapable of doing so themselves. Matters of personal and social care were secondary to this, which contributes to their marginal status within surviving documents. That said, Lunacy Office instructions to receivers almost always included the direction to use a certain amount of money for the incapable person's maintenance and general benefit, which required attention to personal, medical, and social needs, balancing their requirements with the money available. Miss Wortt and her work became extremely important to the Lunacy Office and Official Solicitor for this very reason: it came at virtually no monetary cost. Miss Wortt had originally been recruited with the promise of a salary of one pound per week plus room and board, but this promise dissolved in the deluge of expenses and debts to be settled from Miss Alexander's fixed income.[33] Miss Wortt received a fortnightly allowance from which to pay for all household costs, and there was rarely anything left over for her to take as her wage.

It was not as though the question of Miss Wortt's salary simply slipped from view over the years. Her status became so unclear that the local pensions officer could not fathom, when he called at the Old Rectory in 1946, whether she was an employee or not. Pensions and benefits were in flux: a new state pension was on the horizon, and Miss Wortt had turned sixty, the age of eligibility for pensions for women, the year before. The Official Solicitor had to provide confirmation that, six years into the role, Miss Wortt received no salary and should be considered retired.[34] Although this was useful from the Official Solicitor's perspective, because Miss Wortt's pension could be used to supplement the household income at the Old Rectory, it was not necessarily to Miss Wortt's best advantage. It also underscored the Official Solicitor's understanding by this point that her work was informal, undertaken out of love and loyalty towards Miss Alexander and not in exchange for regular payment.

Miss Wortt's relationship with Miss Alexander remains unclear. The two seem to have quickly developed a close and friendly understanding, if not a relationship of equals. To the outside observer, Miss Alexander was clearly the fortunate recipient of Miss Wortt's diligent care and supervision, and Miss Wortt was very much in charge of the household. Mrs Winder described Miss Alexander as 'lucky' to have such a kindly and efficient companion.[35] 'Miss Wortt is wonderfully good to the patient', Mrs Winder wrote in 1946, 'and by pooling their resources manages to make a very happy home for both of them'.[36] The general practitioner who attended both women in later years also chipped in, commenting with admiration upon Miss Wortt's '25 years [of] devoted service' to Miss Alexander.[37] Miss Wortt herself wrote in increasingly affectionate terms about Miss Alexander, 'a very lovable person' whose happiness brought her 'great joy'. As both women battled with declining health and the challenges of living in an isolated rural spot, Miss Wortt promised that she would 'not give up as long as I can help her', a promise that she valiantly tried to keep.[38] To the matron of the nursing home to which Miss Alexander moved in 1965, Miss Wortt was characterised by the Official Solicitor not as an employee or professional carer whose services were no longer needed, but as a 'very devoted and invaluable companion' and 'friend'.[39]

At the same time, Miss Wortt's care may not have been inspired by this personal commitment and emotional investment alone. It was a responsibility that she took on at first because it provided a welcome alternative to earning her living by running a shop. Although her work at the Old Rectory was unpaid, she did benefit in material ways. She was able to live at the Old Rectory rent free and to benefit from Miss Alexander's income, paying for food, coal, transportation, home help from gardeners and charwomen, outings, a pet dog, and even occasional holidays from their shared resources. Especially as Miss Alexander's income increased in the 1950s when Dr Norton's investments performed well, this afforded Miss Wortt a standard of living that would otherwise have been out of reach. Miss Wortt also came to love the beautiful setting of the Old Rectory almost as much as Miss Alexander, describing it as a 'haven' and her two decades there as 'the happiest years of my life'.[40]

The benefits that Miss Wortt gained raised the question, for the trustees of Dr Norton's will trust, of whether she might be taking advantage of her position. Had this not happened once before, after all? Hadn't Mr and Mrs Humphries grown rather too comfortable at the Old Rectory, living a life of leisure at Miss Alexander's expense? If Miss Wortt had come to enjoy her new lifestyle so very much, might she resist any suggestion that a smaller and more affordable home would really be in Miss Alexander's best interests? The trustees put forward proposals to sell or rent out the Old Rectory quite frequently, to free up more cash for Miss Alexander's living expenses. 'We gather up to now the proposals have been put to [Miss Alexander] through Miss Wortt', the trustees observed. 'Miss Wortt herself is, we understand, a lady over 70 years of age, and may be herself disinclined to make a change'.[41] (She may well have been disinclined to accept the extra decade they added to her age.) Such suggestions were investigated by a member of staff from the Official Solicitor's office, despatched to Dorset to make enquiries. 'There is little doubt in my mind that Miss Wortt holds the purse strings', he concluded, 'but there is no question of domination towards the Patient'.[42] Subsequent reports echo this impression: although Miss Wortt was firmly in control, she was also attentive to Miss Alexander's wishes – and to the requirements of the Official Solicitor to stay within budget, no matter what. Her supervision and management were consistently recognised as sufficient but not excessive, and there was no further intimation that she might ever put her own interests first.

Miss Wortt therefore occupied an uncertain position. She managed Miss Alexander's household budget on behalf of the Official Solicitor, she ran the house, and she provided everyday advice and support, in exchange for some material benefits but mostly because she came to care about Miss Alexander. She was something in between a professional nurse-companion, a housekeeper, and a close friend. This uncertainty, I suspect, is rare only for the clarity with which it is conveyed in the archives, over a period of decades and through her own letters. Elsewhere, paid carers became family, family members became professional carers, and professional helpers of various kinds became involved in the provision of care. After being discharged from an asylum in 1905, Miss Edith Hide lived for thirty-five years with a 'lady-doctor' who provided not only expert supervision but also a home and a place for Miss Hide in her family.[43] Miss Beresford's long-term carer was paid a wage, but was described in terms that echo accounts of Miss Wortt: 'a companion ... who is also a friend'.[44] For the Sims brothers, William and Arthur, the Hole family with whom they had boarded since their adolescence seems to have become an adopted family, with all attendant squabbles and affections. Although the Holes received a modest weekly payment from William and Arthur's income, this was to cover expenses only and was emphatically not meant as payment or profit.[45]

In contrast, where funds were plentiful within the estate of someone found incapable, male family members were paid quite generously for their work. Malcolm Roberts's mother employed her nephew, Valentine Atkin, as her son's companion in exchange for a regular wage and provision for a pension. Peter Stephens received a payment of £20 a week for looking after his mother, plus accommodation in a house specially purchased with his mother's money. Tellingly, although the vast majority of carers and companions were women, there are no examples of female relatives receiving payment. Responsibility for personal care often passed from one generation of women to the next, while the financial responsibility of acting as a receiver was rather more commonly – although certainly not always – held by men. William and Arthur Sims's father and then their cousin Albert acted as their receiver, while several generations of Hole women took care of them on a day-to-day basis. Notably, a male member of the Hole family was refused permission to house Arthur Sims, since he would have 'no woman' to help him.[46] Mary Barnes, who was found incapable in 1931 and needed round-the-clock supervision and help with every aspect of daily life, lived with two female cousins with whom she had been raised, after the death of her aunt, their mother. There is no mention in the archives of their three brothers.[47] After the death of her last surviving sister, Annie Alpass's male relatives became involved in the oversight of her finances (and took her out for drives), but it was her nieces who moved in to live with her and provided daily care and supervision.[48] Unpaid care was largely the responsibility of women, usually family.

The hazy distinction between informal care from family and friends and paid care work is in some respects an inheritance of earlier practices within nursing, domestic psychiatry, and mental capacity law. These practices had emphasised the importance of finding a family member who could sustain a long-term personal relationship with the incapable or unwell person, in order to provide both control and care. When extended family networks failed to yield a suitable person in the eighteenth and nineteenth centuries, the wider family personnel could be adjusted to include a paid servant taking on the role. As historians of mental disability and nursing have made clear, paid care existed long before the arrival of institutional care.[49] The household (rather than the family) included these servants, who might be employed temporarily or for longer periods. With the expansion of asylum care, there was no shortage of servants who had received training in institutions of some kind and could command special payment for their work.[50] Yet, the requirement and expectation that they become something like family in order to deliver successful care and control tended to undermine the notion that care work required special knowledge and skill.

Sociological and feminist work on care has drawn attention to the belief that families, and particularly their female members, are the best or proper providers of care. One of the impacts of this, as Eva Kittay writes, is that the work of caring for those who are significantly dependent on others has 'never occupied a clear place in our economic order'. Even in its salaried iterations, it is poorly valued, not least because it 'competes with a vast unpaid workforce' of mostly female family and friends.[51] Plenty of husbands, sons, and brothers were appointed as receivers, but the small numbers of paid male attendants and companions only emphasises the large numbers of women providing unpaid care. From the perspective of the Lunacy Office, care in the home rather than institutionalisation was perfectly welcome for those found incapable, but it required family involvement to organise it and often the unpaid work of women to deliver it. Even after the mid-1940s and a much larger welfare state, there is little sign in the archives of the prioritisation of this kind of home care through paid services, or very much close enquiry into the kind of care that was actually given and received.

OFFICIAL CARE

Although daily care in the home was largely carried out without notice, this is not to say that there was no official attention paid to matters of care. As Joan Tronto has argued, 'care' has long been seen as something private and somehow feminine, obscuring the many ways in which public, political, and typically 'masculine' activities involve forms of care work.[52] Financial oversight and management was one such way in which care – and its counterpart, control –

was delivered to those found incapable. For Miss Alexander, the Official Solicitor and his staff took pre-emptive steps to increase her income so that she
could afford to stay at the Old Rectory. They repeatedly reviewed her financial
position and applied for regular refunds of income tax; they also carried 'a
considerable adverse balance' on their ledger for many years and used the
weight of their authority to keep irritable creditors at bay.[53] They negotiated
with the trustees of Dr Norton's will trust for the capital to bear some larger
costs associated with the Old Rectory and its upkeep, and for the sale of some
of the extra land and cottages that were more of a drain on Miss Alexander's
income than an asset. While Miss Wortt tackled day-to-day budgeting, the Official Solicitor's office found ways to improve Miss Alexander's finances overall;
while Miss Wortt came up with plans for vegetable plots and paying lodgers,
the Official Solicitor's office gave practical help and moral support.

Relatedly, the Official Solicitor respected Miss Alexander's wishes and remained unerringly supportive of her desire to remain in her own home. Miss
Alexander's attachment to the house where she had lived with her 'dear doctor'
for so many years was clear from the outset of the receivership; Miss Alexander
herself reportedly said in the mid-1940s that she was 'horrified at the thought
of having to be turned out of her present surroundings and she was quite
convinced that she would not "last very long", to use her own words, if this
took place'.[54] That the Official Solicitor's office took time to solicit her views
and worked extremely hard to respect them is worthy of note. It was far from
a foregone conclusion that an official receiver would be quite so involved in
supporting the wishes and wellbeing of the person for whom they acted, although by the 1940s it was becoming more common.

Since the 1930s, the Official Solicitor's office had taken a much more proactive interest in the lives of those for whom it acted as receiver, looking beyond
the purely financial. This engagement seems to have coincided with the appointment of Alexander Gilchrist to the position of Official Solicitor in 1932,
and reflected decades of increasing professionalisation across the civil service.
For the Official Solicitor, such professionalisation included an end to the arrangement that the post-holder would personally keep all of the fees he
charged for acting as receiver: in 1919, a fixed fee payable to the Treasury and
not the post-holder's pocket was introduced instead. 'Now his only interest
in costs', remarked Lunacy Office Master Theobald dryly in the early 1920s,
'is the gratification of contributing to public revenue'.[55]

Shortly after Mr Gilchrist's appointment, the husband-and-wife team of Reginald and Lucy Winder was recruited to pay annual visits to all those for whom the Official Solicitor acted as receiver. This formalised and extended a previously ad hoc process by which the Official Solicitor would occasionally visit those for whom he acted as receiver, if particular problems came up. Mrs Winder had relevant experience of a sort: her father, David Thomson, had been the medical superintendent of the Norfolk County Asylum, so she had grown up around asylums, doctors, nurses, and patients.[56] (Perhaps her childhood in Norfolk gave her a point of connection with Miss Alexander.) The Winders' own fees – which were usually paid by the estates of those being visited – were justified on the basis that the law surrounding lunacy had assumed 'that there would be two sets of Visitors to Patients, the first either from the Board of Control or the Lord Chancellor's Visitors and the second from the Patient's relatives'. The Winders, therefore, were filling the shoes of family, since the Official Solicitor's 'Patients' rarely had relatives on hand to stop by.[57] Mr and Mrs Winder were tasked to discover whether each person's needs were being met or whether they could benefit from anything different, finances permitting, and whether suitable arrangements had been made for their 'spiritual comfort and sustenance'.[58]

Most of the Winders' work (and that of their successors) involved visiting institutions, where the vast majority of those for whom the Official Solicitor acted as receiver were living. Altogether, about 10 per cent of all those found incapable lived at home, but those without family who relied on the Official Solicitor were perhaps even more likely to be institutionalised, since they had no family member able to act as receiver and this often meant no family to organise home care. The Winders would report on the patient's appearance, health, and general wellbeing, and the quality of attention they received from hospital staff, and would make suggestions for any changes that might be of benefit, such as a private room or new clothes.

These visits, along with those carried out by the LCVs plus associated arrangements for companions like Miss Wortt, are examples of that which Peter Bartlett has called 'extra-legal control mechanisms'. They were undertaken to ensure the 'safety and appropriate conduct' of those found incapable, especially amongst those who were not institutionalised and might retain a good degree of freedom.[59] At the same time, the information that flowed back from these visits encouraged the Lunacy Office – and the Official Solicitor, to some degree – to adopt a broader sense of responsibility for the wellbeing of those found incapable.

For the Official Solicitor, Mr and Mrs Winder's annual visits paved the way for a much more engaged style of receivership. As the Winders' first reports about many hundreds of patients began to arrive back in London, Mr Gilchrist felt that there was much that he as receiver could do for those for whom he acted. 'The more I have to go into the lives of my 1700 Patients in detail', he wrote in 1934, 'the more I am convinced that curiously enough it is the small matters that count'.[60] The 'small matters' in mental hospitals that immediately caught his eye included a lack of privacy when bathing, poor diet, and the use of institutional instead of personal underwear – a practice that shocked him considerably. He also complained about poor furnishings in day rooms, and the solitary and dull existence that some patients seemed to endure, without warmth, company, or amusement. Receivers had no direct authority over personal matters, such as where someone lived, what they wore, or how they passed the time. However, for Gilchrist, institutional facilities and practices were all part and parcel of the treatment and care for which he paid, albeit with his patients' money, and for which he was therefore ultimately responsible.[61]

Gilchrist was also keen to find other ways to replicate the informal but essential care that he associated with friends and family, in addition to the visits from the Winders. For those in institutions with no family, he attempted to set up a scheme for members of the Women's Institute (wi) to volunteer as friends, or 'marraines'. This term drew on Gilchrist's encounter during the First World War with the 'marraines de guerre' in France, women who would support a soldier who had no family or whose family was behind enemy lines, 'by writing to him, sending him supplies, and helping him not to feel cut off from family and friends'.[62] The wi 'marraines' were asked to pay visits, write letters, send cards, take patients out on day trips, and generally show an interest in their welfare.[63] The scheme did not get off the ground, despite a degree of willingness from the wi, but it indicates a desire on the part of the Official Solicitor to think in quite expansive terms about the kind of care that those found incapable should receive. It also showed further reliance on the unpaid services of women to provide it.

The impact of this kind of attentive care as part of a receivership emerges in more tangible form at the Old Rectory, and not only in the Official Solicitor's diligent efforts to keep Miss Alexander in her much-loved home. Visitor

Mrs Winder became an important source of support. Miss Wortt in particular appreciated the chance to share the worries that she tried to hide from Miss Alexander about money, lodgers, and eventually their declining health, and wrote to Mrs Winder increasingly frequently between visits as the years passed. Miss Wortt would also write to Mrs Winder directly to share news of a more personal nature, such as a happy visit from the late Dr Norton's nephews, or a thank you for helping them across London on the way to one of their holiday destinations.[64]

Although Mrs Winder seems to have tried to maintain a professional relationship, passing at least some of these letters on to her employer to file, the care that she and the Official Solicitor provided clearly went beyond the strict parameters of Miss Alexander's receivership. This is at its most obvious after Miss Alexander moved to a nursing home in 1965, when Mrs Winder began visiting Miss Wortt as well. At first this was ostensibly to gather information about Miss Alexander's wellbeing, but by 1966 she filed a report about Miss Wortt too. 'I found her in only moderately good health', wrote Mrs Winder, 'and possibly thinking of having to give up her flatlet and go into a[n] Old People's Home. She was very distressed at this idea'.[65] Mrs Winder and the Official Solicitor's office had become keenly aware of Miss Wortt's years of service for limited financial benefit. They sought and were granted permission from the Master of the Court of Protection (as the Lunacy Office had become by this time) to make discretionary payments from Miss Alexander's funds to Miss Wortt, to enable her to maintain some independence. Whether this was conceptualised as back-payment for services rendered or a gift that Miss Alexander would have wanted to make to a dear friend is unclear.[66] In either case, the Lunacy Office and Official Solicitor demonstrated a sense of responsibility towards Miss Wortt: care for Miss Alexander entailed care for Miss Wortt as well.

Although the decision to start looking more closely into the lives of those found incapable may have been in some part down to Official Solicitor Gil - christ's interests and personality, this isn't the whole story. Such scrutiny continued beyond Gilchrist's retirement in 1950, in the form of ongoing annual visits, critical reports on institutional conditions, and irritable letters from medical superintendents who resented this intrusion into their domain.[67] Gilchrist's enquiries from the 1930s also coincided with closer scrutiny on the part of the Lunacy Office as well, suggesting that the care and protection offered through mental capacity law and its administration was being reimagined.

The Lunacy Office began to inspect the activities of receivers much more closely, checking that any 'extra comforts' like chocolates, cakes, fruit, and cigarettes, for which an allowance was made to receivers from the money of those found incapable, were actually purchased and provided. It also started to examine receivers' annual accounts in more detail. This closer scrutiny is suggested by the contents of the leading practitioner's textbook, which included senior Lunacy Office staff among its authors from 1920 onwards. Earlier editions focused on the procedure for the appointment of a receiver, while later editions spent much more time addressing the decisions or activities that might happen afterwards: replacing receivers, conveyancing, litigation, appeals, settlements, and annual accounts.[68] At the start of the twentieth century, the Lunacy Office's primary responsibility had been at the moment of appointing a receiver, but by the 1930s this was only the beginning of its involvement in a person's affairs.

This closer involvement on the part of the Lunacy Office was prompted in part by anxiety about dishonesty and financial abuse. Fears of financial exploitation on the part of Mr and Mrs Humphries had, of course, been the main cause of anxiety about Miss Alexander's situation, but receivers themselves were also suspect. Some within the Lunacy Office felt that fraud was very much on the increase.[69] Such anxiety might have reflected a broader social unease in the interwar years, when 'the difficulties of knowing whom or what to trust' were becoming more acutely felt.[70] There were very many more people taking on the role of receiver without any kind of professional advice and genuine mistakes did happen, but Master Methold reported after seven years in post that he was 'shocked by the number of cases of deliberate fraud' perpetrated by receivers. This was not restricted to those unaccustomed to dealing with complex finances or those in particular financial need, either. Methold emphasised that in the majority of cases, 'the receivers or other persons implicated were educated and fairly well to do people'.[71] This could include professional advisers, too: after Mrs Clara Bathurst's nephew was appointed as her receiver in March 1969, her solicitor was investigated and struck off for having taken advantage of her confused state and misappropriated £11,000 of her money to buy a house for himself.[72]

The Lunacy Office had also been jolted into more proactive attention towards its 'patients' by its involvement in a high-profile case of wrongful confinement, *Harnett v Bond and Adam*, in 1924. This case, in which two doctors were initially found guilty, was one in which there had been a receivership as well as the detention of Mr Harnett as a person of unsound mind. The LCVs had been to see Mr Harnett on numerous occasions and had not raised any concerns about his detention, despite Mr Harnett's letters of complaint. Although technically, the LCVs were not part of the Lunacy Office, the fact that there had been a receivership brought the case close enough to home to cause some sleepless nights. It marked renewed public interest in the issue of wrongful confinement, and prompted a Royal Commission on Lunacy and Mental Disorder before which the Lord Chancellor's permanent secretary had to give evidence concerning the work of the Lunacy Office.[73] No doubt as a direct result of this case, the Lunacy Office conducted a thorough review of all of its institutionalised patients in 1924, requesting confirmation from medical superintendents that these people were without a shadow of a doubt still unwell and incapable of managing their affairs.

This review was a one-off, but it heralded a much greater willingness to engage with the everyday living situation of those found incapable – and the views of those found incapable themselves. Since the gradual obsolescence of the lunacy inquisition in the early twentieth century, the role of 'committee of the person' had all but disappeared, and without this, the Lunacy Office had no jurisdiction over matters of personal welfare.[74] Yet, this could be a grey area. The office had no authority to decide where someone should live, but it *could* recommend or allow receivers to spend set sums of money on particular kinds of accommodation – sometimes resulting in conflict when family members disagreed.[75] It could not dictate what those found incapable did with their days or whom they saw, but it *could* give or withhold permission for receivers to spend money on radios, trips by car, holidays, travel expenses for family, or even the provision of 'pocket money' directly to those found incapable.[76] Complaints or requests on the part of those found incapable also seem to have been investigated more thoroughly from the 1920s onwards.[77] This could include quite lengthy exchanges between the Lunacy Office and those found incapable, and careful consideration of their preferences. When asked directly in the 1930s whether the office was adopting a more interventionist approach, senior Lunacy Office staff were quick to deny that they undertook *too much* detailed investigation. At the same time, they acknowledged implicitly and explicitly that they would no longer simply aim to leave a person's affairs unchanged as much as possible during a receivership.[78] Proactive management of their finances, which could and did include attention to their wellbeing, was becoming much more common.

This sits comfortably alongside a growing welfare state during the interwar years, and the expanding bureaucracies that it required. Such growth may have been piecemeal, but many specialist efforts to address social problems trickled forth from central government, and spending on social services steadily increased.[79] The Lunacy Office was part of the judiciary, not usually considered a social service and not usually connected within historical accounts of state involvement in welfare, but its own staff felt differently. As mentioned in chapter 3, Assistant Master Poyser argued that his office should be considered a public welfare service, funded by central government where necessary; Mr Gilchrist's close interest in the long-term wellbeing of those for whom he acted (and his recruitment of new staff to monitor this wellbeing) also hints at shifting perceptions of the Official Solicitor's role that went beyond the confines of acting as a 'lawyer of last resort'. In the midst of considerable hope that centralised state services might provide a route to a more successful society, a more expansive view of the proper role of these legal bodies and the care that they should provide makes sense.

The Court of Protection today is sometimes criticised for failing to strike the right balance between effective oversight and excessive interference. It is required to provide care and control, without causing harm. This problem is far from new. As both the Lunacy Office and Official Solicitor tried to take a more active interest in their caseload in the interwar years, they sometimes struggled to identify the boundaries of their responsibilities and the best way of fulfilling them. The Lunacy Office sought to provide care for those found incapable by controlling receivers increasingly closely, with mixed results: some receivers were angered and hurt by the implication of dishonesty, while the extra work involved in these checks reduced the office's overall efficiency considerably.[80] On the other hand, it did identify cases of possible fraud, or at least, inattention, and kept a close eye on how much money receivers took for themselves from the estates of those found incapable.[81] As for the Official

Solicitor's office, its work as receiver – at least for Miss Alexander – was onerous but necessary, securing her finances, her home, and her daily care. At the
same time, only rarely did the Lunacy Office (or Official Solicitor) find fault
with or even enquire very closely into matters of daily care, whether in institutions or the home. Those found incapable were acknowledged as needing
care and supervision, entailing an increasing amount of scrutiny and oversight
of those who looked after them, but for the most part, care took place behind
closed doors and its details remained beyond official responsibilities.

In the 1970s, generalised concerns and complaints resurfaced that the Court
of Protection habitually went beyond its brief, 'prying into matters' that were
none of its business, overstepping its jurisdiction, and slowing itself down by
trying to monitor receivers too closely.[82] Even though this coincided with considerable efforts elsewhere to reduce legal controls over those with mental illness or disability and to advocate for their rights, there was very little concern
that those found incapable were too closely supervised, that the care and control they received was harmful, or that this form of legal care and control was
inappropriate.[83] The charity MIND had begun to show a little interest, but in
this it seems to have been a lone voice on a low-profile stage.[84] The role of
this branch of mental capacity law in providing care and control, and its potential for harm, was to remain largely unnoticed until the end of the century.

MATTERS OF INTERPRETATION

On the whole, this chapter paints a rosy picture of Miss Wortt and Miss
Alexander's life together. Unknowables and imponderables still lurk around
the edges, but I, at least, have been persuaded. Letters and reports across the
thirty years of their relationship hint to me that the two were well matched
in terms of personality, and largely enjoyed their years together at the Old
Rectory. Although official records tend to focus more heavily on moments of
stress and difficulty (often financial) that required the receiver or the Lunacy
Office to take action, there are passing references to everyday pleasures at the
Old Rectory, derived from gardening, billiards, the pianola, whist, canasta,
jigsaws, knitting, trips out by car, caring neighbours, holidays with family, and
visits with friends. Miss Alexander was somewhat frail and sometimes nervous, but her health was generally good and her family, when she visited Nor-

folk in her eighty-fifth year, 'think she is wonderful for her age'.[85] There is also the evidence of action: Miss Wortt was loyal and devoted, staying at the Old Rectory for twenty-five years and continuing to visit Miss Alexander regularly in the nursing home, even in the midst of her own serious health problems. Despite paying fairly close attention to life at the Old Rectory, the Official Solicitor went to great lengths not to disrupt it until the frailties of both women made a change unavoidable. By many measures, this companionship and receivership seems to have been a success.

There is barely a hint of criticism of Miss Wortt throughout her many years with Miss Alexander. In addition to the concern from Dr Norton's trustees about whether Miss Wortt enjoyed living at the Old Rectory a little too much, Miss Stevenson of the DVAMW had remarked that Miss Wortt might perhaps 'outrun the constable' when it came to spending Miss Alexander's income.[86] These were fleeting remarks, but perhaps Miss Wortt was not quite as frugal as she might have been, especially in her first months with Miss Alexander when she had been led to believe that her charge was rather well off. Someone who got to know both Miss Wortt and Miss Alexander quite well during an association that lasted nearly thirty years was visitor Mrs Winder; the only word of critique that she ever offered was that Miss Wortt had perhaps 're- tained rather high standards of how work should be carried out', with the re- sult that many of lodgers, gardeners, and charwomen who passed through the Old Rectory's gates were found wanting.[87] Mrs Winder also observed in 1966 that if she had to move into an 'Old People's Home', Miss Wortt would undoubtedly 'very much resent being "Managed"'.[88] Miss Wortt was exacting in domestic matters, and she knew her own mind. She sounds like an excellent match for Miss Alexander.

I could find out very little about Miss Wortt, beyond her role as Miss Alexander's companion. Census data reveals her birth (1885, near Bourne- mouth) and death (1976, near Bournemouth), a note of her father's profession (gas fitter), and the fact that her given first name was Ethel, not the middle name (Kate or Katie) by which she was known. It hints that she may not have been living with her parents any longer by the time she was sixteen, having possibly remained in Bournemouth to work at the hospital there when her family moved to Maidenhead. Nearly forty years later, she was running a wool and embroidery shop, still living near Bournemouth, and was also 'looking after a mental defective girl for the County Authorities'.[89] No doubt this was how she was known to Miss Stevenson of the DVAMW, who recommended her to the Official Solicitor. As someone who travelled little, whose family was not quite as well known in their locality as Miss Alexander's, and who seems to have done nothing to catch the eye of those most energetic producers of historical resources about people – newspapers, courts, and institutions of all kinds – Miss Wortt is only really visible through her connection to Miss Alexander. She is something of a blank page, on which this version of events can appear without complication.

How did Miss Alexander feel about Miss Wortt, or the care and control under which she was placed? From 1940 until her death, Miss Alexander's views and feelings were reported by others. She did not contact the Lunacy Office or Official Solicitor directly, as some of those found incapable certainly did, to express any wishes or concerns.[90] Mrs Winder did not report hearing any complaints, although she did take time during her visits to speak to Miss Alexander as well as Miss Wortt. Miss Wortt conveyed specific wishes to the Official Solicitor on behalf of her charge, such as Miss Alexander's desire to visit family in Norfolk, or to take a holiday, or her fervent hope to remain at the Old Rectory, but there may have been other wishes that were less well aligned with Miss Wortt's own preferences that were not committed to paper. Miss Wortt may also have made use of Miss Alexander's tendency to be over-powered by a stronger personality, when it suited. It was, after all, part of her role to provide Miss Alexander with guidance and encouragement, or per-suasion, or pressure. 'I had to force her to meet people', Miss Wortt later re-flected.[91] 'Force' is a strong word.

On balance it looks as though Miss Wortt delivered excellent care, but part of that was to persuade Miss Alexander to trust her completely. 'I have read what I have written to Miss Alexander & she has agreed to it all', wrote Miss Wortt to the Official Solicitor in 1947, after eight years at the Old Rectory.[92] Would Miss Alexander have been in a position to disagree? Miss Alexander always insisted that she wanted things to stay exactly as they were, but hadn't she said the same before, to the neighbours who insisted that the Humphries family had to go? Did she think fondly of carefree times spent drinking with the Humphries; did she resent her companion's insistence that they go out and about and make new friends? Was she being helped and protected, or ex-cessively controlled? Was this kind of care harmful?

My own interest in these questions reflects several contemporary concerns, historical and otherwise. The harms that can be enacted by current guardianship and mental capacity laws have been highlighted by scholars in Australia, in particular, who have argued that these disability-specific laws can be 'a form of *legal violence*'.[93] Histories of nursing and of care more broadly have begun to address the harms associated with care, and have highlighted the central importance of social and cultural context in determining not only whether harm can easily occur, but how the provision and receipt of care itself is experienced.[94] It is difficult, then, to talk about care without very secure insights into those experiences. Although Miss Wortt struggled at times, on the whole she seemed to derive great pleasure from her place with Miss Alexander. Given that Miss Alexander was far from forthright and had limited opportunity to express herself to the Official Solicitor or Lunacy Office, whether she was happy, dissatisfied, or ambivalent about the care she received and the constraints under which she was placed is harder to say.

It is also unhelpful to put care and control in opposite corners: to ask whether Miss Alexander received care *or* whether her freedoms were curtailed. Research on mental capacity law and vulnerable adults has pointed to the emergence in the late twentieth century of problematic binaries in law and policy, which place concepts like autonomy and paternalism, or empowerment and protection, in opposition. Such binaries assume an independent, rational, disembodied individual, and fail to recognise that all people 'are connected to and reliant upon others to support us, to provide information, to help us to process and create our own sense of self'.[95] Interactions, connections, constraints, opportunities, and experiences of all kinds provide a framework within which everyone develops and modifies their preferences and wishes. The valorisation of autonomy and empowerment risks ignoring this, looking only at individual choice and not the social and structural contexts in which such choices are made. Importantly, the absence of restrictions or constraints, whether from individuals, professionals, or social structures, can be 'experienced as *a failure to care*'.[96] A simple dividing line between care and control, autonomy and paternalism, or empowerment and protection, is not necessarily very useful. There is also little sign that any such tensions were perceived throughout the duration of Miss Alexander's legal incapacity. My suspicion is that Miss Alexander experienced the constraints of the receivership, with supervision and control of herself and her affairs undertaken by Miss Wortt and the Official Solicitor, as mostly beneficial and caring.

I suspect, as well, that my perspective on this has been very much shaped by my own reaction to Miss Alexander's story. It was the drama at the Old Rectory in 1939 that initially caught my attention, but what sustained it through so many hefty files was the relationship between Miss Alexander and Miss Wortt. It came to matter to me that this was a caring relationship, since the happiness of both women seemed to depend upon it to some degree. Miss Wortt's dedicated efforts, her loyalty, and her attention to Miss Alexander's wishes – whether to remain at the Old Rectory, to see her family, or to be buried in the churchyard next to her 'dear doctor' when the time came – all suggest very persuasively to me that she was deeply invested in Miss Alexander's wellbeing. I was moved by her words of regret when Miss Alexander had to go into a nursing home, that she 'was not able to look after her until her end'.[97] I believed that Miss Wortt wanted the best for her, even though this belief does not entirely douse my doubts about whether this was the best possible arrangement for Miss Alexander.

Miss Alexander's experiences were unusual in many respects. The Lunacy Office may have been far more active in the middle of the twentieth century than historians of mental health law have previously noticed, but it was responsible for no more than about 30,000 people at any one time. Most of those were in hospitals or nursing homes of one sort or another, receiving care from medical attendants and nurses. But arrangements similar to those at the Old Rectory were not unheard of, as indicated by the long-term companions of John Brocklehurst, Eileen Beresford, and others who lived in their own homes. These caring and controlling arrangements often sit beyond official interest and leave little trace, but Miss Alexander's experiences point towards their existence and importance. Her story highlights not only individual work and devotion, but also the very practical support, supervision, and advice from the Official Solicitor and Lunacy Office that helped to make her final years at the Old Rectory such happy ones.

5

ENDINGS

After Miss Alexander's admission to a private nursing home in 1964, Miss Wortt's letters and Mrs Winder's annual reports described her increasing frailty and forgetfulness. Never one to enjoy change, the initial move out of the Old Rectory caused Miss Alexander much distress, although those around her led her to believe that it was only a temporary measure while some extra help for the ailing Miss Wortt was obtained. Miss Alexander's short-term memory seemed to deteriorate rapidly at first, and her overriding preoccupation was simply to get back home.[1] The nursing home matron, Mrs Fish, then relocated her business by some fifty miles to Bournemouth: the further upheaval that this entailed caused additional upset (perhaps more for Miss Wortt than Miss Alexander). After a few months in Bournemouth, though, Miss Alexander seemed to settle in, becoming attached to Mrs Fish and much less distressed at the thought of her former home. 'No need for you to worry about me', she wrote to her brother in March 1965, in only slightly shaky handwriting (figure 5.1). 'I am alright & very happy. Mrs Fish is looking after me well. We are real pals. I could not be so happy anywhere out of my own home … Much love from the Old Gander'.[2]

Miss Alexander was by this time in need of much more hands-on care than had been the case decades earlier, when she had first come to Lunacy Office attention. She was physically frail, sometimes forgetful, and affected by bouts of 'nocturnal confusion' that prompted her to get up and dress or walk about at night. Although her 'mind doesn't weaken as much as her body', by 1968 Mrs Winder found her to be 'returning to her youth'.[3] Memories of more recent years and the people associated with them were fading, and she lost track of when and where she was. She sometimes struggled to remember Miss Wortt and Mrs Winder, although she always seemed pleased to see them, and she

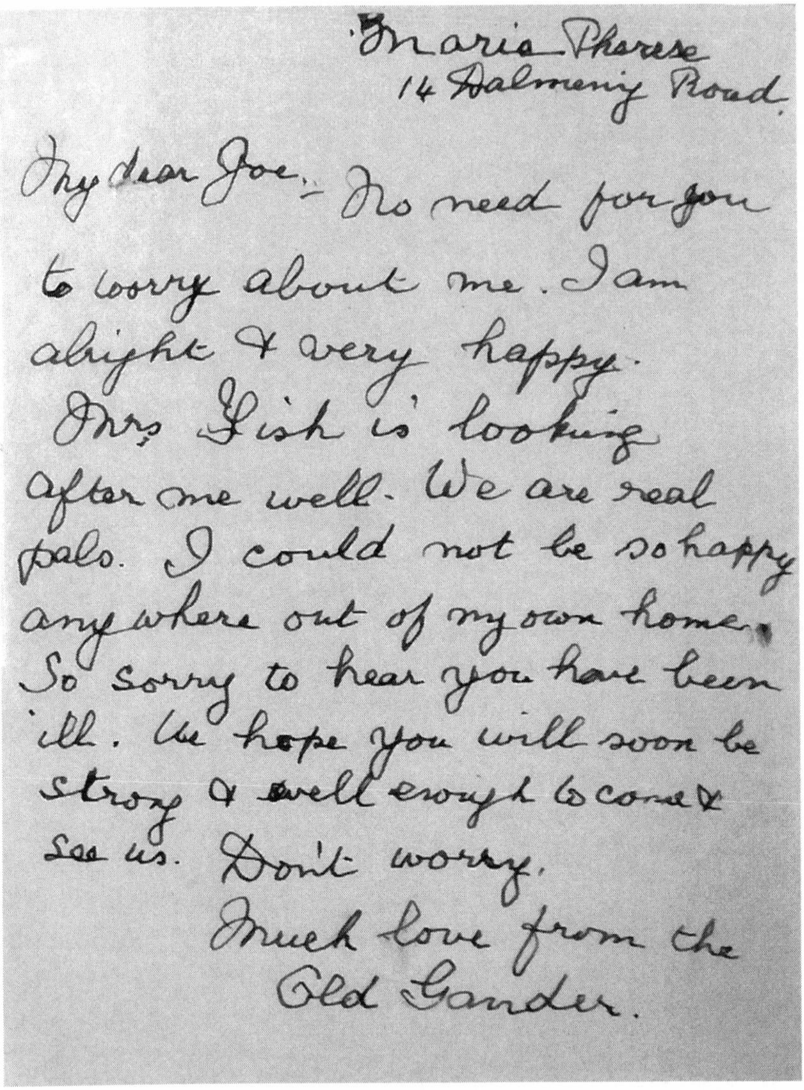

Figure 5.1 Miss Alexander's letter to her brother, from around March 1965.
It is not clear why this came to rest in the Official Solicitor's file.

began to talk about her many brothers and her childhood home in Norfolk instead of her dear doctor and life at the Old Rectory. On 9 September 1969, Miss Wortt paid her regular visit and 'was thankful to see she knew me'.[4] Three days later, at the age of ninety-one, Miss Alexander died.

This was no doubt a great shock to Miss Wortt, even though she had watched her friend's deteriorating health with sadness for a long while and had prepared herself for the inevitable. '[A]lthough it will be a big loss to me after so many years of happiness with her', she had written two years before, 'I would be glad to see her at rest'.[5] Loss, even when expected and to some degree welcomed, still marked the end of a remarkable relationship which had lasted for more than three decades. Thanks to Miss Wortt's conscientious attention, Miss Alexander was buried in the graveyard in Chilfrome right next to the Old Rectory, beside Dr Norton's final resting place. Despite being legally incapable of managing her property and affairs, Miss Alexander was able to make a will and she left £500 – more than half her estate – to Miss Wortt, with the rest going to her surviving family in Norfolk: her sister, Helen, her niece Ruth, and her brothers, Arthur, Ernest, and John.[6] Dr Norton's substantial estate – which included the proceeds of sale from the Old Rectory – passed to his surviving nephew, Victor, himself nearly seventy years of age. The Court of Protection and Official Solicitor balanced the books and closed their files in January 1970.

In one sense, being found incapable had very little impact on Miss Alexander's life. After the initial period of turbulence while Mr and Mrs Humphries were evicted, she continued to live in her beloved home and enjoyed the usual everyday things. She hosted a knitting group during the war; she loved a game of billiards in the evening; she was besotted by the television as soon as she saw one. She re-established contact with her family in Norfolk, and after the end of the Second World War, she took occasional holidays to pay them visits and was visited in return. She developed friendships with neighbours and had a dog, for a short while at least.[7] Daily life was occasionally disrupted by attacks of lumbago or shingles, for which she saw her local doctor, and by the ongoing difficulties of finding reliable people to help take care of the large house and garden. There were also challenges with making ends meet, particularly in the 1940s when costs were high, income was low, and the Old Rectory was in dire need of repairs. Miss Alexander rarely got on well with the lodgers that occasionally came and went, recruited to contribute to the modest household budget and to give a helping hand around house and garden. On the whole, though, and until her health began to fail quite significantly some twenty years later, Miss Alexander seems to have enjoyed the comfortable retirement that Dr Norton had tried to design for her.

In another sense, the events of summer 1939 were transformative. The Lunacy Office declared that she was unable to look after herself, gesturing vaguely to mental weakness as the cause but emphasising her unsatisfactory living situation and apparent vulnerability to exploitation. No longer allowed to receive any money from Dr Norton's will trust directly, Miss Alexander relied on strangers in the form of the Official Solicitor and his staff to manage her finances and to pay out a regular allowance. Mr and Mrs Humphries, with whom she had lived and worked for over fifteen years, were removed entirely from her life. In their place came Miss Wortt, who quickly realised how important the Old Rectory was to Miss Alexander's happiness. She and the Official Solicitor agreed that Miss Alexander should not be institutionalised or otherwise moved from her beloved home, and worked hard to enable her to remain there for as long as possible. Miss Wortt took charge of the household and its budget, and soon grew very fond of her companion, this timid, gentle, lovable woman. Who knows to what extent this affection was reciprocated, but there can be no doubt that Miss Wortt's presence radically altered Miss Alexander's life. She may have resented at times the supervision and control that she experienced, but the interventions of the Lunacy Office enabled a form of caring companionship and allowed at least some of Miss Alexander's priorities to be respected and fulfilled.

THE COURT OF PROTECTION

The Lunacy Office underwent its own transformation during the tenure of its involvement with Miss Alexander. It was renamed the Court of Protection in 1947, and in 1959 the law governing its operation also changed when a new Mental Health Act repealed the Lunacy Act of 1890. The 1959 Act finally abolished the old inquisitions procedure, although it was by this time very rarely used, and simplified the jurisdiction of the Court of Protection. It removed the lingering administrative distinctions between those who were 'certified' in hospital, those who had been found criminally insane, those who had very small estates, and those, like Miss Alexander, to whom none of the above applied but who were nonetheless found incapable. This new Act prompted a new set of official rules to govern procedure, but no great disruption to the daily business of the Court of Protection. It had not been the primary focus of the 1959 Act, and these statutory changes aimed only to tidy up mental capacity law rather than to alter it in any substantive way. Despite persistent grumbles about how slow the Court of Protection was, and occasional complaints about some of its policies, for the most part its activities generated little interest or concern.[8]

The most significant changes were gradual. By the time of Miss Alexander's death, the Court of Protection's cohort of 'patients', as those found incapable were still called, bore increasingly little resemblance to their early twentieth century counterparts. In broad terms, they were older, less wealthy, and less likely to be in hospital. Most of those with receivers in place during the first half of the twentieth century had been in mental hospitals, with an array of diagnoses dominated by mania, melancholia, and delusional insanity. Ages had ranged widely: it was not unusual for someone certified as a person of unsound mind to be found incapable in their thirties and to remain both hospitalised and legally incapable until their death.[9] By 1962, the Master of the Court of Protection painted a slightly different picture. He felt that the most common form of infirmity coming to the court's attention was 'the mental confusion which so often accompanies old age, the difficulty of distinguishing the past from the present, and forgetfulness which leads to bills being left unpaid'.[10] A decade later, investigations undertaken by the Lord Chancellor's department endorsed and fleshed out this picture: just over half of the 20,000 open cases involved people over sixty-five years of age, and were cases of 'gross brain damage' which included dementia. A minority were in hospitals.[11] By 1992, these subtle shifts had become more pronounced: 70 per cent of receiverships involved patients over the age of sixty-nine, and only 24 per cent were in hospital – although a further 40 per cent were in nursing homes.[12] Increasingly, the Court of Protection was dealing with older people in residential, but not psychiatric or narrowly clinical, settings.

The fact that declining numbers of those found incapable were living in hospital is an echo of the widespread move towards deinstitutionalisation from the 1960s onwards. This move has been associated with the postwar attempt to rethink citizenship and the role of the state in terms of universalism and rights: segregating those with mental or cognitive impairments became ideologically difficult to sustain. It was also very expensive.[13] For historian Barbara Taylor, this policy shift in favour of closing institutions coincided with growing hostility towards dependence. To 'need other people', or the welfare state itself, was increasingly positioned as problematic, if not 'inherently pathological; independence is a *sina qua non* of mental health'.[14] The Court of Protection can be seen as part of the welfare state, albeit an unusual part, and one in which dependence was central to every aspect of its work. A finding of incapacity was a declaration of dependence. Those found incapable depended in law on other people and ultimately the courts to make decisions on their behalf. As dependence became politically unpopular, the Court of Protection's caseload decreased significantly in the 1960s and early 1970s, declining sharply by 1984 to its mid-1930s levels.[15]

As described in chapter 1, the Lunacy Office had begun to involve itself in the affairs of many more people of modest means in the interwar years. Unlike the lunacy inquisition, receiverships were not the preserve of the extremely wealthy. Since the office notionally paid for itself by taking a percentage fee from the estates it managed, this inevitably affected its bottom line. Smaller estates did not necessarily mean less work, and sometimes quite the opposite. In many cases, smaller estates meant no fees at all, since the office made frequent use of its discretionary power to waive fees when they were likely to cause hardship. By the mid-1930s, it was receiving over £40,000 in funding from the Treasury to top up its budget (around £2 million in today's money); forty years later, the shortfall between income and expenditure had increased to £735,000 (or £5 million).[16] Behind the scenes, as the decades went by, questions were asked as to whether this 'social service for people with property' was really an appropriate use of state funds.[17]

Amidst much civil service budget tightening in the 1970s, it was a difficult case to make. The Court of Protection appeared large and expensive, slow moving, even anachronistic, prompting hard questions about its future. These questions did not challenge the principles of mental capacity law, but rather the practicalities of the Court of Protection's daily operation. To some, it seemed to be engaged in an odd assortment of duties that did not make much sense together: medical assessments, legal proceedings, investment management, auditing of accounts, and something akin to social work, all on behalf of quite a small number of people. The LCVs were criticised, since their advanced qualifications and very generous salaries did not seem to tally with the nature of their work; the visitors themselves also hinted at dissatisfaction with the running of the Court of Protection. Furthermore, and for the first time in many decades, there were sustained criticisms and concerns aired by members of parliament, including calls for a formal enquiry.[18] Complaints about the ways in which the Court of Protection invested the money of those found incapable had been expressed in the 1950s, but this issue as well as the court's (in)efficiency and questions about its very purpose were taken up with new energy in the 1970s.[19]

In this context, the dissolution of both the Court of Protection and the role of LCV was tentatively discussed. The preferred idea was to place most of the work to do with people found incapable in the hands of the county courts, with regular welfare checks delivered by local authority social services rather than centrally managed and expensive official visitors. But the Court of Protection was excluded from the Review of the Mental Health Act in 1975, putting a stop to any immediate proposals for reform. This exclusion followed the precedent of the 1926 and 1954 to 1957 enquiries into mental health law, which cast mental capacity law as something entirely separate from the central legal issues surrounding mental health: admission to hospital, and involuntary detention there. Efforts to scrutinise and reform mental health law throughout the twentieth century seemed curiously blind to mental capacity law, at least until the very end of the century. This not only meant that the Court of Protection largely evaded criticism, public attention, and statutory reform, but also rendered its work somewhat unknowable. With no comprehensive reviews, public enquiries, or critiques, the 'work of the Court remains a mystery', as one civil servant remarked rather sadly in 1979.[20]

This mystery is itself one explanation for the lack of attention to mental capacity law and the Court of Protection throughout most of the twentieth century, albeit a circular one. No great reforms were proposed and carried through because this branch of the law was poorly understood; this branch of law was poorly understood because no great reforms were proposed and carried out. Vestiges of the very old – the royal prerogative, the lunacy inquisition, the committee of the person or estate – lingered until the end of the 1950s, co-existing relatively comfortably alongside changing models of mental illness, up-to-date (but complex) rules, and sometimes innovative legal precedent as well.

This is not enough as an explanation, though: the same is true of many branches of law. There are two additional factors which help to explain the low profile of the Court of Protection and its long-term survival. Firstly, its opacity was enhanced by the relatively small numbers of people whose affairs it oversaw. Most people, most of the time, would have no interaction with it, and would know nothing about it. And secondly, the bulk of its work concerned the management of the estates of the mentally infirm, not their personal or medical treatment. This was not to do with controversial diagnoses, treatments, and deprivations of liberty, but bank accounts, investments, properties, trusts, and business management. Neither fish nor fowl, it was nobody's main course until the very end of the century.

The Court of Protection was reorganised and slimmed down over the 1980s, but the principle of having a separate entity dealing with those incapable of managing their property and affairs remained. It was largely unaffected – once again – by the mental health legislation of that decade, the Mental Health Act of 1983, which side-stepped the question of mental capacity to manage property and affairs almost entirely. This new law did interact with the elimination of inquisitions and committees of the person in the Mental Health Act 1959 in unexpected ways, but with no immediate ramifications for the Court of Protection itself.[21] The Court of Protection finally found itself scooped up into a larger investigation into mental capacity law reform in the 1990s, but the extent of its existing and anticipated caseload, and its claims to unique expertise, left it well positioned to provide the conceptual foundation for the new mental capacity legislation of the twenty-first century.[22]

Master Theobald, who had taken over as Master of the Lunacy Office in the early 1900s and revitalised this ailing office, would probably have been surprised by its survival. His own preference had been for an amalgamated lunacy department or division, bringing together the LCVs, the Board of Control that oversaw mental hospitals, and the Masters in Lunacy. All lunacy law business would be together, in one place.[23] If Theobald's proposals had been accepted, it seems likely that the office's activities would have caught the attention of policy-makers and historians much earlier, and its approach to determining and dealing with incapacity would have taken a different course. Greater proximity to the Board of Control could have changed the relatively low profile of medical expertise within the Lunacy Office, its continued use of the blunt instrument of capacity law as set out in the Lunacy Act of 1890, and even its willingness to think in very expansive terms about incapacity itself during the interwar years. Would such changes have been for better or worse? Theobald would probably have seen them as a positive development. From the vantage point of the 2020s, and much influenced by my reading of Miss Alexander's experiences, I am not so sure.

THE KEY PLAYERS

Master Theobald would no doubt have approved of the fact that his successors as Masters in Lunacy continued to receive knighthoods. He had been the first to do so, on the occasion of his retirement.[24] Ronald Poyser, whose family was so closely involved in the Lunacy Office and who had been sent the first notification of Miss Alexander's situation, received *his* knighthood in 1952, eight years after becoming Master.[25] Around this time, or possibly a few years later when he retired, he was invited to sit for a portrait by photographer Walter Stoneman for the National Portrait Gallery, making him the only central figure within this story for whom a public photograph exists. Stoneman photographed one or two hundred people each year, mostly military and political figures but also senior civil servants and other men of national importance. It was something of an honour to be invited to sit for one of his portraits: the role of Master of the Court of Protection must have been comfortably established as a significant one within the machinery of the courts.[26] Poyser died after only a year of retirement, at the age of seventy-two.[27]

His friend and relative Dr Humphrey Stephenson survived him by less than a year. Stephenson had been interned in 1940 in Walton Prison as a result of his BUF membership, but had joined the British army sometime soon thereafter. His wife remained in Dorset and had enough contact with Miss Alexander and Miss Wortt to enable her to write to the Official Solicitor as soon as she heard that the cottage in the grounds of the Old Rectory might be available to rent.[28] In the end she did not become Miss Alexander's tenant and next-door neighbour, and after the end of the war the Stephensons relocated to Earl's Court in West London. Their allegiance to the BUF had caused friends to 'cool off' and Mrs Stephenson had worried even in the 1930s that it would affect her husband's ability to earn a living; perhaps by 1946 they were no longer welcome in their small Dorset community, particularly since Dr Stephenson remained a staunch supporter of Oswald Mosley.[29] It is unclear whether they remained in touch with Miss Alexander and Miss Wortt after this move, but possibly not. Neither Miss Wortt nor official visitor Mrs Winder mentioned the Stephensons at all following Dr Stephenson's arrest in 1940. Although Miss Wortt and Miss Alexander certainly did visit friends in London on occasion, they went to Harrow and Ealing, not Earl's Court.[30]

There is no doubt that Miss Alexander and Miss Wortt came to know the Official Solicitor's visitor Lucy Winder very well. Mrs Winder first came to see them in the summer of 1940, after her husband, the official visitor who had faced down Mrs Humphries's frying pan and spirited Miss Alexander away to Corfe Mullen in his car, had enlisted in the army. Mr Winder did not return to his role with the Official Solicitor, but Mrs Winder continued in post throughout the duration of Miss Alexander's receivership. First hired to the position in 1934, this gave her at least thirty-five years of experience visiting hospitals, nursing homes, and private residences around England and Wales, to ensure that those for whom the Official Solicitor acted were well looked after and did not want for anything. Not so very much younger than Miss Wortt, she was seventy-seven at the time of Miss Alexander's death. This could well have been her longest-running case. She may never have officially retired, although by the 1950s another husband-and-wife team of visitors were taking on some of the workload. Mrs Winder clearly admired all that Miss Wortt had done for Miss Alexander, and advocated on her behalf to the Official Solicitor. She was concerned about Miss Wortt's wellbeing and financial security once she was unmoored from the Old Rectory and her full-time role as nurse-companion. Miss Wortt had been in the habit of writing to Mrs Winder on a regular basis during Miss Alexander's final years: I like to imagine that they stayed in touch.

Miss Wortt, just like Miss Alexander, lived to see her ninety-first birthday. Immediately after leaving the Old Rectory she moved around a good deal, finding it hard to establish a home that was close enough to visit Miss Alexander on at least a monthly basis while also meeting her own needs. She had very little money to spend on accommodation and her health was precarious. At first she rented a cottage not far from the Old Rectory, but it was very rural and the journey to Miss Alexander's nursing home, covering some forty miles, was onerous. She eventually found a council 'flatlet' in the New Forest, not too far from her sister and niece, but was not happy there: her room was dark and gloomy; the staff managing the building were unpleasant; she was lonely. The 'Doctor here says I must get away from here as its too isolated + depressing for me + I must live with other people', she wrote in 1966. 'I miss Miss Alexander + the dear Old Rectory more than ever'.[31] The following year she moved to a hotel in Boscombe, near Bournemouth, which had been converted into a home for older people, but moved on again after about six months. 'You see

I have made what I sincerely hope is my last home for life', she then wrote to Mrs Winder. 'The atmosphere here is very friendly all the other Residents are mostly of my own generation. I am quite near shops, church + library + this is a very quiet road. So, I ought to be content'.[32]

This turn of phrase makes me suspect that she was very much not content. Miss Wortt was probably quite a demanding resident, with those high standards that had caused problems for a series of cleaners, gardeners, and lodgers at the Old Rectory. Unreliable staff, mess, and noisy neighbours all caused her considerable annoyance in these shared homes. Money, ill health, and Miss Alexander loomed large in her considerations and caused her to worry and to move, time and again. In 1968 she moved twice more, to a cheaper 'Old People's home' and then to a small council-run nursing home. The latter was 'too relaxing', likely a euphemism for boring, and in 1969 she moved yet again to a home that provided all meals and could also 'cater for my illness'. It was also only two miles from Miss Alexander, the closest they had been in five years.[33]

Miss Wortt said often that she missed the Old Rectory. 'Old people's homes' along the south coast, no matter how comfortable, were unlikely to live up to its spacious rural charms. A neighbour kept an eye on the house after the two women moved out, but it quickly fell into disrepair. The gardens, always demanding, swiftly became wild and overgrown. Damp permeated the house itself, which became a sorry shadow of its former self. Nothing substantial by way of redecoration had been done since Dr Norton and Miss Alexander's arrival some forty years earlier: the wallpaper was peeling away and the removal of Dr Norton's many pictures and possessions left gaping spaces that only highlighted the dirt and decay.[34] It was not a very appealing prospect for tenants and its condition would only get worse. There was no chance at all that Miss Alexander would be able to return. There was really no choice but to sell it.

Miss Wortt dutifully helped to identify and remove Miss Alexander's most treasured possessions from the Old Rectory, including two silver spoons that were family heirlooms, framed photographs of 'her brothers killed in the 14–18 war, a silver rose bowl which was a champion prize for butter making + a half hunter gold watch which was the late Dr Norton's'.[35] Miss Wortt also gratefully accepted as a present two chairs and a painting that Miss Alexander had particularly wanted her to have, but her own reduced circumstances meant that she had to refuse all other gifts of furniture. The Old Rectory and its contents were sold in the autumn of 1965. This represented a 'wrench' for Miss Wortt, after so many happy years there, but it was, she stoically conceded, for the best.[36] Miss Wortt, the Official Solicitor, Mrs Winder, nursing home matron Mrs Fish, and Miss Alexander's family all agreed to conceal the fact of the sale from Miss Alexander, who remained sure that she would one day return home.[37]

To add to her health problems and frequent spells in hospital, Miss Wortt struggled to manage on her state pension. She expressed frequent gratitude for the additional allowance she received from Miss Alexander's surplus income, but this was wholly discretionary and came to an end when Miss Alexander died. Miss Wortt suffered a few months of financial strain at that time, before her pension was increased to cover the rent at her nursing home. The legacy of £500 from Miss Alexander, roughly equivalent to a year's rent, gave her a useful cushion, but as her only source of income besides her state pension it would not last for too long. Hopefully she herself continued to receive care over her last seven years, and finally found a happy enough home.

At one time, I thought that I might find out more about these fascinating people and their extraordinary ordinary lives from surviving family and friends, or even those who came later but remembered hearing stories about them. No such luck. I am no genealogist, for one. I think that there are few, if any, surviving grandchildren and great-nieces and nephews, but there is no doubt that privacy laws protecting the living will have hidden some from view. And of course, one thing that Miss Alexander's story has shown very clearly is that official records are a deeply imperfect account of human relationships: perhaps dear friends and sworn enemies (or their children) could have told me a great deal, but their personal connections took none of the forms that official archives will capture.

Even so, the idea that my efforts to reconstruct these lives might be read by someone who knew those who led them has rarely been far from mind. It has shaped my account for the better, as a sharp reminder of some of the ethical issues that this attention to small stories brings. The impulse to save, to rescue, to restore individual lives from the past – and to pass judgement on those lives, whether explicitly or not – is powerful, but it can be both arrogant in its confidence that this is always a good thing to do, and blind to the limitations that crowd around any such attempt.[38] In presenting these lives, I have tried to recognise and show the central figures in this story as complex people whose lives extended far beyond the narrow confines of state records, and far beyond my grasp. I have tried to evade some of the labels that such records bestow, to make plain my own role and reactions, and to think carefully about the purpose and weight of all my claims (and speculations). Although I have, in the end, still used these lives for my own purpose – to convey something of the complexity of 'lunacy law' and the history of the Court of Protection – I have tried to treat Miss Alexander and those around her with respect, and with care.

MISS ALEXANDER'S SMALL STORY

The events of Miss Alexander's later life were far removed from the cases of disputed testamentary capacity that I first encountered at work in the 2000s, but they prompted similar questions. How can legal processes possibly determine when someone's choices are not 'really' their own? What kinds of protections or interventions should be available when our decision-making somehow fails? Miss Alexander's story offers a glimpse of some possible answers to these questions. The unusual features of this story point towards broader trends within this little-known branch of 'lunacy law', not least of which is the fact that the Lunacy Office was surprisingly active in the middle decades of the twentieth century. Its administration of mental capacity law relied on the blunt tool of an all-or-nothing approach, in which people had to be either wholly incapable or wholly capable of managing their own affairs. Relying on nineteenth-century statute, this was somewhat at odds with the growing recognition of grey areas of mental health that was taking hold elsewhere, as acknowledged in the Mental Treatment Act of 1930. The Lunacy Office had little time for novel or nuanced medical notions of the mind and its misfunctions, which do not appear in its records. At the same time, its work was nonetheless influenced by a growing willingness to see troublesome mental weakness in capacious terms. General agreement that someone like Miss Alexander was incapable of managing her own affairs, even in the absence of any clearly defined illness or disorder, reflected an idea of mental incapacity that extended far beyond self-evident 'lunacy' or 'idiocy'.

This view of mental incapacity can be connected to shifting ideas about the proper role of the state and its citizens. The administration of the law, after all, is part of the workings of the state, and the staff of the offices of the Master in Lunacy, Official Solicitor, and LCVs were civil servants. Law and policy surrounding mental deficiency and mental illness illustrate some of the ideas in circulation about welfare reform, psychological health, and the boundaries of citizenship. Mental defect and mental illness were increasingly seen as national problems requiring state-sponsored solutions, but this was not conceptualised as a right to receive treatment or care. Instead, mental weakness tended to be seen as a condition that could inhibit access to full citizenship. Those whose supposedly biological difference prevented them from exercising their freedoms meaningfully were not seen as being in possession of those freedoms in the first place, while those who failed in practice to fulfil the requirements of a 'healthy mind' were failing to live up to the responsibilities of citizenship. For those found incapable, who straddled boundaries between mental defect, mental illness, and a nebulous mental weakness of the kind attributed to Miss Alexander, these apparent failures enabled quite dramatic interventions into everyday lives and liberties.

Miss Alexander's experience suggests that the Lunacy Office can be seen as a part of the growing welfare state, but a curious part: its intervention implicitly acknowledged that those found incapable required legal protection, and delivered this protection by removing rights. Lunacy Office involvement in Miss Alexander's life came in the midst of significant expansion in terms of its case load, staffing, and activities, and in terms of who was seen as the proper object of its actions. These actions marked out small but growing numbers of people as unable to exercise their freedoms meaningfully or to live up to the responsibilities of modern citizenship. This can be seen as a form of care work, albeit one that runs counter to more usual notions of care as interpersonal and hands on, taking place within families in private settings and between specialists and patients in institutional ones. Much broader conceptualisations of care work have some power to illuminate the politics of care, and the role of states and communities as well as individuals in providing it.[39]

This kind of care work also draws attention to the connections between care and control. The Official Solicitor took control of Miss Alexander's 'property and affairs' and appointed Miss Wortt to take care of her on a daily basis, managing the household, the budget, and to some extent every aspect of Miss Alexander's daily life. This was care and supervision in the community, and specifically in the home, without recourse to hospitals or other institutions.

It involved the Lunacy Office and Official Solicitor, but it relied very much on the mostly unpaid work of Miss Wortt. For nearly twenty-five years at the Old Rectory, Miss Wortt provided care and control in their material and emotional aspects, from sleeping in Miss Alexander's room to bringing her breakfast, from 'forcing' her to meet new people to organising holidays. In being found incapable, Miss Alexander became legally and practically dependent on others. Her own view of this was never made explicit, but her deeply held wish to remain at the Old Rectory was respected and no small amount of attention was given to her health and happiness. It is very possible that she experienced the control and supervision of the Official Solicitor and Miss Wortt as caring and beneficial.

Lunacy Office interventions for Miss Alexander were also symptomatic of a readiness to recognise vulnerability, and to acknowledge the role of social circumstances in creating it. Given the focus of this branch of law on property and affairs, the primary concern was vulnerability to fraud or financial exploitation, and it was slightly more readily identified amongst unmarried women. Miss Alexander's capacity to look after her own affairs was not simply an inherent quality that resulted from mental illness or defect, although certainly her 'character' and its supposed 'weakness' was an important consideration. Just as important was the very particular situation in which she found herself: far away from family, bereaved and isolated, mistress of a large house, and living with a family of doubtful character and conduct. This recognition that her capacity had to be weighed up in light of the specific decisions and circumstances that faced her implicitly acknowledged the role of such circumstances in affecting her capacity and creating vulnerability. Evaluations of her situation were liberally flavoured with assumptions and beliefs about respectability and gender, though. Mrs Humphries fell foul, while Miss Alexander prompted pity, and had Miss Alexander been Mister, recognition of vulnerability and willingness to take control of her affairs would have been much reduced.

Miss Alexander's story also opens up questions about indeterminacy and imagination, in law and history alike. Combining knowledge and the unknowable, this account is full of questions and possibilities that unsettle any impression of certainty or historical realism.[40] Numerous outside observers took imaginative leaps to understand what was happening at the Old Rectory, including me. The great and the good could not imagine why Miss Alexander tolerated the Humphries family; the only satisfactory explanation was that she was weak, bullied, and unable to say or do otherwise. The Official Solicitor and Lunacy Office could not imagine that she might resent their interference, and were confident that Miss Wortt's care was excellent. I have not strayed far from their hostility towards Mr and Mrs Humphries, as well as a broadly positive picture of their intervention. In the end, although I could imagine some alternatives, this was the version that I found most persuasive. The legal story was that Miss Alexander was a person incapable of managing her affairs, that she was just the sort of person the law intended to benefit through its protections. This particular historical story is that her experiences with the Lunacy Office were unusual but not shocking and appalling; that her story is about matters of welfare, vulnerability, and care; that for her, there was a happy ending.

Many people tried to look after Miss Alexander in their different ways, from her beloved employer and friend Dr John Norton to their neighbour Dr Humphrey Stephenson, from the clerks at the Official Solicitor's office to her devoted companion (and prolific letter writer) Miss Wortt. Mental capacity law was itself interested in the business of looking after people, in its own way. These endeavours were shaped by opinions and beliefs, by creative interpretations of puzzling situations, by occasional rule bending, and by plenty of quirks of fate, all set within the legal and social structures that were available.

This account of Miss Alexander's experiences helps to restore an important legal institution, the Lunacy Office, to its rightful place within the history of mental health law in England and Wales. My focus on Miss Alexander has provided a concrete example to illuminate complicated rules, procedures, and institutions, but her story is not simply an illustrative example. It has enabled me to draw attention to the place of creativity, ambiguity, and subjectivity in history writing, even when dealing with apparently certain legal facts, and it has allowed me to present Miss Alexander's life and the lives of those around her as historically important. In making sense of the strangeness of this 'small story', I have opened up for consideration some of the complex issues that surround welfare and citizenship, vulnerability and dependence, care and control, history writing and the law. These are issues that connect past, present, and future, and should concern us all.

NOTES

PREFACE

1   The files about Miss Alexander are in The National Archives in London (hereafter, TNA), catalogue reference J127/24 to J127/36 inclusive.

2   Peter Bartlett, 'Legal Madness in the Nineteenth Century', *Social History of Medicine* 14, no. 1 (2001): 107–31.

3   Ben Griffin, 'Paternal Rights, Child Welfare and the Law in Nineteenth-Century Britain and Ireland', *Past and Present* 246, no. 1 (2019): 109–47.

4   Key examples include Martha A Fineman, 'The Vulnerable Subject: Anchoring Equality in the Human Condition', *Yale Journal of Law and Feminism* 20, no. 1 (2008): 1–23; The Care Collective, *The Care Manifesto: The Politics of Interdependence* (London; New York: Verso, 2020); Eva Feder Kittay, 'The Ethics of Care, Dependence, and Disability', *Ratio Juris* 24, no. 1 (2011): 49–58; and in relation to capacity law, Margaret I Hall, 'Mental Capacity in the (Civil) Law: Capacity, Autonomy and Vulnerability', *McGill Law Journal* 58, no.1 (2012): 61–94.

5   A few examples include Julia Laite, *The Disappearance of Lydia Harvey* (London: Profile Books, 2021); Matt Houlbrook, *Prince of Tricksters: The Incredible True Story of Netley Lucas, Gentleman Crook* (Chicago; London: University of Chicago Press, 2016); Seth Koven, *The Match Girl and the Heiress* (Princeton: Princeton University Press, 2014).

6   This draws on ideas and arguments in Walter Breckman, 'History and Indeterminacy: Making Sense of Pasts Imperfect', in *Indeterminacy: The Mapped, the Navigable, and the Uncharted*, ed Jose V Ciprut (Cambridge, MA: MIT Press, 2008), 267–87; Marisa J Fuentes, *Dispossessed Lives: Enslaved Women, Violence, and the Archive* (Philadelphia: University of Pennsylvania, 2018); Saidiya V Hartman, 'Venus in Two Acts', *Small Axe: A Caribbean Journal of Criticism* 12, no. 2 (2008):

1–14; Houlbrook, *Prince of Tricksters*, amongst others. The call to claim a 'middle ground' where responsibility to evidence and professional standards co-exists with recognition of the role of individual and cultural ideologies in interpretation is made in Hannah R Johnson, *Blood Libel: The Ritual Murder Accusation at the Limit of Jewish History* (Ann Arbor: University of Michigan Press, 2012), 12–13, 18.

INTRODUCTION

1   Alex Ruck Keene, Nuala B Kane, Scott Y H Kim, and Gareth S Owen, 'Taking Capacity Seriously? Ten Years of Mental Capacity Disputes before England's Court of Protection', *International Journal of Law and Psychiatry* 62 (2019): 56–76 (57).

2   Law Commission, *Mental Incapacity* (London: HMSO, 1995), 1.

3   For insight into the kinds of questions that Court of Protection hearings have addressed since 2020, the blog Open Justice Court of Protection Project (https://openjusticecourtofprotection.org) is an invaluable resource. Many decisions are made without hearings, though, particularly where there is no significant disagreement about the course of action to be followed.

4   Some more detailed numbers are available in Janet Weston, 'Managing Mental Incapacity in the 20th Century: A History of the Court of Protection of England and Wales', *International Journal of Law and Psychiatry* 68 (2020): 1–12.

5   The Patients' Estates (Naming of Master's Offices) Order, 1947, available in 'Management and Administration Department: Proposed Change of Name to Court of Protection' [1925-1947], TNA LCO 4/53.

6   The phrase 'small history' is from Julia Laite, 'The Emmet's Inch: Small History in a Digital Age', *Journal of Social History* 53, no. 4 (2020): 963–89, which also inspired many of my reflections on the strengths, challenges, and ethical imperatives of small histories.

7   Clive Unsworth, 'Mental Disorder and the Tutelary Relationship: From Pre- to Post-Carceral Legal Order', *Journal of Law and Society* 18, no. 2 (1991): 254–78; Akihito Suzuki, *Madness at Home: The Psychiatrist, the Patient and the Family in England, 1820–1860* (Berkeley: University of California Press, 2006).

8   Stephen Taylor and Alice Brumby, eds, *Healthy Minds in the Twentieth Century* (London: Palgrave Macmillan, 2020), 6–7; Clive Unsworth, *The Politics of Mental Health Legislation* (Oxford: Clarendon, 1987), 23; Unsworth, 'Mental Disorder and the Tutelary Relationship'; Arlie Loughnan and Tony Ward, 'Emergent Authority and Expert Knowledge: Psychiatry and Criminal Responsibility in the UK', *Inter-*

national Journal of Law and Psychiatry 37, no. 1 (2014): 25–36; John Fanning, *New Medicalism and the Mental Health Act* (Oxford: Hart Publishing, 2018).

9   Bent Flyvbjerg, 'Five Misunderstandings About Case-Study Research', *Qualitative Inquiry* 12, no. 2 (2006): 219–45 (229).

10 Filippo de Vivo, 'Prospect or Refuge? Microhistory, History on the Large Scale: A Response', *Cultural and Social History* 7, no. 3 (2010): 387–97 (391); Matti Peltonen, 'Clues, Margins, and Monads: The Micro-Macro Link in Historical Research', *History and Theory* 40, no. 3 (2001): 347–59 (349).

11 Laite, 'Emmet's Inch', 974–5.

12 John Harrington, Lucy Series, and Alex Ruck Keene, 'Law and Rhetoric: Critical Possibilities', *Journal of Law and Society* 46, no. 2 (2019): 302–27 (308).

13 Laite, 'Emmet's Inch', 965–6.

14 de Vivo, 'Prospect or Refuge?', 394.

15 Imagination and law has attracted recent attention: Richard Mullender, Matteo Nicolini, Thomas D C Bennett, and Emilia Mickiewicz, eds, *Law and Imagination in Troubled Times: A Legal and Literary Discourse* (Abingdon: Routledge, 2020); Amalia Amaya and Maksymilian Del Mar, eds, *Virtue, Emotion, and Imagination in Law and Legal Reasoning* (Chicago: Hart Publishing, 2020). On the failures and limitations in particular of imagination in a legal context, see Adam Morton, 'Imagining Motives,' in Amaya and Del Mar, eds, *Virtue, Emotion, and Imagination*, 199–215.

16 John Harrington, *Towards a Rhetoric of Medical Law* (Abingdon: Routledge, 2017), 5–7.

17 David J Staley, *Historical Imagination* (Abingdon: Routledge, 2021), n.p. [ebook]: introduction. The role of imagination in the work of historians is perhaps most famously addressed in Robin G Collingwood, *The Idea of History* (Oxford: Oxford University Press, 1978); see also William H Dray, *History as Re-Enactment: R G Collingwood's Idea of History* (Oxford: Clarendon Press, 1995).

18 See, for example, 'Microhistory Today: A Roundtable Discussion', *Journal of Medieval and Early Modern Studies* 47, no. 1 (2017): 7–52; Laite, *Disappearance of Lydia Harvey*, ix–x.

19 Carolyn Steedman, 'Intimacy in Research: Accounting for It', *History of the Human Sciences* 21, no. 4 (2008): 17–33 (21). The best known reflections on historical narrative and its multiple possibilities (or possibilities for multiples) may be Hayden V White, *Metahistory: The Historical Imagination in Nineteenth-Century Europe* (Baltimore: Johns Hopkins University Press, 1973); Hayden V White, *The Content*

of the Form: Narrative Discourse and Historical Representation (Baltimore: Johns Hopkins University Press, 1990).

20 Johnson, *Blood Libel*, 5.

21 Suzuki, *Madness at Home*, 21.

22 As stated on the Court of Protection homepage, https://www.gov.uk/courts-tribunals/court-of-protection.

23 Harrington, Series, and Ruck Keene, 'Law and Rhetoric', 316. Denzil Lush, 'Thoughts on the Court of Protection: The ACTAPS Annual Lecture', 2018: copy kindly provided by the author.

24 Section 20 (5) of the Mental Treatment Act of 1930 provided for the elimination of the word 'lunatic' from 'any enactment or in any order, regulation or other document issues under any enactment'. Information about Lunacy Office changes of name can be gleaned from 'Management and Administration Department: proposed change of name to Court of Protection' [1925–1947], TNA LCO 4/53.

25 For a more detailed account of this renaming, see Weston, 'Managing Mental Incapacity'.

26 Christopher Booker, 'The Most Sinister Court in Britain Strikes Yet Again', *Telegraph*, 4 January 2015, 28; Christopher Booker, 'It's Time for Answers about Britain's Secret Court', *Sunday Telegraph*, 16 October 2016, 24.

27 National Council for Civil Liberties (NCCL), *50,000 Outside the Law* (London: National Council for Civil Liberties, 1951); Claire Hilton, *Improving Psychiatric Care for Older People: Barbara Robb's Campaign 1965–1975* (Basingstoke, UK: Palgrave Macmillan, 2017), 37.

28 The treasured rose bowl is mentioned in Mrs Baldry's letter of 3 January 1940, in TNA J127/25, and again in Miss Wortt's letter of 24 September 1964, in TNA J127/33.

29 Fuentes, *Dispossessed Lives*, 27.

30 'The Norwich Shows: Poultry, Dairy Produce, &c', *Norfolk News*, 24 November 1906, 14. 'Miss Beatrice Ruth Alexander, Home Farm, Long Stratton' is named as the winner of Class 62: 'Pot of not less than 5lb. of preserved butter'. Her sister took second place.

31 de Vivo, 'Prospect or Refuge?', 391. See also Claudia Verhoeven, 'Court Files', in Miriam Dobson and Benjamin Ziemann, eds, *Reading Primary Sources: The Interpretation of Texts from Nineteenth and Twentieth Century History* (New York: Routledge, 2009), 90–105 (92).

32 Hartman, 'Venus in Two Acts', 2. As Julia Laite has pointed out, the impulse to

'rescue' historical actors from obscurity also requires interrogation; I return to this briefly in the closing chapter. Laite, 'Emmet's Inch', 976–9.

33 Fuentes, *Dispossessed Lives*, 29.

34 This approach also draws on the work of Saidiya Hartman, particularly 'Venus in Two Acts' and Hartman, *Wayward Lives, Beautiful Experiments: Intimate Histories of Social Upheaval* (London: Serpent's Tail, 2019).

35 Letter from the Official Solicitor to C F Renton of the Board of Control dated 26 January 1934, in '"Marraines": Visits to nursing homes and hospitals by representatives' [1934-1960], TNA J136/134.

36 As I write this, in late 2021, staff at The National Archives are still gamely working their way through my Freedom of Information requests to open Court of Protection and Official Solicitor files relating to individuals who have died, and so this number will be increasing. The work of making files available sometimes involves redacting sensitive information about surviving family members, and has been drastically slowed down by the COVID-19 pandemic.

37 Description on National Archives online catalogue, at https://discovery.national archives.gov.uk/details/r/C9700.

38 Note from 9 March 1973, in 'Court of Protection: General bundles of court papers' [1972-3], TNA PRO 57/3039.

39 These are: 'Boylan, Mildred Roberts' [1968-9], TNA J92/307; 'Golodetz, Michael' [1951-70], TNA J92/221; 'Evans, Helen Martin' [1970], TNA J92/315.

40 Bartlett, 'Legal Madness'; James Moran, 'A Tale of Two Bureaucracies: Asylum and Lunacy Law Paperwork', *Rethinking History* 22, no. 3 (2018): 419–36; James Moran, *Madness on Trial: A Transatlantic History of English Civil Law and Lunacy* (Manchester: Manchester University Press, 2019); Ruth Paley, 'Sources and Resources: Affidavits in Proceedings in Lunacy, 1719–1733 – The Court of Chancery and the Fate of Lunatics in the Long Eighteenth Century', *Social History of Medicine* 33, no. 4 (2020): 1,363–80; Suzuki, *Madness at Home*.

41 Moran, 'A Tale of Two Bureaucracies', 429.

42 Suzuki, *Madness at Home*, 4.

43 Griffin, 'Paternal Rights', 111.

44 Pat Thane, 'Government and Society in England and Wales, 1750–1914', in F M L Thompson, ed, *Cambridge Social History of Britain, 1750–1950: Volume 3: Social Agencies and Institutions* (Cambridge: Cambridge University Press, 1990), 1–62 (48). See also José Harris, 'Society and the State in Twentieth-Century Britain', in

Thompson, ed, *Cambridge Social History of Britain*, 63–118; Brad Beaven and John Griffiths, 'Creating the Exemplary Citizen: The Changing Notion of Citizenship in Britain, 1870–1939', *Contemporary British History* 22, no. 2 (2008): 203–25.

45 Unsworth, *Politics of Mental Health Legislation*.

46 Robert Dingwall, Anne Marie Rafferty, and Charles Webster, *An Introduction to the Social History of Nursing* (London: Routledge, 1988), 135.

47 Unsworth, *Politics of Mental Health Legislation*, chapter 10.

48 Mathew Thomson, *The Problem of Mental Deficiency: Eugenics, Democracy and Social Policy in Britain, c. 1870–1959* (Oxford: Clarendon, 1998), 42, 54.

49 On these two aspects of citizenship, see Kathleen Canning and Sonya O Rose, 'Gender, Citizenship and Subjectivity: Some Historical and Theoretical Considerations', *Gender and History* 13, no. 3 (2001): 427–43; Marilyn Friedman, 'Introduction', in Marilyn Friedman, ed, *Women and Citizenship* (Oxford: Oxford University Press, 2005), 3–11.

50 Taylor and Brumby, eds, *Healthy Minds*, 2. See also Michal Shapira, *The War Inside: Psychoanalysis, Total War, and the Making of the Democratic Self in Postwar Britain* (Cambridge: Cambridge University Press, 2013); Shaul Bar-Haim, '"The Drug Doctor": Michael Balint and the Revival of General Practice in Postwar Britain', *History Workshop Journal* 86 (2018): 114–32.

51 On consumerism and interwar citizenship, see Beaven and Griffiths, 'Creating the Exemplary Citizen', 214.

52 Bar-Haim, 'Drug Doctor', 127.

53 Fineman, 'Vulnerable Subject', 20.

54 Beverley Clough, 'Vulnerability and Capacity to Consent to Sex: Asking the Right Questions?', *Child and Family Law Quarterly* 26, no. 4 (2015): 371–97 (372). See also Beverley Clough, 'Disability and Vulnerability: Challenging the Capacity/ Incapacity Binary', *Social Policy and Society* 16, no. 3 (2017): 469–81; Kirsty Keywood, 'The Vulnerable Adult Experiment: Situating Vulnerability in Adult Safeguarding Law and Policy', *International Journal of Law and Psychiatry* 53 (2017): 88–96.

55 Clough, 'Vulnerability and Capacity to Consent', 375. See also Deborah O'Connor and Martha Donnelly, 'Confronting the Challenges of Assessing Capacity: Dementia in the Context of Abuse', in Deborah O'Connor and Barbara Purves, eds, *Decision-Making, Personhood and Dementia: Exploring the Interface* (London: Jessica Kingsley Publishers, 2009), 106–113, which highlights the importance of context in assessing mental capacity.

56 A point also made in a slightly different context in Jackie Gulland, *Gender, Work and Social Control: A Century of Disability Benefits* (London: Palgrave Macmillan, 2019), 8.

57 A. Szerletics, *Vulnerable Adults and the Inherent Jurisdiction of the High Court: Essex Autonomy Project Briefing Document* (2011), available at https://autonomy. essex.ac.uk/resources/vulnerable-adults-and-the-inherent-jurisdiction-of-the-high-court. See also Mary Welstead, 'Vulnerable Adults: The Inherent Jurisdiction and the Right to Marry', *Denning Law Journal* 19 (2007): 258–69.

58 Ian Hacking, 'The Making and Molding of Child Abuse', *Critical Inquiry* 17, no. 2 (1991): 253–88; Adrian Bingham, Lucy Delap, Louise Jackson, and Louise Settle, 'Historical Child Sexual Abuse in England and Wales: The Role of Historians', *History of Education* 45, no. 4 (2016): 411–29.

59 The care/control paradox is summarised in Pamela Dale, 'Implementing the 1913 Mental Deficiency Act: Competing Priorities and Resource Constraint Evident in the South West of England before 1948', *Social History of Medicine* 16, no. 3 (2003): 403–18. See also, for example, Phil Fennell, 'Balancing Care and Control: Guardianship, Community Treatment Orders and Patient Safeguards', *International Journal of Law and Psychiatry* 15, no. 2 (1992): 205–35.

60 Louise Hide and Joanna Bourke, 'Cultures of Harm in Institutions of Care: Introduction', *Social History of Medicine* 31, no. 4 (2018): 679–87 (684).

61 Meredith Stone, Renata Kokanovic, Felicity Callard, and Alex F Broom, 'Estranged Relations: Coercion and Care in Narratives of Supported Decision-Making in Mental Healthcare', *Medical Humanities* 46 (2020): 62–72.

62 Care Collective, *Care Manifesto*; Susan Reverby, *Ordered to Care: The Dilemma of American Nursing, 1850–1945* (Cambridge: Cambridge University Press, 1987); Joan C Tronto, *Caring Democracy: Markets, Equality, and Justice* (New York: New York University Press, 2013).

63 A few examples include Anne Borsay and Pamela Dale, eds, *Mental Health Nursing: The Working Lives of Paid Carers in the Nineteenth and Twentieth Centuries* (Manchester: Manchester University Press, 2015); Tommy Dickinson, *Curing Queers: Mental Nurses and Their Patients, 1935–74* (Manchester: Manchester University Press, 2015).

64 Joan Tronto, 'Care as the Work of Citizens: A Modest Proposal', in Friedman, ed, *Women and Citizenship*, 130–45 (141).

65 Joan Tronto, 'Care as the Work of Citizens', 141.

66 Hartman, 'Venus in Two Acts', 12; Houlbrook, *Prince of Tricksters*.

67   Hannah Johnson argues something similar in *Blood Libel*, particularly for example at 77–79.

68   On historians, their subjects, and the value of disclosure, see Jill Lepore, 'Historians Who Love Too Much: Reflections on Microhistory and Biography', *Journal of American History* 88, no. 1 (2001): 129–44 (139). On emotional connection as a critical tool that can generate history 'both of the past and the present', see Katie Barclay, 'Falling in Love with the Dead', *Rethinking History* 22, no. 4 (2018): 459–73, especially 468–9.

69   On the study of law as a route to understand some of these aspects, see Harrington, Series, and Ruck Keene, 'Law and Rhetoric'.

CHAPTER ONE

1   Letter from Miss Wortt dated 11 August 1940, in TNA J127/26.

2   Henry Studdy Theobald, *Remembrance of Things Past* (Oxford: Blackwell, 1935), 90.

3   Denzil Lush, 'Lives of the Masters', *Trusts and Estates Law and Tax Journal* 100 (2008): 21–5.

4   Theobald, *Remembrance of Things Past*, 91.

5   Margaret McGlynn, 'Idiots, Lunatics and the Royal Prerogative in Early Tudor England', *Journal of Legal History* 26 (2005): 1–24.

6   Roy Porter, *Mind-Forg'd Manacles: A History of Madness in England from the Restoration to the Regency* (London: Penguin, 1990); Michael MacDonald, 'Lunatics and the State in Georgian England', *Social History of Medicine* 2, no. 3 (1989): 299–313.

7   Useful summaries of these procedures and reforms can be found in Charles Palmer Phillips, *The Law Concerning Lunatics, Idiots, and Persons of Unsound Mind* (London: Butterworths, 1858); Suzuki, *Madness at Home*, 18–22; Chantal Stebbings, 'Protecting the Property of the Mentally Ill: The Judicial Solution in Nineteenth Century Lunacy Law', *Cambridge Law Journal* 71, no. 2 (2012): 384–411.

8   *Lunacy Act 1890*, s.116 (d).

9   Henry Studdy Theobald, *The Law Relating to Lunacy* (London: Stevens & Sons, 1924), 79.

10   Theobald, *Law Relating to Lunacy*, 5–6, 79; N A Heywood and A C Massey, *Lunacy Practice*, 3rd edn (London: Stevens & Sons, 1907), 90.

11   Suzuki, *Madness at Home*, particularly 25–38.

12   Theobald, *Law Relating to Lunacy*, 80; *Royal Commission on the Law Relating to Mental Illness and Mental Deficiency, 1954–1957: Report* (London: HMSO, 1957), 267.

13 'Departmental Committee of Inquiry set up to consider staff, organisation and accommodation in Management and Administration Department' [1934], TNA LCO 4/47. See also 'Organisation and Methods report' [1949-50], TNA LCO 4/55, which reports 130 staff in 1938 and 134 in 1948. Currency conversions are all very approximate and make use of The National Archives' currency converter, https://www.nationalarchives.gov.uk/currency-converter.

14 Suzuki, *Madness at Home*, 22–3.

15 *Report of the Select Committee to Inquire into Operations of Lunacy Law* (London: HMSO, 1877), 522; Theobald, *Law Relating to Lunacy*, 103; *Report of the Royal Commission on the Care and Control of the Feeble-Minded* (London: HMSO, 1908), 266.

16 'Departmental Committee of Inquiry on Management and Administration Department: draft reports' [1934-5], TNA LCO 4/49; 'Departmental Committee of Inquiry' [1934], TNA LCO 4/55; *Royal Commission on the Law Relating to Mental Illness*, 291; Hansard, House of Commons (written answers) 2 May 1991, vol 190. See also T C S Keely, 'One Hundred Years of Lunacy Administration', *Cambridge Law Journal* 8, no. 2 (1943): 195–200.

17 Gerald Mills and Arthur Ronald W Poyser, *Mills & Poyser's Lunacy Practice* (London: Butterworth & Co, 1934). See also Poyser's evidence in 'Departmental Committee of Inquiry set up to consider staff, organisation and accommodation in Management and Administration Department' [1934], TNA LCO 4/48.

18 Hunt and Phillips, *Heywood & Massey's Court of Protection Practice*, 7th edn (London: Stevens & Sons, 1954), 3.

19 *Who Decides? Making Decisions on Behalf of Mentally Incapacitated Adults: A Consultation Paper* (London: HMSO, 1997), 5–6. Law Commission, *Mental Incapacity*, 21–2.

20 Mills and Poyser, *Mills & Poyser's Lunacy Practice*; evidence of Mr Poyser on 9 October 1934, in 'Departmental Committee of Inquiry' [1934], TNA LCO 4/47.

21 Poyser's evidence to the Departmental Committee of Inquiry on 9 October 1934, in 'Departmental Committee of Inquiry' [1934], TNA LCO 4/47.

22 Suzuki, *Madness at Home*, 25; *Report of the Select Committee to Inquire into Operations of Lunacy Law*, 57.

23 Some examples include 'Brocklehurst, John Ogilvy' [1947-1970], TNA J127/189; 'Roberts, Malcolm Atkin' [1916-1940], J92/25; 'Stanley, Herbert' [1915-1942], J92/22; 'Carr, Jean Alison' [1934-1941], J92/77.

24 *Report on the Care and Control of the Feeble-Minded*, 260.

25 Evidence provided by Mills on 8 October 1934, and evidence provided by Poyser on 9 October 1934, both in 'Departmental Committee of Inquiry on Management

and Administration Department: Evidence and minutes of meetings' [1934], TNA
LCO 4/50. Some examples of relatively small estates include 'Lockett, Anna Emma'
[1927-1982], TNA J92/100; 'Mathews, Charles John' [1928-1983], TNA J92/103; 'Hall,
Evelyn Lucy' [1929-1940], TNA J92/60; 'Sampson, Arthur Thomas' [1930-1940],
TNA J92/65.

26 'Future of the Court of Protection and Lord Chancellor's Legal Visitors: Interde-
partmental Steering Group on Review of the Mental Health Act 1959' [1975-9],
TNA LCO 65/178.

27 As characterised in 'Obituary: Norman Turner', *Telegraph*, 21 December 2007.

28 Sarah Castle was the first woman to be appointed to the role of Official Solicitor,
in 2019.

29 For example, the confusion of the receiver in 'Picton, Clara' [1914-1940], TNA
J92/18.

30 Background information about the Alexanders is from census records and local
newspapers, particularly 'Long Stratton', *Eastern Daily Press*, 18 April 1901, 8; 'Long
Stratton', *Eastern Daily Press*, 2 November 1903, 10; 'Correspondence: The County
Council Vacancy: Stratton Division', *Eastern Daily Press*, 6 March 1903, 13 (see also
'County Councils' on the same page, for news of Dennis Alexander's election).
Notice of Mr Alexander's death, including a biographical note, is in 'Depwade
Rural District Council' and 'Depwade Ex-Councillor's Sad End', *Diss Express and
Norfolk and Suffolk Journal*, 22 April 1927, 8.

31 'Waveney Valley Show at Harleston', *Norfolk News*, 27 September 1902, 11; 'Agricul-
tural Show at Harleston', *Diss Examiner*, 1 October 1909, 1; 'The Cattle Show',
Norfolk News, second sheet, 22 November 1902, 10; 'Butter-Making Competition',
Norwich Mercury, 24 June 1905, 6, in which Helen took first place; 'Poultry, Dairy
Produce', *Norfolk News*, 24 November 1906, 14, in which Beatrice was victorious.

32 'The Cattle Show: Prize Awards & Specials', *Norfolk News*, second sheet, 23 November 1902, 10.

33 'County Council Competitions', *Norwich Mercury*, 24 June 1905, 6; and then vic-
tory over Helen is reported in 'The Norwich Shows', *Norfolk News*, second sheet,
24 November 1906, 14.

34 For a report of her enjoyment in later life at meeting another woman from a
'farming background' with whom to share memories, see Miss Wortt's letter dated
18 July 1968, in TNA J127/36.

35 Impressions of Miss Alexander's personality and interests are scattered throughout

the archived files, but are particularly clearly expressed in Miss Wortt's letters dated 7 April 1940 in TNA J127/25; 11 August 1940 in TNA J127/26; 12 December 1941 in TNA J127/27; 10 April 1952 in TNA J127/30; Mr Winder's report dated 20 November 1939 in TNA J127/24; Letter from Barclays Bank Yeovil dated 14 September 1940 in TNA J127/26. The direct quote is from Mrs Winder's report of 6 October 1956, in TNA J127/31.

36   UK Medical Registers, 1859–1959; Notice of appointment to the Metropolitan Police in *Times*, 16 July 1901, 9; various newspaper reports of inquests in which Dr Norton gave evidence are available, including 'A Woman's Despair', *London Daily News*, 14 December 1910, 7; 'Suicide of a Prince's Footman', *Times*, 6 January 1913, 13; 'Notting Hill Murder and Suicide', *West London Observer*, 25 June 1915, 2; 'Army Doctor Severely Criticized', *Evening Mail*, 12 May 1920, 8 (Dr Norton was the one doing the criticising here).

37   Gail L Savage, 'Divorce and the Law in England and France Prior to the First World War', *Journal of Social History* 21, no. 3 (1988): 499–514 (503, 511).

38   'Motor Drive by Night', *Essex Newsman*, 19 February 1910, 1; 'Divorce Court File: 9882. Appellant: John Norton. Respondent: Mabel Norton. Co-respondent: Robert S W Brewer' [1909], TNA J77/984/9882.

39   Lucy Delap, *Knowing Their Place: Domestic Service in Twentieth-Century Britain* (Oxford: Oxford University Press, 2014), 32.

40   Letter from Miss Wortt dated 10 July 1965, in TNA J127/34; letter from Miss Wortt dated 24 September 1964 in TNA J127/33; Dr Norton's last will dated 7 August 1928.

41   Information gleaned from the census, from the online digital archives of Brighton College, and from his army file, 'Lieutenant Richard Legge Norton, Norfolk Regiment' [1916-1919], TNA WO 374/50923.

42   Delap, *Knowing Their Place*, 83.

43   Tessa Boase, *The Housekeeper's Tale: The Women Who Really Ran the English Country House* (London: Arum Press, 2015); Delap, *Knowing Their Place*.

44   Leonore Davidoff, *Worlds Between: Historical Perspectives on Gender and Class* (New York: Routledge, 1995), 33.

45   'Lieutenant Richard Legge Norton, Norfolk Regiment' [1916-1919], TNA WO 374/50923.

46   'Sales by Auction', *Western Gazette*, 7 September 1923, 1.

47   'Dorset Field Club', *Western Gazette*, 22 August 1924, 9.

48   Mr Winder's report dated 20 November 1939 in TNA J127/24.

49 Mrs Winder's report dated 20 May 1965 and letters from Miss Wortt dated 3 June 1965 and 19 January 1965, in TNA J127/34; Mrs Winder's report dated 8 March 1968 in J127/36.

50 After Miss Alexander's death, his estate was to be divided between his sister's five sons, his god-daughter Cynthia, and his ex-wife if she could be traced. Miss Alexander outlived all but one of these, Dr Norton's youngest nephew, Victor Parkhouse. Victor himself died in his seventies in 1976.

51 Pat Thane, *Happy Families? History and Family Policy* (London: British Academy, 2011), 25.

52 Davidoff, *Words Between*, 34.

53 Undated statement provided to the Official Solicitor in around late June 1939, in TNA J127/24.

54 Letter dated 6 September 1948 from Midland Bank, in TNA J127/29.

55 Letter from Helen Baldry dated 22 January 1940, in J127/25.

56 Visitor's report dated 20 November 1939 in TNA J127/24. See also assorted correspondence from Dr Stephenson in the same file.

57 Mr Winder's report dated 22 January 1940, in TNA J127/24.

58 Jonathan Toms, *Mental Hygiene and Psychiatry in Modern Britain* (Basingstoke, UK: Palgrave Macmillan, 2013), 28. See also Jonathan Toms, 'Citizenship and Learning Disabled People: The Mental Health Charity MIND's 1970s Campaign in Historical Context', *Medical History* 61, no. 4 (2017): 481–99 (483).

59 Letter from Miss Stevenson dated 29 December 1939, in TNA J127/24.

60 Ibid.

61 For more on this, see Jan Walmsley, 'Women and the Mental Deficiency Act of 1913: Citizenship, Sexuality and Regulation', *British Journal of Learning Disabilities* 28, no. 2 (2000): 65–70; Thomson, *Problem of Mental Deficiency*; Mark Jackson, *The Borderland of Imbecility: Medicine, Society, and the Fabrication of the Feeble Mind in Late Victorian and Edwardian England* (Manchester: Manchester University Press, 2000). For attitudes in Dorset in particular, see Graham Chester and Pamela Dale, 'Institutional Care for the Mentally Defective, 1914–1948: Diversity as a Response to Individual Needs and an Indication of Lack of Policy Coherence', *Medical History* 51, no. 1 (2007): 59–78.

62 Dr Stephenson's letter of 2 July 1939, in TNA J127/24.

63 Mr Winder's report of 20 November 1939; Mr Meysey-Thompson's report of 11 May 1939; Dr Stephenson's letters dated 28 April 1939, 24 May 1939, 3 October 1939; Miss Stevenson's letter of 25 November 1939, all in TNA J127/24.

64 Thomson, *Problem of Mental Deficiency*, 34, 272.

65 Shelley McSheffrey, 'Detective Fiction in the Archives: Court Records and the Uses of Law in Late Medieval England', *History Workshop Journal* 65, no. 1 (2008): 65–78 (74).

66 McSheffrey, 'Detective Fiction in the Archives', 74.

67 For legal recognition of the impact of bereavement on decision-making capacity, see *Key v Key* [2010]; *Clitheroe v Bond* [2020].

68 Mrs Humphries reports this request from Dr Norton in her undated letter received on 8 February 1940, in TNA J127/24.

CHAPTER TWO

1 Letters from Dr Stephenson dated 24 May and 2 July 1939, in TNA J127/24.

2 Barclay, 'Falling in Love with the Dead', 468.

3 Suzuki, *Madness at Home*.

4 'Phillips, Edith' [1910-81], TNA J92/95; 'Perry, Doris Mildred' [1944-81], TNA J92/151.

5 'Cohen, Esther Eugenie' [1920-40], TNA J92/36.

6 'Bathurst, Clara: Court administration papers' [1968-70], TNA J92/308.

7 'Ross, Mary' [1936-9], TNA J92/85.

8 'Down, Andrew' [1913-39], TNA J92/15; 'Nightingale, Ann Eugenie' [1916-40], TNA J92/24; 'Brothers, Emma Rosa' [1922-40], TNA J92/43.

9 'Stein, Ada' [1936-81], TNA J92/117; 'Stevens, Alice Constance' [1937-9], TNA J127/123; 'Rigby, Mabel' [1939], TNA J127/54; 'Trounson, Leslie Powers' [1944-80] TNA J92/159. On poor law and public assistance institutions, see Lyn Hollen Lees, *The Solidarities of Strangers* (Cambridge: Cambridge University Press, 1998), 331–5; Martin Gorsky, 'Creating the Poor Law Legacy: Institutional Care for Older People Before the Welfare State', *Contemporary British History* 26, no. 4 (2012): 441–65.

10 'Parker, Constance Mary Louisa' [1935-40], TNA J92/82; 'Hoskins, Elizabeth' [1943-51], TNA J92/148; 'Millar, Henry James' [1938-83], TNA J92/118.

11 'Jones, Ernest Edward' [1934-82], TNA J92/111. See also 'Knights, George David' [1954-82], TNA J91/240, where the Court was notified by the Air Ministry of funds they held for a former serviceman.

12 Examples include, in 1953, 'Middleton, Arthur' [1935-1982], TNA J92/116; 'Leach, Mary Ann' [1948-82], TNA J92/205; 'Newman, Amy Annie Lilian Ida' [1948-81], TNA J92/206; 'Williamson, Margaret May' [1952-81], TNA J92/239; ' Williams, Maria' [1956-81], TNA J92/247.

13 'Knock, Bertha' [1954-82], TNA J91/241.

14 'Gilliam, Annie' [1961-75], TNA J127/220; Walmsley, Mary Jayne' [1969-70], TNA J92/313; 'Rees, Edith Emily: 1968-9 September and minute notes 1968-73', J92/310; 'Grant, Beatrice Eliza' [1973-4], TNA J127/217.

15 Examples include 'Nightingale, Ann Eugenie' [1916-40], TNA J92/24; 'Crank, William' [1924-40], TNA J92/49. See also the case of re TRM [1939].

16 Hunt and Phillips, *Heywood & Massey's Court of Protection Practice*, 134–7.

17 'Quigley, Ellen Mary' [1928-9], TNA J127/39.

18 'Evans, Basil Edward' [1927-83], TNA J92/102.

19 'Gwynne, Sir Roland Vaughan' [1967], TNA J92/295.

20 Oral evidence from Poyser on 9 October 1934, in 'Departmental Committee of Inquiry on Management and Administration Department: Evidence and minutes of meetings' [1934], TNA LCO 4/50.

21 Letter from Barclays Bank dated 14 September 1940, in TNA J127/26.

22 The 1959 Act removed the administrative distinction between those who had been found incapable and were also hospitalised involuntarily, and those who were not involuntarily detained; the archived records also become very much more patchy.

23 Examples include 'Longhurst, Victoria Mary' [1928-1941], TNA J92/59; 'Evans, Mary Annie' [1935-40], TNA J92/80; 'Hopkins, Obadiah' [1929-39], TNA J92/63; 'Carr, Jean Alison' [1934-1941], J92/77.

24 'Ward, Emma Canwell' [1921-39], TNA J92/40; 'Raggett, Frances Jane' [1926-41] TNA J92/54.

25 Suzuki, *Madness at Home*, 4.

26 Editors' introduction, in Peter Bartlett and David Wright, eds, *Outside the Walls of the Asylum: The History of Care in the Community, 1750–2000* (London: Althone Press, 1999), 7.

27 Those receiving constant care in their home included 'Willard, Emily' [1932-41], TNA J92/72; 'Grove, Sidney Bertram Cole' [1937-40], J92/88; 'Roberts, Herbert' [1937-9], J92/86; and 'Nicols, John Bowyer Buchanan' [1938-9], J92/91. Those receiving close supervision include 'Beresford, The Hon Eileen Theresa de la Poer' [1921-41], TNA J92/39; 'Alpass, Annie Laura' [1927-41], TNA J92/57; 'Barnes, Mary Elizabeth Prescot' [1931-80], TNA J92/108; 'Brocklehurst, John Ogilvy' [1947-74], TNA J127/189.

28 The 1891 census has most of the Poyser family in Suffolk with Isabella, who is recorded as a lunatic by inquisition. Mrs Alice Poyser is noted as her committee.

29 On Gerald Mills, see George Barker and Alan Stenning, eds, *Record of old Westminsters*, vol 2 (London: Chiswick Press, 1928), 647.

30 Gerald Mills and Arthur Poyser, *Management and Administration of Estates in Lunacy*, 2nd edn (London: Butterworth & Co, 1927); Mills and Poyser, *Mills & Poyser's Lunacy Practice*.

31 Note to Visitor with pencilled date of 22 January 1940, in TNA J127/24.

32 The original copy of Dr Stephenson's letter has not been retained and the copy does not record the name of the addressee, but it is signed informally as 'Humphrey', and Poyser's identity as the addressee is mentioned elsewhere: TNA J127/24.

33 Note to Visitor with pencilled date 22 January 1940, in TNA J127/24.

34 His older brother was killed in 1935 in a Royal Air Force aeroplane, at the age of 21. 'R.A.F. Machines in Collision: Pilot Officer Killed', *Times,* 2 October 1935, 16. His younger sister moved to Norway in 1945 and then to Canada, where she died in 2010.

35 John Fendley, 'The Little Company of Hope and the Tradition of Spiritual Healing at Brownshill', *Gloucestershire Catholic History Society* 41 (2002): 3–21 (16). See also the Chalfont local history group website, https://www.chalfordparishlocalhistory group.org.uk/parish/brownshill.

36 Will of Humphrey Meigh Stephenson dated 23 August 1957 and admitted to probate on 24 September 1958, available from the England and Wales probate records service.

37 Martin Pugh, *'Hurrah for the Blackshirts!': Fascists and Fascism in Britain between the Wars* (London: Pimlico, 2006), 140.

38 Correspondence from Mrs G Stephenson in the Robert Saunders Collection, Sheffield Special Collections (hereafter SSC), A1/393-395; A2/366-373; A3/306-320; A4/182; Letter from Robert Saunders dated 18 May 1938, A7/331.

39 G C Webber, 'Patterns of Membership and Support for the British Union of Fascists', *Journal of Contemporary History* 19, no. 4 (1984): 575–606.

40 Letter from Robert Stephenson to Dick Bellamy dated 19 April 1964, in the Robert Saunders Collection, SSC D3/8 (1); Correspondence between Robert Saunders and the Stephensons, in the Robert Saunders Collection, SSC C10/348, C11/326-7, C15/559-562.

41 David Redvaldsen, '"Science Must Be the Basis": Sir Oswald Mosley's Political Parties and Their Policies on Health, Science and Scientific Racism, 1931–1974',

Contemporary British History 30, no. 3 (2016): 368–88; Gary Love, "'What's the Big Idea?": Oswald Mosley, the British Union of Fascists and Generic Fascism', *Journal of Contemporary History* 42, no. 3 (2007): 447–68; Michael A Spurr, "'Living the Blackshirt Life": Culture, Community and the British Union of Fascists, 1932–1940', *Contemporary European History* 12, no. 3 (2003): 305–22.

42 Pugh, *Hurrah for the Blackshirts!*, 5, 35.

43 Mrs Stephenson's letters in the Robert Saunders Collection, SSC A4/184 and A3/321.

44 Anonymous editorial, 'The Feeble-Minded Control Bill: House of Commons Meeting, December 5th, 1911', *Eugenics Review* 3, no. 4 (1912): 355–8 (358). Quoted in Simon Jarrett, *Those They Called Idiots: The Idea of the Disabled Mind from 1700 to the Present Day* (London: Reaktion Books, 2020), 266.

45 Thomson, *Problem of Mental Deficiency*, 35.

46 Dr Stephenson's application form to join the British Union of Fascists dated December 1934, in the Robert Saunders Collection, SSC 119/A2/118.

47 Mrs Stephenson's letters dated 27 October 1937 and 30 November 1937 in the Robert Saunders Collection, SSC 119/A3/314 and 119/A3/313.

48 Stephenson's publications are mentioned within his later medical directory entries. The book in question is H M Stephenson, *On the Highest Hill* (London: John Long, 1927). He also wrote something called 'Yo Ho & a Bottle of Rum', apparently published in 1930 but sadly untraceable, and 'Light Anaesthesia in Transporting Wounded from the Field,' published in the *British Medical Journal* in 1918. Perhaps these are a better read.

49 Mr Winder's report of 20 November 1939, in TNA J127/24.

50 'D'Aguilar, Emily Gertrude' [1919-40], TNA J92/32; 'Cohen, Esther Eugenie' [1920-40], TNA J92/36. Similar examples include 'Bolton, Alice Worswick' [1922-40], TNA J92/41; 'Chabot, Sarah' [1923-38], TNA J92/44; 'Stone, Henry Samuel' [1924-39], TNA J92/47.

51 'Kendall, Florence Adeline' [1932-83], TNA J92/109; 'White, The Rev Verner Moore' [1939-40], TNA J92/92.

52 'Gladstone, Robert Theodore' [1939-40], TNA J92/94.

53 'Roberts, Herbert' [1937-39], TNA J92/86.

54 'Barnes, Mary Elizabeth Prescot' [1931-80], TNA J92/108.

55 Peter Bartlett and David Wright, 'Community Care and Its Antecedents', in Bartlett and Wright, eds, *Outside the Walls of the Asylum*, 1–18 (10).

56 'Kendall, Florence Adeline' [1932-1983], TNA J92/109.

57 'Mathews, Charles John' [1928-83], TNA J92/103.

58 Suzuki, *Madness at Home*, 99.

59 Oral evidence from Master Methold on 19 November 1934, in 'Departmental Committee of Inquiry on Management and Administration Department: Evidence and minutes of meetings' [1934], TNA LCO 4/50.

60 'Higgins, Joseph' [1918-40], TNA J92/30.

61 'Alpass, Annie Laura' [1927-41], TNA J92/57; 'Whitehouse, Gladstone Power' [1951-81], TNA J92/233.

62 'Carr, Jean Alison' [1934-1941], J92/77; 'Short, Arthur Reginald Terry' [1921-39], TNA J92/38.

63 'Whitehouse, Gladstone Power' [1951-81], TNA J92/233.

64 Suzuki, *Madness at Home*, 66–7.

65 Ibid., 66.

66 'Dowdy, Alice Blanche' [1939-40], TNA J92/93; 'Taylor, Anne Jane' [1968-74], TNA J127/190. Miss Taylor's name is usually spelt as Ann within the file.

67 There is no mention in the evidence given to the Committee of Inquiry appointed in 1934, nor in the Organisation and Methods Report of 1949: TNA LCO 4/47-50; LCO 4/55.

68 'Mower, George Henry Graham' [1966-74], TNA J92/293.

CHAPTER THREE

1 This phrasing borrows from Raymond Jennings, 'Mental Disorder and the Court of Protection', *Lancet* 279 (1962): 855–6.

2 Peter Bartlett, 'Sense and Nonsense: Sensation, Delusion and the Limitation of Sanity in Nineteenth-Century Law', in Lionel Bently and Leo Flynn, eds, *Law and the Senses: Sensational Jurisprudence* (London: Pluto Press, 1996), 21–41. See also Peter Bartlett and Ralph Sandland, *Mental Health Law: Policy and Practice*, 1st edn (London: Blackstone Press, 2000), 349.

3 Harrington, *Towards a Rhetoric of Medical Law*, 2, 6.

4 Mills and Poyser, *Mills and Poyser's Lunacy Practice*, 16.

5 Dr Stephenson's letter of 28 April 1939, in TNA J127/24.

6 It is hard to be exact, as diagnostic terms were flexible and document retention haphazard. The fifteen I have identified are: 'Alpass, Annie Laura' [1927-41], TNA

J92/57; 'Barnes, Mary Elizabeth Prescot' [1931-80], J92/108; 'Beresford, The Hon Eileen Theresa de la Poer' [1921-41], TNA J92/39; 'Brocklehurst, John Ogilvy' [1947-74], J127/189; 'Evans, Basil Edward' [1927-83], TNA J92/102; 'Fenwick, Robert' [1940-83], TNA J92/127; 'Gilbert, Jemima Peck' [1925-38], TNA J92/50; 'King, May' [1949-1981], TNA J92/210; 'Lane, Thomas' [1940-82], TNA J92/128; 'Newman, Amy Annie Lilian Ida' [1948-81], TNA J92/206; 'Parrish, Blanche Ivy Irene' [1948-81], TNA J92/207; 'Pringle, Claude Mark Elliott' [1913-1941], TNA J92/14; 'Scotney, Thomas' [1928-1941], TNA J92/61; 'Sims, Arthur Palmer' [1912-40] (which includes some mention of his brother William as well), TNA J92/12; 'Trounson, Leslie Powers' [1944-1980], TNA J92/159.

7   Medical affidavit dated 4 July 1912, in 'Sims, Arthur Palmer' [1912-40], TNA J92/12. See also the medical certificate in 'King, May' [1949-1981], TNA J92/210.

8   Medical statement of 20 January 1927, in 'Alpass, Annie Laura' [1927-41], TNA J92/57; medical certificate from June 1930, in 'Scotney, Thomas' [1928-1941], TNA J92/61.

9   Miss Wortt's letter dated 11 August 1940 in TNA J127/26; Letter from Barclays Bank dated 14 September 1940, in TNA J127/26.

10 Instructions to Lord Chancellor's Visitor, in TNA J127/24.

11 Inner Temple Admissions Database; Wartime diary held by the Imperial War Museum, catalogued as 'Private papers of Captain H C Meysey-Thompson CBE'; 'News in Brief', Times, 21 November 1928, 11. His grandfather was Sir Harry Meysey-Thompson, 1st Baronet of Kirby Hall; his father was old Etonian, barrister, and semi-professional footballer Albert Childers Meysey-Thompson QC; his uncles included Henry Meysey-Thompson, MP and then peer, and Ernest Meysey-Thompson, MP for Birmingham Handsworth until 1922.

12 Letter from Frederick Ward, in 'Ward, Emma Canwell' [1921-1939], TNA J92/40.

13 Report of visit on 11 May 1939, in TNA J127/24.

14 Chester and Dale, 'Institutional Care for the Mentally Defective'.

15 Mr Winder's report dated 31 January 1940, in TNA J127/24.

16 For example, see Dr Curran's remarks in his October 1970 report, in 'Evans, Helen Martin' [1970], TNA J92/315.

17 'Statistics of cases and visits made' [1866-1960], TNA LCO 11/2; 'Proposed increase in the number of Visitors' [1936], TNA LCO 11/4.

18 'Proposed increase in the number of Visitors' [1936], TNA LCO 11/4.

19 Report of visit on 11 May 1939, in TNA J127/24.

20 Memorandum dated 19 May 1939, in TNA J127/24.

21 Harrington, Series, and Ruck Keene, 'Law and Rhetoric', 308.

22 Simon Jarrett, "'Belief', "Opinion", and "Knowledge": The Idiot in Law in the Long Eighteenth Century', in Patrick McDonagh, C F Goodey, and Timothy Stainton, eds, *Intellectual Disability: A Conceptual History, 1200–1900* (Manchester: Manchester University Press, 2018), 162–89; Bartlett, 'Sense and Nonsense'; Joel Peter Eigen, *Witnessing Insanity: Madness and Mad-Doctors in the English Court* (New Haven; London: Yale University Press, 1995); Loughnan and Ward, 'Emergent Authority and Expert Knowledge'.

23 Specified in Heywood and Massey, *Lunacy Practice* (1900).

24 N A Heywood and Ralph C Romer, *Heywood & Massey's Lunacy Practice*, 5th edn (London: Stevens & Sons, 1920), 54.

25 Mills and Poyser, *Management and Administration of Estates in Lunacy*, 31; Mills and Poyser, *Mills & Poyser's Lunacy Practice*, 16. On more involved case management, see Weston, 'Managing Mental Incapacity'.

26 Griffin, 'Paternal Rights'.

27 As well as the Poyser-Mills-Stephenson family network, the 1911 census records Thomas Alexander Southwell Keely of Twickenham as chief clerk of the Office of Masters in Lunacy and his son (later to be Assistant Master) as third class clerk at the same office. See also Keely, 'One Hundred Years of Lunacy Administration', 197.

28 Dr Stephenson's letters dated 2 July and 24 May 1939, in TNA J92/24.

29 Greta Jones, *Social Hygiene in Twentieth Century Britain* (London: Croom Helm, 1986), 20.

30 'Carr, Jean Alison' [1934-1941], TNA J92/77.

31 'Waite, Emily Fraser' [1930-1941], TNA J92/67.

32 'Short, Arthur Reginald Terry' [1921-39], TNA J92/38.

33 Mr Winder's report of 20 November 1939, in TNA J127/24.

34 Letter to Dr Stephenson of 18 December 1939, in TNA J127/24.

35 Procedural notes in 'Departmental Committee of Inquiry set up to consider staff, organisation and accommodation in Management and Administration Department' [1934], TNA LCO 4/47; Mills and Poyser, *Mills & Poyser's Lunacy Practice*, 27 (1934, and earlier editions).

36 Medical statement sworn on 20 June 1939, in TNA J92/24.

37 Mrs Willard's undated letter and her doctor's letter of 18 July 1932; Dr Raw's report of 19 July 1932, in 'Willard, Emily' [1932-41], TNA J92/72.

38 Mr Kilbey's petition to the Lunacy Office of November 1944, in 'Kilbey, William' [1944-81], TNA J92/193.

39 Mr Cook's letter dated 4 February 1931, in 'Cook, Thomas' [1917-1939], TNA J92/28.

40 A B Macfarlane, 'The Court of Protection', *Medico-Legal Journal* 60, no. 1 (1992): 25–43 (35). Mrs Macfarlane was the first woman (and first Solicitor) to head up the Court of Protection, but chose to retain the title of 'Master'. See Denzil Lush, 'Anne Bridget Macfarlane, 1930–2019', *Journal of Elder Law and Capacity* 1 (2020): 95–101 (97).

41 Ruck Keene, et al., 'Taking Capacity Seriously', 60.

42 These reported cases include *Re Walker* [1905]; *Re Marshall* [1920]; *re Freeman* [1927]; *re XY* [1937]; *re TRM* [1938]; *re CWM* [1941].

43 *Masterman-Lister v Brutton & Co* [2002].

44 *Banks v Goodfellow* [1870].

45 Wendy J Turner, 'Mental Health as a Foundation for Suit or an Excuse for Theft in Medieval English Legal Disputes', in Sara M Butler, ed, *Medicine and the Law in the Middle Ages* (Leiden: Brill, 2014), 157–74 (162).

46 Cited in a memorandum from Sir Boggis-Rolfe dated 20 December 1957, in 'Cost of administering patients' estates: Proposed increase in lunacy percentage and fees in connection with reduction of the Supreme Court vote' [1957-8], TNA LCO 2/7695.

47 NCCL, *50,000 Outside the Law*; *Royal Commission on the Law Relating to Mental Illness*.

48 The case is unreported; it is described but not named in Hunt and Phillips, *Heywood & Massey's Court of Protection Practice*, 83. It is then described *and* named from the next edition of the textbook onwards. Further detail about the case is available in TNA LCO 2/5714, as it raised concerns about the role of Lord Chancellor's Visitors as witnesses.

49 For example, *Banks v Goodfellow* [1870].

50 *Royal Commission on the Law Relating to Mental Illness*, 292.

51 The case is unreported but described in Donald G Hunt, Maurice E Reed, and Ronald A Whiteman, *Heywood & Massey's Court of Protection Practice*, 9th edn (London: Stevens, 1971), 22. It is cited in later editions of the textbook and in later cases, including *Re WLW* [1972], and *PY v RJS* [1982] in New South Wales. My thanks to Denzil Lush for sharing his notes and insights about this case.

52 Described in Ruck Keene, et al., 'Taking Capacity Seriously', 56–7.

53 'Carr, Jean Alison' [1934-1941], TNA J92/77; 1932 application from Ellen Freeman in 'Willard, Emily' [1932-41], TNA J92/72.

54 Keywood, 'Vulnerable Adult Experiment', 89; Clough, 'Vulnerability and Capacity to Consent'; Clough, 'Disability and Vulnerability'.

55 Information about it survives thanks to a later dispute over Mrs Wilson's testamentary capacity: 'Requests for the Lord Chancellor's consent to the Visitors giving evidence in legal proceedings concerning certain lunatics' [1919-71], TNA LCO 2/5714.

56 Outline of procedure in 'Departmental Committee of Inquiry set up to consider staff, organisation and accommodation in Management and Administration Department' [1934], TNA LCO 4/47.

57 Letter from Thomas Coombs and Morton dated 26 September 1939; letter from Miss Stevenson dated 29 December 1939, both in TNA J127/24; 'Test of Civil Defence', *Times*, 10 July 1939, 9.

58 Official Solicitor's memorandum dated 24 July 1939 in TNA J127/24.

59 Mr Winder's report of 20 November 1939; Miss Stevenson's letter dated 29 December 1939, in TNA J127/24. On Miss Alexander's fear of mental hospitals in a different context, see Miss Wortt's letter dated 30 August 1964, in TNA J127/33.

60 Miss Stevenson's letter dated 19 March 1940, in TNA J127/25.

CHAPTER FOUR

1 Letters from Official Solicitor dated 26 September 1939 to Thomas Coombs and Morton and to Dr Stephenson in TNA J127/24.

2 Taylor and Brumby, eds, *Healthy Minds*, 5. See also Bartlett and Wright, *Outside the Walls of the Asylum*; Peter Rushton, 'Lunatics and Idiots: Mental Disability, the Community, and the Poor Law in North-East England, 1600–1800', *Medical History* 32, no. 1 (1988): 34–50; Pat Thane, 'Social Histories of Old Age and Aging', *Journal of Social History* 37, no. 1 (2003): 93–111; David Thomson, 'The Welfare of the Elderly in the Past: A Family or Community Responsibility?', in Margaret Pelling and Richard Michael Smith, eds, *Life, Death, and the Elderly: Historical Perspectives* (London; New York: Routledge, 1991).

3 For example, Thomson, *Problem of Mental Deficiency*, chapter 4; Toms, 'Citizenship and Learning Disabled People'.

4 Lydia Hayes, *Stories of Care: A Labour of Law* (London: Palgrave Macmillan, 2017), 65.

5 On rethinking the place of care in public or political life, see Tronto, 'Care as the Work of Citizens', 141–2.

6 Hide and Bourke, 'Cultures of Harm'. A useful study of nursing interventions that occupy an uncertain place between care and harm can be found in Dickinson,

Curing Queers. An exception to the negative portrait of the asylum is Barbara Taylor, 'The Demise of the Asylum in Late Twentieth-Century Britain: A Personal History', *Transactions of the Royal Historical Society* 21 (2011): 193–215. See also Barbara Taylor, *The Last Asylum* (London: Penguin Books, 2015).

7   For example, Stone, et al., 'Estranged Relations'; Clough, 'Disability and Vulnerability'.

8   Mr Winder's report dated 20 November 1939 and memorandum dated 1 December 1939 in TNA J127/24; Memorandum dated 3 January 1940 in TNA J127/25.

9   Hearing on 16 November 1939 for a receiver ad interim, in 'Gladstone, Robert Theodore' [1939-1940], TNA J92/94.

10   Letter from Stonham and Sons dated 8 January 1963, in 'Golodetz, Michael' [1963-1964], TNA J92/222.

11   Assorted correspondence from 1933–34 in 'Froud, Alice Sarah Parker' [1933-1940], TNA J92/76.

12   Note of telephone call with Mr Winder dated 9 January 1940, in TNA J127/25.

13   Undated letter from Mrs Humphreys received 8 February 1940; letter from Private Humphries received 23 January 1940, both in TNA J127/25.

14   Mrs Winder's report of her visit on 3 June 1940, in TNA J127/25.

15   Miss Stevenson's letter dated 23 November 1939, Mr Winder's report dated 20 November 1939, in TNA J127/24; Mrs Winder's report from November 1959, in TNA J127/32.

16   Letter from Miss Stevenson to Mr Winder dated 23 November 1939 in TNA J127/24.

17   Mr Winder's report dated 22 January 1940 in TNA J127/25.

18   Letter from Miss Wortt dated 12 February 1940 in TNA J127/25.

19   Mrs Winder's report from 3 June 1940 in TNA J127/25.

20   Louise Westwood, 'A Quiet Revolution in Brighton: Dr Helen Boyle's Pioneering Approach to Mental Health Care, 1899–1939', *Social History of Medicine* 14, no. 3 (2001): 439–57 (450).

21   Letter from Miss Wortt dated 11 August 1940, in TNA J127/26.

22   'Barnes, Mary Elizabeth Prescot' [1931-80], J92/108; 'Alpass, Annie Laura' [1927-41], TNA J92/57; 'Gilbert, Jemima Peck' [1925-38], J92/50; 'Chabot, Sarah' [1923-38], TNA J92/44 (prior to the receivership).

23   'Beresford, The Hon Eileen Theresa de la Poer' [1921-41], TNA J92/39.

24   'Brocklehurst, John Ogilvy' [1947-74], J127/189.

25   This is particularly clear in 'Middleton, Arthur' [1935-82], J92/116; 'Longhurst, Victoria Mary' [1928-41], J92/59.

26 Rosemarie Tong, 'Love's Labor in the Health Care System: Working toward Gender Equity', *Hypatia* 17, no. 3 (2002): 200–13 (207); Eva Feder Kittay, '"Love's Labor" Revisited', *Hypatia* 17, no. 3 (2002): 237–50.

27 Mrs Winder's report from 21 March 1946, in TNA J127/28; Miss Wortt's letter of 12 December 1941 in TNA J127/27; Mrs Winder's report dated 24 November 1944 in TNA J127/28; Miss Wortt's letter of 19 October 1941 in J127/27; Miss Wortt's letter of 28 March 1945 in TNA J127/28.

28 Miss Wortt's letter of 4 December 1966, TNA J127/35. See also the references to friendly and helpful neighbours, and visits and cards from 'Chilfrome friends': Mrs Winder's report of 15 July 1952, TNA J127/30; Mrs Winder's report of 29 November 1961, in TNA J127/32; Miss Wortt's letters dated 4 January 1966 TNA J127/34; 18 June 1967, TNA J127/35.

29 Mrs Winder's report of 8 November 1960; Miss Wortt's letter dated 14 May 1961, in TNA J127/32.

30 Miss Wortt's letter of 19 February 1962, in TNA J127/32.

31 On the invisibility of unpaid work, see Arlene Kaplan Daniels, 'Invisible Work', *Social Problems* 34, no. 5 (1987): 403–15.

32 Kerry Harman, 'Sensory Ways of Knowing Care: Possibilities for Reconfiguring "the Distribution of the Sensible" in Paid Homecare Work', *International Journal of Care and Caring* 5, no. 3 (2021): 433–46 (440); Hayes, *Stories of Care*, 70.

33 Letter from Miss Stevenson dated 11 December 1939, in TNA J127/24.

34 Letter from Miss Wortt dated 31 October 1946; correspondence between Official Solicitor and Local Assistance Board, in TNA J127/28.

35 Mrs Winder's report dated 22 January 1941, in TNA J127/27.

36 Mrs Winder's report dated 21 March 1946, in TNA J127/28.

37 Letter from Dr Hereward dated 3 September 1964 in TNA J127/33.

38 Miss Wortt's letter dated 12 December 1941, in TNA J127/27; Miss Wortt's letter dated 7 April 1962, in TNA J127/32.

39 Letter from Official Solicitor to Mrs Fish, January 1965, in TNA J127/34.

40 Letter from Miss Wortt 4 January 1966, in TNA J127/34.

41 Letter from Midland Band dated 22 December 1947 in TNA J127/28.

42 Attendance note from visit on 14 January 1948, in TNA J127/29.

43 'Hide, Edith Jane' [1902-1939], TNA J92/3.

44 'Beresford, The Hon Eileen Theresa de la Poer' [1921-41], TNA J92/39.

45 'Sims, Arthur Palmer' [1912-40], TNA J92/12.

46 Dr Rotherham's report dated 23 May 1933, in 'Sims, Arthur Palmer' [1912-40], TNA J92/12.

47 The Barnes brothers were living at home with their parents, sisters, and cousin Mary according to the 1911 census. By the time of their parents' death, it is the two sisters who take Mary in: 'Barnes, Mary Elizabeth Prescot' [1931-80], J92/108.

48 'Alpass, Annie Laura' [1927-41], TNA J92/57.

49 Borsay and Dale, *Mental Health Nursing*, 6–7; Dingwall, Rafferty, and Webster, *Introduction to the Social History of Nursing*, 8.

50 Suzuki, *Madness at Home*, 109–11.

51 Kittay, '"Love's Labor" Revisited,' 238.

52 Tronto, 'Care as the Work of Citizens,' 141–2.

53 Handwritten note on Mrs Winder's report of her 22 January 1941 visit, in TNA J127/27; annual accounts to Lunacy Office; letter from local general store dated 8 August 1942 and Official Solicitor's response, in TNA J127/27.

54 Report of official visit on 14 January 1948, in TNA J127/29.

55 Theobald, *Law Relating to Lunacy*, 136.

56 Memorandum from Mrs Winder dated 10 March 1934 in '"Marraines": Visits to nursing homes and hospitals by representatives' [1934-60], J136/134.

57 Letter from the Official Solicitor to C F Penton of the Board of Control dated 6 March 1934, in '"Marraines": Visits to nursing homes and hospitals by representatives' [1934-1960], TNA J136/134.

58 A standard turn of phrase; for example, the instructions to Mrs Winder on the Visitor's Report of May 1934, TNA J92/11.

59 Bartlett, 'Legal Madness', 109.

60 Letter from Official Solicitor to C F Penton of the Board of Control dated 21 February 1934, in '"Marraines": Visits to nursing homes and hospitals by representatives' [1934-1960], TNA J136/134.

61 See, for example, Official Solicitor letter to P Barter of the Board of Control dated 15 March 1938, in '"Marraines": Visits to nursing homes and hospitals by representatives' [1934-1960], TNA J136/134.

62 Susan R. Grayzel, 'Mothers, Marraines, and Prostitutes: Morale and Morality in First World War France', *International History Review* 19, no. 1 (1997): 66–82 (70).

63 Letter from Official Solicitor to Secretary of Norfolk Federation of Women's Institutions dated 30 January 1934, in '"Marraines": Visits to nursing homes and hospitals by representatives' [1934-1960], TNA J136/134.

64 Miss Wortt's letter dated 1 July 1957, in TNA J127/31; Miss Wortt's card from May 1963, in TNA J127/32.

65 Mrs Winder's report from November 1966, in TNA J127/35.

66 Correspondence from September–October 1964, in TNA J127/33; Memorandum of
    1 April 1965 and correspondence from December 1965 in TNA J127/34.

67 See for example the correspondence with the Medical Superintendent of Carlton
    Hayes Hospital, 29 September 1952, 14 October 1952; 10 April 1953; reports on Kent
    institutions under cover of Mrs Winder's letter dated 10 May 1960, in in '"Mar-
    raines": Visits to nursing homes and hospitals by representatives' [1934-1960],
    TNA J136/134.

68 Heywood and Massey, *Lunacy Practice* (1900, and later editions).

69 Mr Mills's evidence of 15 October 1934, in 'Departmental Committee of Inquiry
    on Management and Administration Department: Evidence and minutes of meet-
    ings', TNA LCO 4/50.

70 Houlbrook, *Prince of Tricksters*, 4.

71 Written evidence from Master Methold and his oral evidence given on 19 Novem-
    ber 1934, both in 'Departmental Committee of Inquiry on Management and Ad-
    ministration Department: Evidence and minutes of meetings', TNA LCO 4/50.

72 'Bathurst, Clara: Court administration papers' [1968-72], TNA J92/308.

73 'Harnett v Bond and Adam', *Lancet* (8 March 1924): 503; 'Lunacy Law: The Harnett
    Case Appeal', *Lancet* (19 April 1924): 815; 'Lunacy Law and Administration: Open-
    ing Sittings of the Royal Commission', *Lancet* (1 November 1924): 909–14. The 1924
    requests for confirmation of incapacity are present throughout the archived files.

74 There was a small and declining number of committees of the person, who were
    answerable to the Lunacy Office/Court of Protection, right up until inquisitions
    were finally abolished in 1959.

75 'Ward, Emma Canwell' [1921-1939], J92/40; correspondence from 1932, in 'Hill,
    Sarah Warren' [1919-40], J92/34; correspondence from 1928 and 1932 in 'Coburn,
    Emma Florence' [1904-1939], J92/4; arrangements made for housing in 'Stephens,
    The Hon Isobel Muirman Young: Court administration papers' [1967-8], J92/300.

76 Minutes from 1928 in 'D'Aguilar, Emily Gertrude' [1919-40], J92/32; visitors' re-
    ports from 1924, 1925, 1926, and 1929 in 'Beresford, The Hon Eileen Theresa de la
    Poer' [1921-41], TNA J92/39; correspondence about holidays throughout 'Hide,
    Edith Jane' [1902-39], J92/3; refusal of more pocket money in August 1931 'Hop-
    kins, Obadiah' 1929-39], J92/63.

77 Compare for example the response to Isabella Clay's letter of 24 February 1915 in
    'Clay, Bella' [1915-42], TNA J92/20 and the response to Thomas Cook's letters in
    1931 and 1932, in 'Cook, Thomas' [1917-1939], TNA J92/28.

78 Poyser's oral evidence on 14 October 1934; criticism of over-involvement from Sir Roger Gregory of the Law Society in his letter of 3 November 1934 and Mr Medley of Field Roscoe & Co in his evidence; all in 'Departmental Committee of Inquiry on Management and Administration Department: Evidence and minutes of meetings', TNA LCO 4/50.

79 See, for example, Jameel Hampton, *Disability and the Welfare State: Changes in Perception and Policy 1948–1979* (Bristol: Policy Press, 2016); Bernard Harris, *The Origins of the British Welfare State: Society, State, and Social Welfare in England and Wales, 1800–1945* (Basingstoke, UK: Palgrave Macmillan, 2004).

80 See letters from Sarah Wilson, receiver and sister, in 'Lewis, Walter' [1926-82], J92/99.

81 Possible financial mismanagement: 'Picton, Clara' [1914-40], J92/18; very heated disagreements about how much Mrs Bradley's daughter should receive from her hospitalised mother: 'Bradley, Kate' [1924-38], J92/48.

82 Extracts from paper prepared by Joe Jacob for Labour Human Rights Sub-Committee, under cover of letter dated 7 October 1977 in 'Future of the Court of Protection and Lord Chancellor's Legal Visitors' [1975-9], TNA LCO 65/178.

83 On the campaigns of the 1970s, see Jonathan Toms, 'MIND, Anti-Psychiatry, and the Case of the Mental Hygiene Movement's "Discursive Transformation"', *Social History of Medicine* 33, no. 2 (2020): 622–40; Toms, 'Citizenship and Learning Disabled People'; Phil Fennell, *Treatment without Consent: Law, Psychiatry and the Treatment of Mentally Disordered People since 1845* (London: Routledge, 1991).

84 Memorandum dated 6 September 1977, in 'Future of the Court of Protection and Lord Chancellor's Legal Visitors' [1975-9], TNA LCO 65/178.

85 Letter from Miss Wortt to Mrs Winder in May 1963, in TNA J127/32.

86 Letter from Miss Stevenson dated 10 July 1940, in TNA J127/26.

87 Mrs Winder's report from November 1959, in TNA J127/32.

88 Mrs Winder's report of 29 October 1966, in TNA J127/35.

89 Mr Winder's report of 22 January 1940, in TNA J92/245.

90 For example, 'Quigley, Ellen Mary' [1952-4], TNA J127/48 and J127/49; 'Allnut, Albert William' [1974-6], J127/226.

91 Miss Wortt's letter to Mrs Winder dated 4 December 1965, in TNA J127/35.

92 Letter from Miss Wortt dated 15 September 1947, in TNA J127/28.

93 Claire Spivakovsky and Linda Steele, 'Disability Law in a Pandemic: The Temporal Folds of Medico-Legal Violence', *Social and Legal Studies* 31, no. 2 (2022): 175–96 (176), italics in original. See also Claire Spivakovsky, Kate Seear, and Adrian Carter,

eds, *Critical Perspectives on Coercive Interventions: Law, Medicine and Society* (London: Routledge, 2018), particularly part 2 and chapter 14: John Chesterman, 'Adult Guardianship and its Alternatives in Australia', 225–35.

94 Barbara Mortimer and Susan McGann, eds, *New Directions in the History of Nursing: International Perspectives* (London: Routledge, 2005). See also the special issue 'Cultures of Harm in Institutions of Care', *Social History of Medicine* 31, no. 4 (2018).

95 Beverley Clough, 'New Legal Landscapes: (Re)Constructing the Boundaries of Mental Capacity Law', *Medical Law Review* 26, no. 2 (2018): 246–75 (262).

96 Stone, et al., 'Estranged Relations', 69, italics in original. On the problematic valorisation of choice within healthcare: Annemarie Mol, *Logic of Care: Health and the Problem of Patient Choice* (London: Routledge, 2008).

97 Letter from Miss Wortt dated 4 January 1966, in TNA J127/34.

CHAPTER FIVE

1 Miss Wortt's letters of 4 and 24 September 1964, in TNA J127/33.

2 Miss Alexander's letter from March 1965 and Miss Wortt's letter of 14 April 1965, in TNA J127/34.

3 Lord Chancellor's Visitor report of 17 March 1966 and Miss Wortt's letter from August 1967 in TNA J127/34; Report of Mrs Winder's visit, 8 March 1968, in TNA J127/36.

4 Miss Wortt's letter of 9 September 1969, in TNA 127/36.

5 Miss Wortt's letter of 18 September 1966, in TNA J127/35.

6 For information about her last will and the LCV's assessment of her testamentary capacity, see notes from 17 March 1966 and subsequent correspondence in J127/34; discussion of an earlier will in May 1946 is in J127/28.

7 Miss Wortt's letter and account dated 4 September 1946, in J127/28.

8 Grumbles about delays can be found in 'Departmental Committee of Inquiry set up to consider staff, organisation and accommodation in Management and Administration Department' [1934], LCO 4/47; 'Departmental Committee of Inquiry on Management and Administration Department: Evidence and minutes of meetings' [1934], LCO 4/50; 'Complaint of delays caused by archaic procedure' [1947], LCO 4/54; 'Future of the Court of Protection and Lord Chancellor's Legal Visitors' [1975-9], LCO 65/178; *Royal Commission on the Law Relating to Mental Illness*, 293.

9   Examples of these life-long 'patients' include 'Goddard, Thomas Harry Clarence' [1920-1967], TNA J92/1 and J92/104-106; 'Lewis, Walter' [1926-82: he died in the 1950s], TNA J92/99; 'Lockett, Anna Emma' [1927-1982: she died in 1960], TNA J92/100; 'Quigley, Ellen Mary' [1928-70], TNA J127/39-53; 'Richard, Dorothy Madeline' [1931-1973], TNA J127/175-77.

10 Jennings, 'Mental Disorder and the Court of Protection', 855.

11 Letter from Martin Cuthbert of the Royal College of Psychiatrists to DHSS dated 18 January 1976, in 'Future of the Court of Protection and Lord Chancellor's Legal Visitors' [1975-9], TNA LCO 65/178.

12 Macfarlane, 'Court of Protection', 30, 32.

13 Toms, 'Citizenship and Learning Disabled People'. See also Thomson, *Problem of Mental Deficiency*.

14 Taylor, 'Demise of the Asylum', 198.

15 More detail on these numbers is available in Weston, 'Managing Mental Incapacity'.

16 Correspondence from February 1935, in 'Departmental Committee of Inquiry on Management and Administration Department: Draft reports' p. 1934-5], TNA LCO 4/49; letter from Mr Kelsey dated 27 April 1976. See also minutes of 6 July 1977 meeting, both in 'Future of the Court of Protection and Lord Chancellor's Legal Visitors' [1975-9], TNA LCO 65/178.

17 September 1969 letter from Mr Cartwright Sharp of the Law Commission to Mr Boggis-Rolfe, in 'Possible changes in function' [1967-9], TNA LCO 4/409.

18 Hansard, HC 1 March 1973, vol. 851, col. 1833; 'Future of the Court of Protection and Lord Chancellor's Legal Visitors' [1975-9], TNA LCO 65/178.

19 On concern about investments in the 1950s: 'Investment of funds in court in Court of Protection cases: Policy' [1956], TNA LCO 2/5710.

20 Memorandum from 26 January 1979, in 'Future of the Court of Protection and Lord Chancellor's Legal Visitors' [1975-9], TNA LCO 65/178.

21 This is well explained in Brenda Hoggett, 'The Royal Prerogative in Relation to the Mentally Disordered: Resurrection, Resuscitation, or Rejection?', in Michael D A Freeman, ed, *Medicine, Ethics, and the Law: Current Legal Problems* (London: Stevens, 1988), 85–101.

22 Law Commission, *Mentally Incapacitated Adults and Decision-Making: An Overview* (London: HMSO, 1991); *Making Decisions: The Government's Proposals for Making Decisions on Behalf of Mentally Incapacitated Adults* (London: HMSO, 1998).

23 Theobald, *Remembrance of Things Past*, 94; Theobald, *Law Relating to Lunacy*, 91–2.

24 Theobald, *Remembrance of Things Past*, 98.

25 The New Year Honours, *Times*, 1 January 1952, 2.

26 Susanna Brown, 'Stoneman, Walter Ernest (1876–1958), Photographer', *Oxford Dictionary of National Biography*, 2006. It is unclear exactly when Poyser sat for the portrait: the National Portrait Gallery's catalogue gives a date of 1958, but this is after his death.

27 'Sir Ronald Poyser', *Times*, 2 July 1957, 10.

28 Mrs Stephenson's letter dated 26 August 1944, in TNA J127/28.

29 Mrs Stephenson's letters dated 27 October 1937 and 30 November 1937 in the Robert Saunders Collection, SSC 119/A3/314 and 119/A3/313; correspondence between Robert Saunders and the Stephensons, in the Robert Saunders Collection, SSC C10/348, C11/326-7, C15/559-562.

30 Miss Wortt's letter of 21 July 1945, in TNA J127/28; of July 1948 in J127/29.

31 Miss Wortt's letter from April 1966 in TNA J127/34.

32 Miss Wortt's letter of 27 May 1967 in TNA J127/35.

33 Correspondence throughout J127/34; Miss Wortt's letters of 16 and 28 October, 10 November, 4 December 1966 in TNA J127/35; Miss Wortt's letters throughout TNA J127/36.

34 Miss Wortt's letters of 30 April and 13 May 1965; correspondence with Ensors and Midland Bank, in TNA J127/34.

35 Miss Wortt's letters dated 26 February 1965 in TNA J127/34, and 24 September 1964 in TNA J127/33.

36 Miss Wortt's letters dated 27 May, 20 July, 31 October 1965, in TNA J127/34.

37 Correspondence from May to July 1965, in TNA J127/34.

38 These issues are summarised beautifully in Laite, 'Emmet's Inch'. See also the reflections on ethics in Cora Salkovskis, '"Queer Mind and Body": Hallucinations, Delusions, and the Experiences of the Body in the British Asylum, c. 1840–1914' (unpublished PhD thesis: Birkbeck, University of London, 2022).

39 Tronto, 'Care as the Work of Citizens'. See also Care Collective, *Care Manifesto*.

40 Hartman, 'Venus in Two Acts', 12.

INDEX